Heartsick and Astonished

New Perspectives on the Civil War Era

SERIES EDITORS
Judkin Browning, Appalachian State University
Susanna Lee, North Carolina State University

SERIES ADVISORY BOARD
Stephen Berry, University of Georgia
Jane Turner Censer, George Mason University
Paul Escott, Wake Forest University
Lorien Foote, Texas A&M University
Anne Marshall, Mississippi State University
Barton Myers, Washington & Lee University
Michael Thomas Smith, McNeese State University
Susannah Ural, University of Southern Mississippi
Heather Andrea Williams, University of Pennsylvania
Kidada Williams, Wayne State University

Heartsick and Astonished

Divorce in Civil War–Era West Virginia

Edited by
Allison Dorothy Fredette

The University of Georgia Press
ATHENS

© 2023 by the University of Georgia Press
Athens, Georgia 30602
www.ugapress.org
All rights reserved
Set in 9.75/13 Baskerville 10 Pro
by Kaelin Chappell Broaddus

Most University of Georgia Press titles are
available from popular e-book vendors.

Printed digitally

Library of Congress Cataloging-in-Publication Data
Names: Fredette, Allison Dorothy, editor.
Title: Heartsick and astonished : divorce in Civil War–era
West Virginia / edited by Allison Dorothy Fredette.
Other titles: New Perspectives on the Civil War Era.
Description: Athens : University of Georgia Press,
[2023] | Series: New perspectives on the Civil War era
| Includes bibliographical references and index.
Identifiers: LCCN 2022053796 | ISBN 9780820364278 (hardback)
| ISBN 9780820364285 (paperback) | ISBN 9780820364292
(epub) | ISBN 9780820364308 (pdf)
Subjects: LCSH: Divorce suits—West Virginia—Ohio County—
History—19th century. | Divorce suits—West Virginia—Ohio
County—Cases. | Divorce suits—West Virginia—Wheeling—
Cases. | Marriage—West Virginia—Ohio County—Public
opinion. | Sex role—West Virginia—Ohio County—Public
opinion. | United States—History—Civil War, 1861–1865—
Influence. | LCGFT: Trial and arbitral proceedings.
Classification: LCC HQ835.W43 2023 |
DDC 306.89—dc23/eng/20230110
LC record available at https://lccn.loc.gov/2022053796

*To my father, Kevin Leo Fredette—
librarian, archivist, finder of hidden histories*

Contents

Acknowledgments   ix
Introduction. Humbly Complaining   1

PART 1. ANTEBELLUM

Chapter 1. Adultery: Her Skin Should Never Touch His   49
Chapter 2. Abandonment: I Would Not Give Up My Wife for the World   77
Chapter 3. Cruelty: Encouraging the Disobedience of His Wife   94
Chapter 4. Jail: Imprisoned for Criminal Offense   106

PART 2. WARTIME

Chapter 5. Wartime Cases: Catharine Shall Not Marry Her Said Paramour   113

PART 3. POSTBELLUM

Chapter 6. Adultery: Since His Discharge, She Has Been Living a Lewd and Adulterous Life   125
Chapter 7. Abandonment: She Had Never Lived Happier in Her Life   167
Chapter 8. Cruelty: How Far in the Streets Could He Be Heard?   203

Appendix A. The Code of Virginia, 1849   263
Appendix B. The Code of West Virginia, 1870   266
Bibliography   271
Index   283

Acknowledgments

I FIRST ENCOUNTERED THESE DOCUMENTS ABOUT FIFTEEN YEARS ago, and I was quickly fascinated by them. At the time, I was working on my master's thesis, and I was more focused on property law than divorce. Still, the stories in these cases stuck with me, and before long, they formed the foundation of my doctoral dissertation. I have spent so long with these stories that the people in them almost seem real to me, and I am so excited to share their lives with you. I couldn't have done that, though, without the help of so many.

I would like to acknowledge and thank the people in these cases for sharing their stories with the courts in the first place. None of these couples could have known that a nosy historian would stumble on their divorces a century and a half after they happened, and it was obviously never their intention to have their personal lives published about in a book. Still, they felt strongly enough about their needs to make intimate details of their lives public in their own community in the mid-nineteenth century. Regardless of the reasons, I think that takes a certain amount of bravery (or arrogance), and I appreciate and acknowledge that.

Of course, I have to thank the staff at the West Virginia and Regional History Center at West Virginia University. Their work is vital to the preservation of West Virginia's history. For a state that cares deeply about its past, many have let the records of it slip away. Few documents like these from West Virginia still exist. Some have disappeared from lack of care. Some have been burned or thrown out to save money over the years. Others still sit molding in courthouse basements. I feel extremely fortunate to have found these records preserved on microfilm at the WVRHC, and I am even more grateful that the center generously allowed me to publish them and share them with the world. Special thanks go to Lori Hostuttler, Jessica Eichlin, and Lemley Mullett for their help securing permission to publish, answering my research questions, and helping obtain images for the manuscript. I would also like to thank W. Hal Gorby, Adam Zucconi, Elisabeth Moore, and my mom, Hilary Fredette, for rescanning documents for me after a very important external hard drive disappeared during a move in graduate school.

I would also like to thank my advisors at both WVU and the University of Florida, Ken Fones-Wolf, Bill Link, and Matt Gallman, for encouraging me to analyze these cases for their valuable insights. They continue to be my supporters, as well as generous colleagues now that I am a professor myself.

Everyone knows that the academic job market is a nightmare right now, and yet, somehow I landed my dream job at Appalachian State. My colleagues, friends, and students in the department and at the university make my job a true pleasure. I would especially like to thank Sheila Phipps for supporting me as I stepped into the position of American women's historian. Her class on the history of women and the law in the United States not only allowed me to continue to explore these cases (and craft the assignments found in the online materials that accompany this book) but reminded me of the continued importance of understanding the legal history of women in the United States. At a moment when women are still fighting for recognition of their full equal rights, understanding how the law and legal experiences like those found in this book shaped their history and their current lives is even more vital.

When I first came to App State, Judkin Browning helped me secure an adjunct position. Without his support, I could never have made it all the way to the tenure track. In addition to all that, he generously asked me if I would like to contribute to this series. He has been a fantastic person to lead me through this process, although I'm sure he regrets editing a book for someone who can easily walk to his office and ask for advice. Thank you for all your help and for your friendship.

I would also like to thank Susanna Lee, the coeditor on this series, for her thoughtful critiques and support. This book is better for her contribution. Everyone at the University of Georgia Press has been unfailingly helpful. Without their help, I would still be procrastinating on a deadline, and there would be no book. Mick Gusinde-Duffy has been a fantastic editor, leading me through this process in the midst of a global pandemic (and the accompanying work delays). I would also like to thank Jon Davies, Bethany Snead, Christina Cotter, and all of the advisory board, marketing team, editing department, and production team for their hard work on this book. I would especially like to thank Anne Coulling, my copy editor, for her careful reading of this document. She saved me from so many errors. Two anonymous readers took their valuable time to read and critique this work, and I truly appreciate their efforts. They challenged me to expand my arguments and showed me the value in this work. Any mistakes left are, of course, my own.

If the last two years have taught me anything, it's the continued importance of my family. Somehow my husband, Will, always finds a way to provide me extra time to work, while also caring for our kids and getting his own articles and book published. Thank you for your support, your love, and your sense of humor. I want to thank my two children, Henry and Walter, for bringing sheer joy into my life. Also, whether on Zoom or in person, my sister (and her family), my in-laws, and my whole extended family support and revive me. And of course, I want to thank my mom. As a mother, a spouse, a cook, and an academic, she is my role model. I am truly in awe of her strength, intelligence, generosity, and grace.

Finally, I want to thank my dad, Kevin Fredette, without whom, quite simply, this book would not exist. As an archivist at the West Virginia and Regional History Center, he was the one who first handed me the drawer from the card catalog containing these cases. "Do you think you could use these for your thesis?" he asked. As a parent and as a librarian, he has always quietly helped me on my path—supporting me in every endeavor, guiding me to valuable resources, and modeling a passion for history I strive to emulate every day. Although his struggle with Lewy body dementia means that he is less likely to read these cases in their book form now, he read them with me fifteen years ago, and he was the first one to truly recognize their importance.

Heartsick and Astonished

INTRODUCTION

Humbly Complaining

AS THE SUMMER OF 1865 DREW TO A CLOSE, JACOB STROBLE RETURNED to his adopted hometown, Wheeling, West Virginia, after more than three years of absence.[1] The state of Virginia had seceded in April 1861, and shortly thereafter, western Virginians had declared their intention to remain with the Union. Statehood proceedings began in the northern panhandle's largest city, Wheeling. Those living in the western counties of Virginia now had to decide whether their loyalty lay with the new state of West Virginia and the Union or with their former state of Virginia and the Confederacy. In the summer of 1861, Jacob, a German immigrant, made his decision and enlisted as a private in what would become the First Regiment of the West Virginia Light Artillery. He was eager to do his part "fighting rebels."[2] During the war, his regiment served mostly in the area that became West Virginia, as well as in western Virginia, seeing action at Cheat Mountain, fighting in the Battle of Kernstown near Winchester, and serving almost a year in the defenses of Washington, D.C.[3] Like many returning soldiers at the end of the war, he was likely exhausted, homesick, and lonely—ready to see his wife of six years after being so long apart.

He would be disappointed.

Sometime after Jacob went off to war, Ellen met another man—John Hunter. Although he also served in the war as a member of an Ohio regiment, John seems to have spent less time than Jacob in service. Certainly by 1863, he was living in Wheeling and spending most of his time with Ellen Stroble. The couple made no secret of their relationship. At

---

1. For simplicity and fluidity, I have chosen to refer to any counties that eventually became part of West Virginia as "West Virginia" throughout all my editorial content, even if I am referring to the antebellum era.

2. *Stroble, Jacob v. Stroble, Ellen* (1865), Records of the Circuit Court of Ohio County, West Virginia and Regional History Center (WVRHC), env. 259 b-5.

3. "Battle Unit Details," National Park Service, https://www.nps.gov/civilwar/search-battle-units-detail.htm?battleUnitCode=UWV0001RAL, accessed June 12, 2019.

one point, they ate oysters together at a saloon on Main Street, where the owner spotted John with "his arm around Stroble's waist with his hand in an improper place." They also attended market days together, sharing hot whiskey punches in a back room. After they finished, John would stand up and turn to Ellen. "Let us go home now," he would say to her.[4] Some residents of Wheeling even thought they were husband and wife.

Within a week or two of returning home, Jacob discovered the affair and moved out. Within a month, he filed a divorce petition with the Ohio County Circuit Court, asking for a divorce and any "further relief" the court deemed necessary.[5] This was certainly not the welcome he had anticipated, but before Christmas, the court granted his wish. He and Ellen were divorced.

The Strobles' story is hardly unique. Divorce, separation, and heartbreak are often the unintended consequences of war, and as historians have argued, the Civil War had an especially profound impact on households in the United States. In the South, for instance, the war challenged the hierarchies that had previously defined household relationships. Emancipation freed enslaved men and women from bondage and shattered the white southern myth of slaveholder benevolence. Slaveholders who had told both themselves and the nation that enslaved people were part of their family, "white and black," now had to explain the eagerness with which those "family members" fled.[6] As they fled plantations, Black southerners sought to reconnect with family members, long separated, and to assert their right to a legal recognition of their marriages.[7]

Emancipation revealed that household ties were fluid and potentially impermanent. Some worried that white southern women, many

---

4. *Stroble, Jacob v. Stroble, Ellen*.
5. Ibid.
6. Genovese, "Our Family, White and Black." For books on the impact of emancipation on households, see Taylor, *Embattled Freedom*; Bercaw, *Gendered Freedoms*; Edwards, *Gendered Strife and Confusion*; Frankel, *Freedom's Women*; Glymph, *Out of the House of Bondage*; Hunter, *To 'Joy My Freedom*; Jacqueline Jones, *Labor of Love, Labor of Sorrow*; Morsman, *Big House after Slavery*; Schwalm, *Hard Fight for We*; Silkenat, *Moments of Despair*; Whites, *Civil War as a Crisis*.
7. Hunter, *Bound in Wedlock*, 196–232; Edwards, "Marriage Covenant," 99–102.

of whom had spent the war surviving without male assistance or had defended their homes and families against marauding armies and guerrilla bands, might see a similar opportunity to break the bonds that held them to their husbands.[8] Certainly, some white women seized the moment. We will never really know Ellen Stroble's reasons for leaving Jacob, but she may have seen the chaos of the war as a perfect chance to start afresh with a new partner. Some white women even explicitly stated that they were "free" as they gleefully abandoned their former husbands.[9] Yet, these women remained a minority. Far more white southern women chose to shore up their husbands' and fathers' shaken masculinity by confirming their commitment to be good dependents. Many of these women would form the vanguard of the future United Daughters of the Confederacy and Ladies' Memorial Association.[10] Their story tells us much about dominant gender roles, race, and the ways in which white southerners strove to maintain their "way of life" in the wake of the war.

Likewise, although northern white women experienced the war less directly than their southern counterparts, their lives were nonetheless disrupted by the conflict. While a smaller percentage of northern white men fought and died in the war, many northern white women still had to care for farms and households without male support for four long years. Others lost husbands, sons, and fathers in a war fought hundreds of miles from their own homes. A smaller minority of white northern women traveled south to help in the war effort, serving most often as nurses. An even smaller group of white women traveled south to help formerly enslaved people in the wake of the war. Far from home, these women served, for example, in Freedmen's Bureau schools as teachers, another occupation that was commonly held by women but that still allowed them to make some lasting social impact.[11] An even smaller group of activist women seized upon the passage of the Reconstruction amendments to push for greater legal rights for women.[12]

The stories of the war's impact on these small groups of white south-

---

8. Faust, *Mothers of Invention*, 122–23, 137, 234–35, 242; Censer, *Reconstruction of White Southern Womanhood*; Rable, *Civil Wars*.
9. Fredette, *Marriage on the Border*, 182–83.
10. Janney, *Burying the Dead*; Whites, *Civil War as a Crisis*, 160–98; Cox, *Dixie's Daughters*.
11. Glymph, *Women's Fight*; Attie, *Patriotic Toil*; Giesberg, *Army at Home*; Schultz, *Women at the Front*; Currie-McDaniel, "Northern Women in the South; Jacqueline Jones, *Soldiers of Light and Love*.
12. DuBois, *Feminism and Suffrage*; Newman, *White Women's Rights*.

ern and northern women have dominated the historical narrative, leaving little room for the stories of complicated and lesser-known women like Ellen Stroble. But the Ellen Strobles also have a story to tell, even if—and maybe especially if—that story diverges from the common experience during this era. This book shares some of those stories—stories of men and women who did not quite fit the model of nineteenth-century life; stories of people who made choices that challenged social norms and values, not to make a statement, but rather out of their own selfish needs and desires; stories of unhappy couples who manipulated a conservative legal system to meet their personal needs; stories of men and women who lived on the edge of the South, not on plantations or small farms, but in a bustling industrial city; stories of southerners who were barely southerners, who lived on the very edge of the North and who came from Massachusetts, New York, Ohio, Ireland, England, and Germany; stories of a community on the edge, balanced precariously between slave and free and built on the banks of the Ohio River, a gateway to the expanding American West.

This is the story of Ohio County, part of the "Virginia peninsula thrusting northward into the heartland of Yankeedom."[13] Even more, it is the story of Wheeling, a nineteenth-century city so prominent that it would be the destination for the National Road but that has largely been forgotten by Americans today. Perched on the edge of the Ohio River, it was part of Virginia when this book begins in 1850, and by 1873, when this book ends, it was the largest city in the newly created state of West Virginia. Wheeling was an industrial powerhouse with trade connections to many northern cities around it and was home to only one hundred enslaved people on the eve of the Civil War.[14] And yet, until 1863, it was still a part of the Old Dominion.

Studying the divorce records of Ohio County, West Virginia, sheds new light on regional variation in the Civil War–era South and on the evolution of divorce and attitudes toward household gender roles in the United States. Specifically, Ohio County, an industrialized community in a southern state, perched on the knife's edge between two northern states, helps historians understand life and community in the greater border South, a region with overlapping and conflicting political, economic, and religious ideologies, as well as in the urban South, a region often neglected when scholars focus on the rural and plan-

---

13. Williams, *West Virginia*, 49.
14. Williams, *West Virginia*, 52.

tation South. Furthermore, as legal historians have shown, the nineteenth century formed a pivotal period in the shift toward a more modern understanding of family law and divorce. Women's rights activists fought for greater access to divorce for women, and ideas of contractualism and individualism meant that judges and legislators increasingly gave unhappy couples greater latitude to determine their own marital destiny. Still, society remained hesitant to accept divorce, and some courts saw the home as a private sphere that should be unsullied by judicial interference.[15] These Ohio County divorce cases show the ways in which everyday people fought for their heart's desire—a separation and marital freedom—while confronting a legal system that did not always match their needs. The cases also reveal the ways in which West Virginia, as it broke away from Virginia, adopted some of the less restrictive attitudes of its northern and midwestern neighbors, moving the state toward a twentieth-century understanding of divorce.

In the mid-nineteenth century, Wheeling lay at the heart of a complex borderland. The states that lay along this quickly deepening regional divide between slave states and free developed a unique identity in this era, one that grew out of their status as a middle ground. Wheeling, and the future state of West Virginia itself, reflected many of the attitudes of this region, alternately labeled by historians as the border South, the middle border, or the border states.[16] This was a fluid border, one that was as much a reflection of western and eastern differences as northern and southern ones. It was a region of connection, as well as divergence.[17] Migrants flowed in, out, and through the states along the Ohio River, blending their cultural values as they went. Much like that of other international and intranational borders, the region's role as a place of contact and exchange, as well as its mixture of economic, po-

---

15. Grossberg, *Governing the Hearth*, ix, xi–xii, 7–9; Stanton, "Need of Liberal Divorce Laws"; Thomas, *Elizabeth Cady Stanton*, 109–57.

16. In his book on the border, Christopher Phillips uses both "middle border" and the "West" and includes states "bordering the Ohio and Missouri Rivers west of the Appalachian Mountains and south and east of present-day Nebraska, Iowa, Wisconsin, and Michigan." In her recent book, Bridget Ford calls it the "Ohio-Kentucky borderland." Other border scholars, such as Aaron Astor and Diane Mutti Burke, employ both the terms "border" and "border states." In my own study of the border, I prefer the term "border South" to specify those parts of this region that were slaveholding states before the Civil War. Phillips, *Rivers Ran Backward*, xvii; Ford, *Bonds of Union*, xi–xv; Astor, *Rebels on the Border*, 3–7; Burke, *On Slavery's Border*, 1–4; Fredette, *Marriage on the Border*, 4–9.

17. Fones-Wolf and Lewis, "Introduction," ix.

litical, social, racial, and ethnic differences, helped create its uniquely blended culture.

Untangling the regional connections of Wheeling residents is a complicated business. The city was a multiethnic and multiracial mosaic. Just one city block might contain people from a dozen states, as well as a handful of European countries. Thousands of Germans flocked to the city after the failed 1848 revolutions, mingling with Irish and English immigrants. As much as a quarter of the city was foreign born in 1860.[18] Those who lived in the city often did so temporarily. Riverboats carried people in and out of the city and quickly helped them escape if they were unhappy. Marriages took place on all sides of the Ohio River, in small communities throughout Ohio, Virginia, and Pennsylvania. Wheeling was both in the South and outside it. These northern and midwestern connections would prove too strong to sever when Virginia seceded in 1861. And yet, Wheeling was still distinct from its neighbors in Pennsylvania and Ohio, especially with regard to its laws.

As its divorce laws reveal, Wheeling was a city created by Virginians, and before the war, residents followed Virginia laws. Their lives—and loves—were bound by statutes created by a predominantly slaveholding legislature in Richmond.[19] While it is clear that Wheeling was greatly influenced by its northern neighbors and by northern inmigration in the antebellum era, it was nonetheless ruled by southern law. This is what makes these particular divorce cases unique. Since West Virginia is the only state to secede from another state in the way it did, no other state can show us so clearly the divergence between social attitudes and the formal law.[20] This book provides cases to help readers answer a number of questions: How did southern law shape the identity of residents in Ohio County? Did they abide by it? Did they break it? What does it mean if they did break it? How did their experience with divorce change once West Virginia seceded from Virginia, and how does that reveal southerners' complex, varied, and changing attitudes toward marriage and gender in the Civil War era? What was the impact of the Civil War itself on divorce? In other words, what can we learn about this border community, the larger region it inhabited, and

---

18. Fones-Wolf, "Caught between Revolutions."
19. For a good resource on divorce in Virginia, see Buckley, *Great Catastrophe of My Life*.
20. Many considered West Virginia's "divorce" from Virginia to be an unconstitutional act, and the split was so dramatic it would become a Supreme Court case after the war, *Virginia v. West Virginia*.

Map of Ohio County, West Virginia, with detail of
Wheeling and the Ohio River; by Josh Platt.

the war's impact on gender roles and marriage by studying divorce records? Ultimately, many of these cases reveal the complicated mindset of Ohio County residents. These men and women lived on the border, and their lives and choices reflected that. While many southern states, especially Virginia, worked to prevent divorces, many in Ohio County saw little wrong with a divorce, if the circumstances warranted it.[21]

This book contains twenty-seven divorce suits from Ohio County, West Virginia, beginning in 1850 and ending in 1873.[22] Although this sampling does not include every divorce suit filed in Ohio County during this period, it does give a snapshot of the common charges, issues, and people involved in divorce in Wheeling and its surrounding communities.[23] Certainly, the suits reveal the changing attitudes to-

---

21. Fredette, *Marriage on the Border*, 55–82.
22. This time period, chosen in part because of the limitations of the case records, also allows researchers to compare divorces before, during, and after the war.
23. From 1850 to 1873, Ohio County residents filed sixty-six divorce cases, with the vast

ward marriage, gender, and divorce in a border city and its hinterlands at a pivotal moment in American history. But they reveal much more. Each case contains a bill and depositions from witnesses. Some of these depositions are lengthy and would have taken hours, even days, to complete. As the witnesses tell their stories—spying on illicit affairs, protecting battered wives, and intervening with intoxicated husbands—they also describe their city, their lives, their jobs, their homes, and the history happening around them. Divorce cases, such as the ones in this book, are rich primary documents for scholars hoping to learn about the everyday history of those in the past.

"Nail City"

The Ohio River is born in Pittsburgh, a city famed as the confluence of three rivers. Splitting from the Monongahela and the Allegheny, the Ohio flows down from the Steel City, along a meandering path that forms the modern-day northern border of West Virginia. Wheeling, the county seat of Ohio County, sits where the river slips along the edge of West Virginia's Appalachian Mountains before descending down the northern border of Kentucky, eventually meeting the Mississippi River at the southernmost tip of Illinois. In the seventeenth century, as with much of the Ohio River Valley, the area around Wheeling was contested ground, deep in a region disputed by Indigenous people, as well as by English and French settlers. Permanent European settlement began around 1769, and soon after, the English began construction of a fort along the Ohio River, near modern-day Wheeling. With the creation of the United States, the region became part of the state of Virginia, and Congress soon established the Ohio River as the southern boundary of the Northwest Territory.[24] From the earliest moments of European influence, Ohio County was a borderland, resting on a watery line between various cultures and regions.

By the time it was officially incorporated in 1805, Wheeling was already imbued with this long history of conflict and borders. In 1818, the National Road was completed and arrived in Wheeling. The town

---

majority of those coming after the war's end and West Virginia's creation. See the note about editorial procedure at the end of this introduction for more information about how to find the cases not included in this book.

24. Otis Rice, *West Virginia*, 29, 33, 45.

Frontispiece to the Wheeling and Belmont Bridge Company's argument for the U.S. Supreme Court in *Pennsylvania v. Wheeling and the Belmont Bridge*, 54 U.S. 518 (1852).

became a hub of transportation, as goods flowed from Washington, D.C., along the National Road, onto the riverfront wharfs and docks, and down the Ohio and Mississippi Rivers.[25] During the antebellum era, the population boomed. In 1849, the city completed construction on the Wheeling Suspension Bridge, which connected it to Wheeling Island. The bridge would help facilitate movement west, and it also makes an appearance, along with Wheeling Island, in a few of this book's divorce suits. Residents quickly spilled out of the crowded city proper and moved to the Island. For a time, the bridge was the longest suspension bridge in the world and typified Wheeling elites' hopes for the growing city. On top of all of this, in 1852, Wheeling became the Baltimore and Ohio Railroad's western terminus, contributing further to Wheeling's prominence in the region.[26]

---

25. Ambler and Summers, *West Virginia*, 217–18.
26. Williams, *West Virginia*, 50–51; Ambler and Summers, *West Virginia*, 253–54, 257, 288. Upon completion of the suspension bridge, Pittsburgh sued Wheeling over the structure, upset that it gave Wheeling more control over high-water travel upstream. The Supreme Court ruled in Pittsburgh's favor, but Congress sided with Wheeling. A storm destroyed the bridge in 1854. However, thanks to Wheeling congressman George W. Thompson, Congress designated the bridge as a post road and rebuilt it before the start of the war. Thompson served as a circuit court judge and oversaw a number of the divorce cases in this book. See Monroe, *Wheeling Bridge Case*.

Since it was situated at the center of so many transportation systems, it is not surprising that Wheeling also served as a center of slave trading in the Upper South. As the salt mining industry took off in western Virginia's southern counties, enslaved people left Wheeling for this dangerous new work. Enslaved people were sold at weekly auctions in Ohio County, many boarding boats to travel "down river" to slave auctions in New Orleans, eventually making their way throughout the Deep South.[27] Although few enslaved people lived in Wheeling permanently, the community was deeply involved with slavery itself. Famously, Henry Ruffner, an antislavery critic from Kanawha County, argued that Wheeling's ties to slavery and Virginia's slave system held the city back from truly competing with free-labor Pittsburgh.[28]

Still, Wheeling became known as an industrial city, perched on the edge of the more agrarian South. Smog filled the air, as factories dotted the skyline. A glance through the occupations of many of the participants in these divorce suits reveals the increasing importance of manufacturing in this community—brick manufacturers, factory laborers, iron factory mechanics, and glass workers fill these pages. By 1860, two thousand of the town's fourteen thousand residents worked in a factory. On the eve of the Civil War, Wheeling was commonly known as "Nail City," because of its prominent iron manufacturing. The Wheeling Iron Works, for instance, made "nails and bar, boiler, sheet, and hoop iron."[29] The city was also home to a large milling industry, as well as a number of pulp and paper mills and eight glass plants.[30]

Wheeling boosters liked to brag that it was Virginia's second-largest city, if you counted only the white population, and it was far larger than any other city in "transmontane Virginia." In the Valley region of Virginia, Staunton and Winchester had about four thousand white residents, while in western Virginia, Martinsburg and Parkersburg had about twenty-five hundred. For a time, Wheeling elites thought the city might challenge Pittsburgh for regional prominence, but a lack of financial and political support from Richmond stymied their hopes. This frustration would fester until the outbreak of the Civil War.[31]

---

27. Dunaway, *African-American Family*, 10, 21–22, 117–19; Stealey, "Slavery and the Western Virginia Salt Industry," 51.

28. Conley and Doherty, *West Virginia History*, 231.

29. Howe, "Patient Laborers," 121–24; Fones-Wolf, "Caught between Revolutions"; Otis Rice, *West Virginia*, 81–84; Ambler and Summers, *West Virginia*, 486.

30. Conley and Doherty, *West Virginia History*, 183–84.

31. Williams, *West Virginia*, 50–51; Ambler, *Sectionalism in Virginia*, vii–viii, 150; Otis Rice, *West Virginia*, 95–96.

In the mid-nineteenth century, the Ohio River was a potent symbol of the growing divide between North and South. Runaway slaves made their way toward the Ohio River, knowing that crossing it meant entering free territory. Harriet Beecher Stowe made the frozen Ohio River a centerpiece of one of *Uncle Tom's Cabin*'s most harrowing scenes—Eliza's escape from Kentucky to Ohio with her young infant.[32] Yet, as the war approached, the river's boundary became blurry. The passage of the Fugitive Slave Act and the Supreme Court's ruling in *Dred Scott* meant that crossing the Ohio River was no guarantee of freedom. And as the country fractured politically, the region along the Ohio River struggled to define itself. Residents north of the river were no more likely to sympathize with abolitionists than those south of it. Many south of the river were reluctant to secede from the Union, facing off against fire-eaters farther south.[33] And yet, Wheeling residents were not abolitionists, either. Local papers routinely printed critiques of the antislavery movement, including promotions for the proslavery books published in response to *Uncle Tom's Cabin*.[34] Lying along the northern border of the South, Wheeling in many ways reflected its northern neighbors more than its southern counterparts, and yet residents still considered themselves southerners. Its hybrid identity is part of what makes the city so fascinating to historians. It was a city of free Blacks, enslaved people, and immigrants, of industry and agriculture, southern by geography and northern by nature. According to writer Rebecca Harding Davis, "We occupied the place of Hawthorne's unfortunate man who saw both sides."[35]

In the early months of 1861, it was by no means clear whether Virginia would secede. Its secession convention was dominated by conditional Unionists and steadfast Unionists, and debate raged in the state over its course of action.[36] The events at Fort Sumter in April, however, tipped the scales, and Virginia delegates voted to secede and join the Confederacy. Western Virginians fled the convention, descending on Wheeling with a new plan. There, they founded a breakaway government, the Restored State of Virginia, and began the process of creating a new state. West Virginia would officially become a state in 1863, with Wheeling as its first capital. West Virginia's creation reflected decades

---

32. Stowe, *Uncle Tom's Cabin*, 50–53.
33. Astor, *Rebels on the Border*, 3–8; Taylor, *Divided Family*, 3; Link, *Roots of Secession*; Ford, *Bonds of Union*, 252–55.
34. Henwood, "Slaveries 'in the Borders,'" 570–75.
35. Davis, *Bits of Gossip*, 109.
36. Link, *Roots of Secession*, 215–32.

of tension between eastern and western Virginia and an opportunity created by the Union's early occupation of the westernmost counties of Virginia.[37] Wheeling elites were among the leaders of the movement, seeing a chance to crystallize their power and accrue benefits to their industrial city.

As they formed the new state, legislators rewrote Virginia's laws, creating a new state constitution.[38] Legislators redesigned county administration and revised the tax system, but they also had an opportunity to review social differences between the two states. Slavery would be the first major debate. Even though the majority of delegates to the constitutional convention did not own slaves, the men proved reluctant to abandon the "peculiar institution." Most hoped that the state would be able to reenter the Union with its slaveholding status intact.[39] When one delegate proposed an emancipation clause, another delegate wrote, "I discovered on that occasion as I never had before, the mysterious and overpowering influence 'the peculiar institution' had on men otherwise sane and reliable. Why, when Mr. Battelle submitted his resolutions, a kind of tremor—a holy horror, was visible throughout the house."[40]

Still, the United States Congress was not about to allow a new slave state into the Union in the midst of the Civil War and so required the passage of the Willey Amendment before granting statehood. The Willey Amendment stated that the "children of slaves born within the limits of this State after the fourth day of July, eighteen hundred and sixty-three, shall be free." Enslaved people who were under ten at that time would become free at the age of twenty-one; enslaved people between ten and twenty-one would become free at the age of twenty-five. The amendment forbade the importation of new enslaved people. Abraham Lincoln declared that West Virginia had met the requirements for statehood and welcomed the thirty-fifth state into the Union on June 20, 1863. In the end, the Willey Amendment would not have freed a single enslaved person before 1867, and it said nothing about enslaved people over the age of twenty-five.[41] As with other southern states, slavery ended in West Virginia with the passage of the Thirteenth Amendment in 1865.

---

37. Williams, *West Virginia*, 75–76; Ambler and Summers, *West Virginia*, 326–33; Otis Rice, *West Virginia*, 116–23.
  38. Ambler and Summers, *West Virginia*, 372; Fredette, *Marriage on the Border*, 112.
  39. Williams, *West Virginia*, 54.
  40. Curry, *House Divided*, 91.
  41. Curry, *House Divided*, 129; Ambler and Summers, *West Virginia*, 386–99. Additionally, the counties that made up the new state of West Virginia were exempt from the Emancipa-

Legislators at the constitutional convention also wrestled with women's rights in the new state. During the antebellum era, a number of states had passed married women's property laws, protecting women's land and property from their husbands. While Mississippi was the first to do so, most of these laws passed in northern states, spurred on by a growing women's rights movement.[42] At the time of secession, Virginia had no such law. Some delegates to the West Virginia constitutional convention worried about this fact. Daniel Lamb, a lawyer from Ohio County, argued that property was "made common by transferring everything to the husband and leaving no right to the wife" and that "a wife ought to have some rights." Boldly he stated, "When the law assumes that a wife is nobody I take the liberty of saying that is not a fact." After much debate (and one failed vote), delegates passed a Married Women's Property Law modeled on New York's 1860 law. Delegates urged one another to seize the opportunity to change Virginia's code. One legislator argued that the legislature should pass laws for the protection of married women because "it has never been done, I think, in this State."[43]

While this convention debate about married women's legal rights became a surprisingly lively one, no record exists of the delegates' thoughts on divorce. And yet, West Virginians also modified Virginia's divorce law, easing some restrictions and paving the way for a bump in postwar divorces. At a time when divorce was a controversial and unpopular topic, West Virginians signaled a slightly greater willingness to consider marital separation than their eastern counterparts.

---

tion Proclamation, meaning that slavery still very much existed in the state at the time it joined the Union in the middle of the war.

42. For information on the fight over married women's property rights both before and after the Civil War, see Hoff, *Law, Gender, and Injustice*, 377; Warbasse, *Changing Legal Rights of Married Women*, 176; Lebsock, "Radical Reconstruction," 204; Stanley, *From Bondage to Contract*, xi–xiii, 10, 18, 197; Chused, "Married Women's Property Law"; Shammas, "Reassessing the Married Women's Property Acts." Mississippi passed the law to protect patriarchal property from the interference of fortune-hunting husbands, not to give southern women more rights. McCurry, *Masters of Small Worlds*, 60, 72, 89.

43. Ambler, Atwood, and Mathews, *Debates and Proceedings*, 2:52, 61, 63.

"You May Get a Divorce as Soon as You Please"

Divorce law in the English colonies reflected the religious divisions of the early settlers. While all the English settlements adopted the common law and its accompanying dim view of married women's rights, differences emerged in attitudes toward divorce. The Anglican Church, for instance, dominated the Chesapeake colonies, which inherited the church's resistance to divorce. Meanwhile, in New England, Calvinists, such as the Puritans, took a much more liberal view of divorce than their Anglican counterparts did. It seems ironic in many ways, but in the colonial era, if people found themselves in an unhappy, abusive, or unfaithful marriage, their best hope was to live in New England. While the Puritans certainly earned their reputation as morally rigid, they more readily accepted the necessity and possibility of divorce than Anglicans.[44]

This division dates back to the Protestant Reformation. Among his many critiques of Catholic doctrine, Martin Luther argued that marriage was not a sacrament.[45] He was insistent that marriage was still a religious institution—not only recommended but vital for good Christians. Marriage helped prevent sin, provided men with critical domestic help, and led to the birth of more congregants.[46] And yet, by taking away the sacramental status of marriage, Luther made divorce ever so slightly more acceptable. In Protestant eyes, marriage was a contract, and as with any contract, once one party violated its terms, it could be broken.[47]

The Church of England adhered to a more Catholic interpretation of marriage's sacramental status, despite the fact that England's Protestant conversion famously began with King Henry VIII's fervent desire to divorce his aging wife, Catherine, and marry his younger mistress, Anne Boleyn.[48] By the eighteenth century, English spouses who

---

44. Salmon, *Women and the Law of Property*, 12–13, 60. Studies of divorce in early New England include Cott, "Divorce and the Changing Status of Women"; Cott, "Eighteenth-Century Family and Social Life"; Cohn, "Connecticut's Divorce Mechanism."

45. Kolb, "Martin Luther," 136.

46. Luther, *Martin Luther's Table Talk*, 297–308.

47. For more on the contractual nature of marriage, see Cott, "Divorce and the Changing Status of Women," 588–60, 589; Mary Jones, *Historical Geography*, 17–18, 20; Stanley, *From Bondage to Contract*, xii–xiii, 18, 24, 175–77; Basch, *In the Eyes of the Law*, 71.

48. By the end of the sixteenth century, England was the only Protestant country that did not allow divorce. Stone, *Road to Divorce*, 141, 183–210, 301–19.

wanted to divorce had to petition Parliament for a special act granting their wish. Obtaining such a divorce was expensive, time consuming, and nearly impossible for anyone who was not a wealthy man. In the American colonies, places such as Virginia, North Carolina, and South Carolina followed suit, substituting their general assemblies for Parliament. While states such as Massachusetts, Connecticut, and Rhode Island also required couples to petition legislatures for their divorce, New England legislators were far more likely to grant these requests than those elsewhere. In fact, during the colonial era, Massachusetts had five times as many divorces as the entire country of England.[49]

As the American Revolution approached, many colonies pushed for divorce reform, despite resistance from England. In response to rising divorce rates in Pennsylvania, New Jersey, and New Hampshire, in 1773 the British government told royal governors to stop approving divorce acts passed by colonial legislatures. In declaring their political independence, many American revolutionaries saw their actions "as a familial separation, not merely one akin to a fractured paternal relationship but also a marital one."[50] With the founding of a new nation, many legislators also revised their divorce laws, expanding the requirements for divorce.[51]

Yet, while some legal reform occurred, the new United States largely retained English common law.[52] Legal statutes labeled husbands and wives "baron and feme," or lord and woman.[53] Most importantly, as in England, women in the early United States lost most of their legal rights upon marriage. The law considered married women "feme covert," which meant that their legal identity was subsumed to their husband's. In the early United States, a married woman could not sue or be sued in her own name, could not own property, and could not write

---

49. Mary Jones, *Historical Geography*, 18, 24, 175; Basch, *In the Eyes of the Law*, 71; Bardaglio, *Reconstructing the Household*, xii–xiv; Buckley, *Great Catastrophe of My Life*, 17; Cott, "Divorce and the Changing Status of Women," 589; Schweninger, *Families in Crisis*, 1–5; Norton, *Founding Mothers and Fathers*, 89; Cohn, "Connecticut's Divorce Mechanism," 36–40; Kerber, *Women of the Republic*, 160–63; Dayton, *Women before the Bar*; Riley, "Legislative Divorce in Virginia."

50. Basch, *Framing American Divorce*, 22; Fredette, "Breaking Vows," 104.

51. Meehan, "'Not Made Out of Levity,'" 441.

52. Kerber, *Women of the Republic*, xxi–xxiv, 8–15. For scholarship on the failures of the Revolution to improve women's status, see Wilson, "Illusion of Change"; Kann, *Republic of Men*; Zagarri, *Revolutionary Backlash*.

53. Reeve, *Law of Baron and Femme*, 1–226.

a will.⁵⁴ It goes without saying that women had no political rights, but the lack of legal rights for married women would be astonishing to most people today. Coverture, as this status was also known, dramatically shaped the role married women played both inside and outside the household. Without the legal ability to own or control property or even represent themselves in court, how could women take part in public life? The restrictions of coverture also influenced public attitudes toward divorce. Opponents of divorce argued that it would leave helpless women vulnerable and unprotected.⁵⁵ Society expected women to become wives and mothers, and in many places, that role was expected to be permanent.⁵⁶

When the women's rights movement began to take shape in the 1840s, supporters considered addressing married women's lack of legal rights as one of the movement's primary concerns. The Declaration of Sentiments, written by Elizabeth Cady Stanton and ratified at the 1848 Seneca Falls Convention, listed the "injuries and usurpations" that men had perpetuated against women, including that "he has made her, if married, in the eye of the law, civilly dead" and that "he has taken from her all right in property, even to the wages she earns." Stanton also wrote, "He has so framed the laws of divorce, as to what shall be the proper causes of divorce; in case of separation, to whom the guardianship of the children shall be given, as to be wholly regardless of the happiness of women—the law, in all cases, going upon the false supposition of the supremacy of man, and giving all power into his hands."⁵⁷ A few years later, she noted that women seemed more responsive to critiques of the marriage system than to those of the political system. "I feel as never before that this whole question of women's rights turns on the pivot of the marriage relation," she wrote to Susan B. Anthony.⁵⁸

Stanton was not the first—or the last—to tackle married women's rights. Nine years before the Seneca Falls Convention, Mississippi became the first state in the country to pass a married women's property law, protecting women's property from their husbands' control (and creditors). However, Mississippi legislators passed this law not to give married women more power or independence but rather to "chival-

---

54. Cott, *Public Vows*, 11–12; Basch, *In the Eyes of the Law*, 54–55.
55. Cott, *Public Vows*, 64–67.
56. Doyle, *Maternal Bodies*.
57. Lerner, "Meaning of Seneca Falls." See also Stanton, "Need of Liberal Divorce Laws," 242–43.
58. Quoted in Cott, *Public Vows*, 67.

rously" guard wealthy slaveholders' daughters from fortune-hunting men or dissipated husbands.[59] Written almost a decade later, the Declaration of Sentiments had very different goals in mind when it urged men to pass laws protecting women's ownership of property. In 1860, New York State would pass the first married women's property law to align more closely with the goals described in Stanton's declaration, including giving wives control over wages.[60]

Like changes in married women's property laws, divorce reform happened slowly but surely throughout the early United States. As new states joined the Union in the antebellum era, they expanded access to divorce for both residents and nonresidents. Divorce law was complex in the antebellum United States, and states differed in their approaches along both a North-South and a West-East axis. In an era when western states were quickly democratizing and expanding access (for white men) to the franchise, they also challenged hierarchies in the home by giving both men and women more access to legal separations. For example, by the mid-nineteenth century, Indiana was a known "divorce haven," and desperate spouses needed only move to the state for six months to obtain a divorce from a spouse back East. This option was especially popular with New Yorkers, whose strict divorce law granted a divorce only on the basis of adultery.[61] Kentucky was one of only three states in the antebellum era to allow for a divorce based on "mutual separation," a forerunner of today's "irreconcilable differences."[62] Reflective of their understanding of hierarchy and power, western states showed a greater acceptance of contractualism than their eastern counterparts.

Meanwhile, southerners, especially those living in the oldest southern states, remained obstinately opposed to divorce, unwilling to challenge the permanence of household relationships in any capacity. South Carolina, for instance, held the distinction of being the only

---

59. McCurry, *Masters of Small Worlds*, 60, 72, 89. For more on the history of married women's property laws in the United States, see Lebsock, *Free Women of Petersburg*, 57; Stanley, *From Bondage to Contract*, xi–xiii, 10, 18, 197; Chused, "Married Women's Property Law"; Shammas, "Re-assessing the Married Women's Property Acts"; Zeigler, "Uniformity and Conformity," 467; Basch, *In the Eyes of the Law*; Hoff, *Law, Gender, and Injustice*.

60. Basch, *In the Eyes of the Law*, 162–99.

61. Basch, *Framing American Divorce*, 9–10, 48–49; Goodheart, Hanks, and Johnson, "'Act for the Relief of Females'"; Censer, "'Smiling through Her Tears,'" 26; Schweninger, *Families in Crisis*, 6.

62. Fredette, *Marriage on the Border*, 65.

state to forbid divorce entirely in the antebellum era.[63] Like most things in southern life, southern resistance to divorce had a lot to do with slavery. If the marriage bond was impermanent and could be severed by those with less power than white male household heads, what other bonds could be broken? Divorce "represented a threat to power, control, and the slave system itself."[64] Ultimately, divorce laws reflected a variety of influences, including religion, legal culture, attitudes toward women's rights, resistance to social change, and understandings of traditionalism and contractualism.[65]

As the nineteenth century progressed, legislatures also expanded access to divorce by allowing petitioners to file in their local courts, instead of requiring them to petition the state legislature itself.[66] Virginia allowed judicial divorce beginning in 1849. As Laura Edwards has shown, local courts were more likely to be responsive to residents, to listen to voices outside the elite, and to take an expansive view of the law in order to maintain a community's sense of order and justice.[67] The cases in this book were among the first filed in circuit courts in the state of Virginia and serve as an interesting test of that notion. Western Virginians continually maintained that laws written by eastern Virginians did not adequately reflect their needs and desires. Residents of Ohio County received three-quarters of the divorces for which they petitioned in the ten years before the war. Their success had a lot to do with their manipulation of the divorce law and the seeming willingness of judges to accept that manipulation.[68] When legislators revised di-

---

63. Hartog, *Man and Wife in America*, 63–64; Basch, *Framing American Divorce*, 3.

64. Fredette, *Marriage on the Border*, 57; McCurry, *Masters of Small Worlds*, 86–91; Basch, *Framing American Divorce*, 24, 29, 48; Buckley, *Great Catastrophe of My Life*, 51. For studies on divorce in the South, see Censer, "'Smiling through Her Tears,'" 114–34; Schweninger, *Families in Crisis*; Chused, *Private Acts in Public Places*; Buckley, *Great Catastrophe of My Life*; Boswell, *Her Act and Deed*; Silkenat, *Moments of Despair*; Sachs, "Myth of the Abandoned Wife"; Bardaglio, *Reconstructing the Household*, 5.

65. "Contractualism" simply means that people saw marriage as "potentially impermanent—under the right circumstances." Fredette, *Marriage on the Border*, 6–7. See also Stanley, *From Bondage to Contract*, np, x, xii, 10, 33.

66. Historians debate the impact of this shift. Some say it gave petitioners easier access to divorce and made the process simpler, while others argue that the change had little meaning since the grounds for divorce did not change. Buckley, *Great Catastrophe of My Life*, 8–9; Basch, *Framing American Divorce*, 51, 57.

67. Edwards, *People and Their Peace*.

68. I have argued elsewhere that residents of Ohio County used an unusually high proportion of adultery charges, one of the few charges that would get them an absolute divorce under Virginia law. Fredette, *Marriage on the Border*, 67–73.

vorce statutes following statehood, they confirmed West Virginians' differing understandings of divorce.

Throughout the United States, the number of divorces rose in the years following the Civil War. With new Republican-led state governments during the Reconstruction era, even some southern states (including long-resistant South Carolina) liberalized their divorce laws.[69] Legal scholars have argued that the state needed good reason to interfere with the private sphere before the war. The war itself and federal Reconstruction increased the size and power of the federal government, and governments at federal, state, and local levels began to intervene more in household affairs.[70] Still, West Virginians had a different Reconstruction experience than other southern states. Without federal Reconstruction, they did not have the same pressures to adapt their laws. Additionally, much of the push for change came before the end of the war, rather than because of it. West Virginians' attitudes toward divorce had as much to do with their border world as with the impact of the war itself.

To obtain a divorce, unhappy spouses had to follow certain procedures. Although it was not a requirement, all of the people in this sample obtained a lawyer to represent them. These lawyers helped craft a bill of divorce, or the initial request for divorce. This document laid out who the couple was, when they married, who wanted the divorce, why that person wanted a divorce, what kind of divorce that person sought, and any other requests, such as alimony and custody.[71] The person who filed for divorce was the orator (the term used for a male) or oratrix (female) and sometimes the plaintiff. The spouse was the defendant. In the nineteenth century, few states allowed for "no-fault" divorce, which meant that one person had to have done something wrong for the couple to get a divorce.[72] Additionally, people filing for divorce then had to prove to the court that they had not condoned their spouse's behavior and that they had not committed any marital sins themselves.

---

69. Silkenat, *Moments of Despair*, 2, 75, 105–6. The two best article-length analyses of Reconstruction conventions and gender are Bynum, "Reshaping the Bonds of Womanhood," and Lebsock, "Radical Reconstruction."

70. Hartog, *Man and Wife in America*, 24; Bardaglio, *Reconstructing the Household*.

71. Grossberg, "Who Gets the Child?"; Zainaldin, "Emergence of a Modern American Family Law"; Wright, "*De Manneville v. De Manneville*."

72. Hartog, *Man and Wife in America*, 70–73.

In fact, in the nineteenth century, if both husband and wife had committed a marital fault (adultery, for instance), the court might rule that they deserved each other and could therefore not obtain a divorce. Similarly, in most places, couples had to show that they had not "colluded" in filing for a divorce. In other words, there could be no agreement by the couple to obtain a divorce.[73]

Divorce laws varied by state, and therefore, so did the charges couples used. In most states, people could get a divorce if their partner had committed adultery (and if they had not lived with their partner after discovering this). Other states allowed couples to divorce if one of them had abandoned the other for a set period of time (usually three to five years). Some states had statutes that granted divorces for cruelty or lewd and lascivious behavior, but those were often gendered. Wives charged their husbands with cruelty, and husbands charged their wives with behaving in a lewd or lascivious manner. In addition, the type of divorce a person could get depended on where that person lived. For example, in Kentucky in 1855, a person could get a divorce *a vinculo matrimonii*, or absolute divorce, if that person had been abandoned by the spouse for three or more years, but in Virginia in the same year, that would result in a divorce *a mensa et thoro*, or a divorce from bed and board. A divorce from bed and board resulted in a legal separation, economically dividing the couple and protecting their current and future property from one another but forbidding either partner from remarrying. For remarriage, a divorce *a vinculo matrimonii* was necessary. In most states, the requirements for an "absolute divorce" were much more stringent.[74]

Inevitably, state law shaped a bill of divorce. This is perhaps one of the most interesting and complex features of divorce suits. While all primary sources have bias, divorce cases are often deliberately misleading, if not full of outright lies. These are constructed narratives, intended "to persuade."[75] Historians perusing these documents have to ask themselves: what is truth and what is fiction? Nineteenth-century Americans who wanted a divorce had to satisfy certain legal requirements to get one, and they had to present a compelling story to judges who would often be resistant to allowing a divorce at all. And yet, even

---

73. Mary Jones, *Historical Geography*, 53; Hartog, *Man and Wife in America*, 70; Censer, "'Smiling through Her Tears'," 37; *Bailey v. Bailey*, 62 *Supreme Court of Virginia* 43 (1871).

74. Schweninger, *Families in Crisis*, 2–3; Chused, *Private Acts in Public Places*, 56–69; Hartog, *Man and Wife in America*, 35–36.

75. Buckley, *Great Catastrophe of My Life*, 6; Schweninger, *Families in Crisis*, 15–16; Carlson, *Crimes of Womanhood*, 1; Berry, *Pig Farmer's Daughter*.

if these petitions are wholly fiction, what can we learn from the specific fiction these litigants choose to tell? In this case, the lie can tell us as much as the truth.

Wheeling is a fascinating example. In the ten years before the war, residents charged their partners with adultery more frequently than did residents of neighboring southern states.[76] What does this mean? Were residents of Ohio County more likely to cheat on their spouses? Did something about the urban environment encourage or allow affairs? Or did the charge of adultery serve a more specific legal purpose? Before the war, Virginia law granted a divorce *a vinculo matrimonii* for only a few reasons—adultery, incurable impotency, and imprisonment.[77] Two of these could be proven only by a doctor's examination or documents from a state penitentiary. Therefore, if people wanted to make sure that they divorced their spouse and could remarry, few options were available.

Whatever the factors leading up to it, once the court received a bill of divorce, the case began. First, the court issued a summons for the offending spouse. All the circuit courts in the state of Virginia used the same form (see illustration 3). An officer of the court or a local sheriff usually delivered the summons and required defendants to sign it, stating they had accepted it.[78] As historians, we must consider what it meant that some people signed these summonses but never appeared in court to respond to the often damning and salacious accusations levied against them. Interestingly, while other counties in Virginia threatened to charge nonrespondents with a one-hundred-dollar fine if they did not appear or answer the charges by a certain date, no such provision exists in the Ohio County summons records. Perhaps because of that, very few defendants in Ohio County chose to file a formal answer, even when charged with adultery. Their reasoning may have been simple— they were long gone—or it may have been that they were more legally savvy. Uncontested (and unanswered) petitions met with a higher rate of success in the courts.[79]

If defendants could not be found, the sheriff or another person testified that they were no longer "in this bailiwick," or jurisdiction. In

---

76. Fredette, *Marriage on the Border*, 67–73.
77. *Code of Virginia* (1849), title 31, chap. cix.
78. In each case in this book, I noted whether the summons was successfully delivered.
79. Angela Boswell found that in Texas, adultery cases were the most contested. Boswell, *Her Act and Deed*, 76; Silkenat, *Moments of Despair*, 79–80.

Image of three unidentified young women, ca. 1860s; West Virginia and Regional History Center.

other words, they had left the state. In these cases, plaintiffs had to advertise their divorce suit in a local paper for at least four weeks. At the end of that period, the plaintiff took depositions from witnesses. Each case had to have at least two witnesses, but there were no requirements beyond that. Sometimes plaintiffs served as their own witness, often repeating the facts already in evidence from the bill itself. Other times the plaintiffs' witnesses were members of their own family—mothers, fathers, siblings, and children all make an appearance in these pages. Most often, the witnesses were neighbors and friends, who had seen so much in a community where privacy was minimal.

After the depositions, the court made its ruling. If the court granted the divorce, it might follow up with property divisions, custody settlements, or alimony requirements. It might also stipulate that a woman could return to using her unmarried name or that one partner could not remarry. Rarely did courts rule outright against petitioners. Rather the court merely dropped cases from the docket or dismissed them with no clear statement about who was making the decision to dismiss: the court itself, the plaintiff, or the couple. More often than not, in Ohio County, unhappy spouses who sued for divorce got their wish. Given that most Americans opposed divorce in this era, why did 70 percent of Ohio County residents who petitioned for divorce get their desired separation? This question requires us to explore the complex relationship between law, society, and region. By providing an extensive sample of cases for one community, as well as the state statutes, this book helps scholars continue that study.

Simply put, divorce was anything but common in the nineteenth century. Indeed, it was considered shameful and avoidable, and most unhappy couples, unwilling to air their most private troubles to perfect strangers, never found themselves in a courtroom. And yet, as the nineteenth century wore on, the divorce rate in the United States slowly crept up. A variety of factors led to this change. Throughout the late eighteenth and early nineteenth centuries, companionate marriage became the norm. Marriage, once more likely to be an economic arrangement, now became a bond of love between two suitably matched partners. As society placed more emphasis on marrying for love, divorce rates rose. If love was the bedrock of a successful marriage, divorce was a more logical option when that love faded.[80] Social transformations such as the Industrial Revolution, the women's rights movement, the spread of slavery, and the rise of abolitionism all shaped changing understandings of family roles.[81] Divorce rates also rose because of changes in state laws, as well as the disruptions brought on by a devastating civil war. Attitudes about the role of the court in regulating family life also shifted, as many courts no longer regarded the home as a solely private space, beyond their power or control.[82]

The divorce suits in this book provide a critical snapshot of this slow social change, tracking one community's divorces over the twenty-year

---

80. Coontz, *Marriage*.

81. For a description of the development of marriage see Cott, *Public Vows*, 56–76; for an article on the correlation between companionate marriage, divorce, and manhood see Griswold, "Divorce and the Legal Redefinition."

82. Michael Grossberg argues that these innovations challenged power relations within the household, decreased "paternal authority," and increased the state's involvement in family life—creating a new judicial patriarchy. See Grossberg, *Governing the Hearth*, ix, xi–xii, 7–9.

period before, during, and after the Civil War. Ohio County's border position makes it an excellent place to study this shift. This community, living between so many contested regional divides, absorbed both northern and southern attitudes toward marriage. Therefore its divorce laws and practices differed from those of other southern states, often progressing more quickly toward a more modern approach. Analyzing divorce in Ohio County also gives historians a unique opportunity to study the impact of state law, since the county was part of two states during those twenty years. Finally, Ohio County, although less directly affected by war than other southern places, still allows historians to determine the impact of this disruptive event on marriages, households, and understandings of divorce.

Following the war, Jacob Stroble showed little hesitation in filing for divorce, a mere month after returning home to his wife. His friends and neighbors, now deponents in the divorce case, sided with him and urged the court to grant his request. Repeatedly, they insulted Ellen, calling her a prostitute and a lewd woman.[83] For communities such as Wheeling, divorce was a desirable and necessary way to free men (and women) from relationships with those whose behavior the community deemed immoral. Of course, couples in Wheeling may have manipulated the law, charging adultery more often than elsewhere in order to obtain a desired divorce. In the Strobles' case, both Jacob and Ellen quickly remarried. Jacob married Caroline Seabright within a year of his divorce, going on to have five children with her. Ellen married John Hunter, the man with whom she had spent the war. The Strobles' divorce must be understood as a moment when divorce was in flux—still frowned on by many but increasingly sought by others, less available than in the no-fault twentieth century but more possible than in the era of petitioning colonial legislatures.

"Like a Lady"

When Jacob Stroble filed for divorce from his wife, Ellen, he assumed the court would agree with him that a good wife would not have a sexual relationship with another man. At their core, divorce cases, and the laws that frame them, reveal much about gendered expectations

---

83. *Stroble, Jacob v. Stroble, Ellen.*

for husbands and wives. Should husbands support their families financially? Should wives and husbands be faithful to their partners? How important is it that a husband or wife be able to have children? Should wives be obedient and submissive to their husbands? Is it a husband's role to punish his wife? These questions are at the heart of these cases and can help historians learn about how different communities expected men and women to behave at specific points in history.

By the antebellum era, the ideology of separate spheres dominated the American household. According to this philosophy, the public sphere (the place of business and politics) was the natural world of men, and the private sphere (the home) the domain of women. Women, seen as natural caregivers and nurturers, were biologically and divinely intended for a life in the domestic realm.[84] This belief influenced the educational system, household roles, and legal and political rights for men and women. Even women who pushed for more rights often did so by deploying the language of domesticity and the private sphere.[85] The ideology of separate spheres also erased the productive labor that women still did both inside and outside the household. Women's household work, such as child-rearing, homemaking, and sewing, was seen as an extension of their natural domesticity, rather than an important economic contribution to the family. Similarly, the hegemony of the separate spheres ideal ignored the reality that many women still worked outside the household, whether because of financial necessity or desire.[86] In the middle of this contradiction, working women lost respect, wages, and recognition. Work was unfeminine, and therefore women who worked were less womanly than those who did not. In places such as Wheeling, these ideas clashed in fascinating ways. Certainly, as these divorce cases reveal, many residents of Ohio County saw women as best suited to the home, with men as their expected providers. On the other hand, in a community with a large number of working-class women, petitioners challenged the courts to recognize and reward women *as labor-*

---

84. Welter, "Cult of True Womanhood"; Smith-Rosenberg, "Female World of Love and Ritual"; Kerber, "Separate Spheres, Female Worlds"; Cott, *Bonds of Womanhood*, 63–65; Ryan, *Cradle of the Middle Class*; Sklar, *Catherine Beecher*.

85. For an example in reform, see Ginzberg, *Women and the Work of Benevolence*. For works on education and domesticity, see Kelley, *Learning to Stand and Speak*; Kerber, *Women of the Republic*; Farnham, *Education of the Southern Belle*.

86. Barton, "'Good Cooks and Washers,'" 448; Strasser, *Never Done*, 182–90; Boydston, *Home and Work*, 144.

ers, who often provided more for their families than their male counterparts did.[87]

In the nineteenth century society expected women to remain in the home, cultivating a "haven in a heartless world" for their hard-working husbands.[88] While failing to create an adequate domestic sphere was not grounds for divorce anywhere in the United States, accusations to that effect commonly found their way into divorce suits. Husbands who charged their wives with abandonment usually made sure to portray them as failed wives even before they left, suggesting that they did not make meals for their husbands or properly care for their homes. Others defended themselves against accusations of cruelty or adultery by suggesting that their wives had not upheld their end of the marital obligations. Many judges saw it as their duty to uphold social values, and these narratives allowed judges, resistant to divorce, to rationalize breaking up a marriage as a defense of "family values." Divorce records allow historians to see the extent to which men and women accepted, rejected, or reinforced the standard of separate spheres in the household—and in the courtroom.

The ideology of separate spheres also saddled men with certain gendered expectations, and divorce cases frequently reveal the ways in which society expected men to be adequate providers and firm but gentle patriarchs. In some places, courts granted divorces to women whose husbands failed to provide for the household or had forced their wives to work.[89] On the other hand, some historians have argued that the boundaries of these "separate spheres" were more fluid than previously thought. For example, scholars of Victorian masculinity see male domesticity as a pivotal element of the newly ascendant companionate marriage.[90] Whereas previously courts forgave men accused of domestic violence, arguing it was their prerogative and duty as heads of household to discipline and "correct" their dependents, now courts (and communities) began to punish husbands who used violence or even forms of psychological abuse against their wives. The Victorian husband still ruled the roost, but he did so through love, rather than fear. Debates over spousal abuse took on an additional meaning in the slave South,

---

87. Howe, "Patient Laborers," 131.
88. Lasch, "Family as a Haven."
89. Boswell, *Her Act and Deed*, 51–52.
90. Tosh, *Man's Place*, 1–4, 39, 56–57; Rotundo, *American Manhood*; Johansen, *Family Men*.

a place where household violence was the norm.⁹¹ Reading the depositions and characterization of local witnesses regarding domestic violence in Ohio County sheds light on western Virginians' regional identity as they sought to define themselves separately from Virginia.

Divorce law in the nineteenth-century United States also reflected assumptions about sexuality and femininity. Before 1860, Virginia allowed divorce only for adultery, abandonment, and imprisonment, all gender neutral, but after the legislature updated the laws in 1860, a husband could also obtain an absolute divorce if he could prove that his wife was pregnant by another man at the time of their marriage or had been "notoriously a prostitute." In Kentucky, the law stated that either a husband or wife could have a divorce for adultery, abandonment, separation, imprisonment, "concealment of a loathsome disease," or fraud, but only a wife could obtain a divorce for intemperance and neglect or cruelty. Interestingly, West Virginia's first divorce laws stated that either a husband *or* a wife could get a divorce if their partner had been "licentious" before their marriage.⁹²

Nevertheless, society viewed middle- and upper-class white women in the nineteenth century as inherently "chaste" or "purer" than men. While medieval Europeans had considered women the more sexual gender, likely to be tempted to sin the way that Eve had been tempted in the Garden of Eden, in the Victorian era, middle-class Americans saw women as "passionless."⁹³ Women who failed to meet this grand expectation were castigated and vulnerable. Divorce law, as with much law in the nineteenth-century United States, punished and controlled female sexuality while ignoring male sexual behavior. Certainly women charged their husband with adultery and, in places like Wheeling, could even be successful in their suits, but husbands who accused their wives of adultery were more likely to succeed. Wives had a higher burden of proof as well.⁹⁴ In some parts of the United States, husbands could divorce their wives for supposed flirtations, while women often

---

91. Wyatt-Brown, *Southern Honor*, 281. Wyatt-Brown argues that the "general level of violence" in the South could have led to a greater rate of domestic violence. See also Schweninger, *Families in Crisis*, 51–52; Bardaglio, *Reconstructing the Household*, 34; Edwards, "Law, Domestic Violence"; Sager, *Marital Cruelty in Antebellum America*.

92. *Code of Virginia* (1860), chap. 109, sec. 6; *Revised Statutes of Kentucky*, vol. 2, chap. 47, art. iii, sec. I; *Code of West Virginia* (1870), chap. 64, sec. 5.

93. Cott, "Passionlessness."

94. D'Emilio and Freedman, *Intimate Matters*, 95–96; Clinton, *Plantation Mistress*, 206–7.

had to prove that their husband had carried on an active affair for a lengthy period of time.

Additionally, class and race shaped the experiences of married women in the courtroom. Working-class white women and Black women were viewed as more "sexual" than their middle-class white counterparts, and this supposed sexuality defined them as less feminine than other women.[95] In Wheeling, women of a variety of classes and races fought to claim the benefits of mainstream femininity, even as their husbands or society tried to deny it to them. Other women, though, shunned traditional values, instead behaving boldly and proudly in a way that defied expectations.[96] In some ways, this may have upheld racist, classist, and nativist assumptions about them, but in other ways, it shows a commendable ability to defy social norms and live their best lives.

Stereotypes about the sexuality and behavior of working-class women may also have shaped their access to divorce in ironic ways. For the most part, nineteenth-century working-class women and women of color faced a legal system stacked against them, in which the courts invalidated and silenced their voices and their stories.[97] However, negative assumptions about their relationships may actually have allowed them greater access to divorce than middle-class white women had. Whereas judges were reluctant to end middle-class marriages for moral reasons, they may not have seen the marriages of working-class women and women of color as worth defending. In other words, the divorce of a freed Black couple in Wheeling only validated the racist assumptions that elite white judges made about the people of color in their courtrooms. For example, after the Civil War, Virginia judges firmly opposed divorce and worked to maintain marriages as a defense against social changes such as emancipation. Yet, in Amelia County, when half a dozen Black couples stood before the court and asked for divorces, the court readily granted them.[98] The cases in this book, featuring a surprisingly large sample of working-class women (although fewer women of color), allow historians to ask how class and race shaped assumptions about gender, marriage, and sexuality.

Americans from every region subscribed to the ideology of separate

---

95. White, *Ar'n't I a Woman?*, 27–46.
96. Hunter, *Bound in Wedlock*, 110–11; Fredette, *Marriage on the Border*, 176–92.
97. Block, "Lines of Color, Sex, and Service." See also Perrone, "'Back into the Days of Slavery.'"
98. Fredette, *Marriage on the Border*, 170–74.

spheres, but women's and men's lives differed in the North and South, nonetheless. The literal distinction between home and work meant far less in a society that was as agrarian as the South. Plantations, for instance, functioned as both home and workplace for dozens of people, including the plantation master and mistress.[99] Additionally, one prominent group of people in the South could not follow the ideology of separate spheres, even if they desired. Brutal conditions on plantations often prevented enslaved people from maintaining permanent households and claiming the rights and responsibilities of husbands, wives, mothers, and fathers.[100]

Similarly, historians of divorce have noted differences in how southern couples defended their behavior in marriage from how couples in other parts of the country did. For example, in his book on divorce in California during the mid-nineteenth century, Robert Griswold argues that petitioners rarely seemed to demand obedience from their wives. He writes, "What emerges from the divorce evidence is not a picture of submissive women at the beck and call of their husbands but rather one in line with the assumptions of domesticity and the companionate ideal."[101] On the other hand, white southern men often firmly defended their right to chastise all household dependents and demand obedience from them. In his 1852 court case, one Virginia man wrote that he hoped "the laws of his country will not be made the engine of his oppression or the means of encouraging . . . the disobedience of his wife." Peter Bardaglio has argued that antebellum southern divorce cases actually increased patriarchal power in the household, as well as women's dependence on their husbands.[102]

Whereas northerners emphasized the rule of mutuality, if not equality, in their marriages, white southerners remained proudly patriarchal. Marriage was not a contract between mutually consenting parties but an arrangement in which men swore to protect and provide for the fam-

---

99. Cott, *Bonds of Womanhood*, 6–9; Fox-Genovese, *Within the Plantation Household*, 61–66; Edwards, *Scarlett Doesn't Live Here Anymore*, 165–66. See Barton, "'Good Cooks and Washers,'" for a discussion about how these views differed for yeoman farmwives.

100. White, *Ar'n't I a Woman?*, 146–56; Hunter, *Bound in Wedlock*, 294–95; Jacqueline Jones, *Labor of Love, Labor of Sorrow*, 29–43.

101. Griswold, *Family and Divorce in California*, 49–50.

102. *Jackson, Elizabeth B. v. Jackson, John F.* (1852), Fauquier County Circuit Court Records, Library of Virginia, no. 1852-002; Bardaglio, *Reconstructing the Household*, 34–35. More recently, however, some historians have challenged this view and pointed out the ways in which marital violence was common throughout the country. Sager, *Marital Cruelty in Antebellum America*.

ilies, while women promised to honor and obey their husbands. But what did it mean for a wife to obey her husband? What power did he have to chastise her for failing to obey him? What was the line between maintaining his power as a patriarch and sheer cruelty? Divorce cases in the mid-nineteenth-century United States reflected these debates. Friends, family, and neighbors testified about marital cruelty, revealing as they did so their beliefs about the proper power dynamics between husbands and wives. By the mid-nineteenth century, feminist women had begun to question patriarchy itself and pointed to the ways that tyrannical men brutalized their wives.[103] Although not every person who testified against an abusive husband intended to dismantle the patriarchy, they did reveal cracks in its façade as the nineteenth century moved toward a more progressive twentieth century. Analyzing divorce cases allows historians to see changing attitudes toward marital violence, the role of the state in stopping such violence, assumptions about male power and privilege, and the community's role in protecting women.

Nineteenth-century Americans lived in a world where men and women faced strict behavioral expectations and stiff opposition if they defied them. Gendered assumptions are deeply internalized and therefore difficult to study. It is deeply ironic that one of the best sources to uncover these private beliefs and assumptions is so seemingly public, but it speaks to the fact that these beliefs operated at both an individual and a societal level. Divorce suits reveal the gendered values of communities in different parts of the United States during this era, and we must read them with this in mind.

"He Enlisted as a Private Soldier"

Not surprisingly, western Virginians' loyalties were divided at the outset of the Civil War. Debate still rages over the number of West Virginians who served on either side of the conflict. Recent studies suggest that about twenty thousand West Virginians served in the Union forces and twenty thousand in Confederate forces.[104] In the northern-

---

103. Edwards, "Law, Domestic Violence"; Nadelhaft, "'Public Gaze and the Prying Eye'"; Sager, *Marital Cruelty in Antebellum America*.

104. Earlier historians estimated that anywhere from twenty-eight to thirty-six thousand West Virginians served in the Union forces, while only about seven to twelve thousand

most part of the state, Wheeling did not experience the war directly, although the city sent two companies to war—one to the Union military, one to the Confederate.[105]

During the war, the number of divorce cases declined; however, the close of the war saw a spike in divorce cases in Wheeling. The reasons for the increase are both universal (reflecting war's continued ability to disrupt household life and create turmoil in marriages) and specific (reflecting the creation of the new state, the writing of new laws, and the tumultuous postwar atmosphere during Reconstruction and emancipation). With the passage of a new divorce law, as well as new judges taking positions in circuit courts, West Virginians had more opportunity to divorce than before the war. Notably, the divorce rate in Ohio County rose 284 percent following the end of the war. However, while the war and its accompanying disruptions and displacements certainly played a role in the rising divorce rate, it cannot solely explain this dramatic increase. In West Virginia, the war's impact was always complicated by the state's dramatic midwar creation and its complicated ties to northern, midwestern, and southern states, including the former "eastern Virginia."

Throughout the South, the Civil War brought sweeping change, although it affected certain regions differently from others. Hundreds of thousands were dead, millions were freed from bondage, and the land lay in ruins. But on a smaller, more intimate level, it also reshaped homes and the relationships of those within them. At the most striking level, the emancipation of four million formerly enslaved people challenged the entire established hierarchy and structure of southern households. Additionally, in many places, the divorce rate rose alongside the war's end and emancipation. It was no coincidence. The end of one hierarchical relationship called into question others.[106]

During the Civil War, southern men left for battle by the thousands, leaving behind women and children to care for farms and plantations. Historians differ on the impact this absence had on white women's gender roles after the war. Some argue that the change emboldened white women. With their husbands gone, white women took on new respon-

---

served in the Confederate military. Otis Rice, *West Virginia*, 124–25; Curry, *House Divided*, 167–68; Snell, *West Virginia and the Civil War*, 28.

105. Otis Rice, *West Virginia*, 123–26.

106. Bardaglio, *Reconstructing the Household*, xi–xv; McCurry, *Masters of Small Worlds*, 219–24.

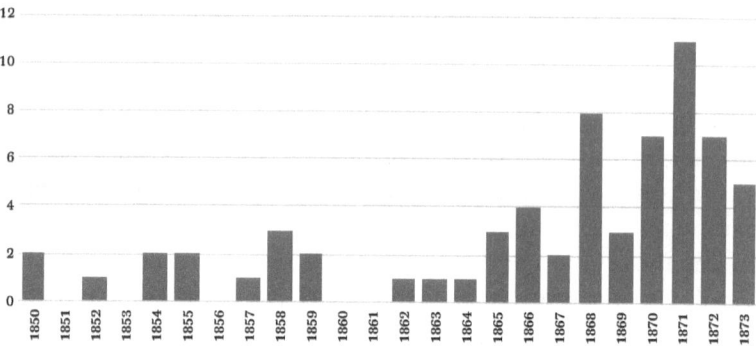

Number of Divorce Petitions in Ohio County.

sibilities and tasks. Additionally, they grew frustrated at the Confederacy, for taking away their husband's protection, and at their husbands themselves. As women did so, they challenged the traditional southern marital bargain. If husbands no longer could protect and provide for their wives, did their wives still owe them obedience? At the same time, the loss of so many young southern men created a marital crisis of its own after the Civil War. No longer could white southern women expect that marriage would bring them support and comfort. Increasingly, in the postbellum period, some white southern women made their way into professions such as teaching and nursing to support themselves without a husband.[107]

Other historians have argued that the loss of the war and Black emancipation was a devastating blow to white southern masculinity. Antebellum white southern men had built their identities as "masters of small worlds," charged with protection and control of dependents in their household, both Black and white. With Black emancipation and the demoralizing loss of the war, white southern men questioned whether they remained the masters they once were. As their enslaved people left or challenged their authority, white men had only one group of dependents left to reaffirm their manhood—white women. White women glorified white southern masculinity and their wartime sacrifices with new women's groups and the creation of Confederate monuments, thereby reaffirming their commitment to the antebellum patriarchal household

---

107. Scott, *Southern Lady*, 106–7, 118–19, 129–33; Massey, *Bonnet Brigades*; Censer, *Reconstruction of White Southern Womanhood*; Morsman, *Big House after Slavery*, 4–8.

arrangement.[108] In this world, women's rights, education, and even the ability to more easily divorce their husbands were a grave threat to masculine authority. In Virginia, for instance, the Supreme Court made clear its hesitation to grant divorces, especially to women, in the years following the war. In an opinion rejecting Georgiana Bailey's divorce from her husband, James, Judge Joseph Christian wrote:

> Amid the whelming tide of social and political revolutions which threaten to sweep away all the forms of our cherished southern civilization, one pillar at least of the social fabric may still stand firm, and that the time may never come when the sacred bond of matrimony can be lightly broken, or the holy duties and high obligations it imposes, can be disregarded with impunity; but that marriage may be in the future, as it has been in the past, be ever recognized in Virginia as an institution to be cherished by law and sanctified by religion, as one upon which alone the happiness and purity of social and domestic life must ever depend.[109]

Yet, while white Virginians fought against divorce in the postwar period, other southern states slowly liberalized their laws. North Carolina, for instance, during the early Reconstruction years, passed a new divorce law to allow for easier separations.[110] West Virginia was part of this group. As with many things, it is difficult to determine if West Virginia's divorce law resulted from the opportunities of Reconstruction in the South or if it reflected the separation between the two Virginias instead. Certainly, Wheeling's story does not fit neatly into this Reconstruction narrative anyway, since the state was never actually a part of federal Reconstruction.

Whether because the law changed or their relationships did, in many southern states, more people filed for divorce after the war than they did before. Especially in the first one to three years after the war, a number of people came before the courts to reveal the ways in which the war had destroyed their marriages. Some had married quickly before they went off to war, only to come home and find their partner no longer loved them or had found another lover in their absence. In the

---

108. Faust, *Mothers of Invention*, 250–54; Rable, *Civil Wars*; Whites, *Civil War as a Crisis*, 2–5; Edwards, *Gendered Strife and Confusion*, 27–30; Cox, *Dixie's Daughters*; Janney, *Burying the Dead*.
109. *Bailey v. Bailey*, 62 Supreme Court of Virginia 43 (1871).
110. Bynum, "Reshaping the Bonds of Womanhood."

Second Wheeling Convention, Wheeling, Va., June 1861;
West Virginia and Regional History Center.

working-class neighborhoods of Wheeling, women struggled to survive without the financial assistance of their husbands. Rosanna Long, for example, lived with James Hays while her husband fought for the Union. As proof of Rosanna's affair, her husband, Lewis, pointed out that "she is obtaining groceries on the credit of the said James L. Hays and that said James L. Hays pays the rent to the house in which she now lives."[111] Sometimes men took advantage of the war to abandon or neglect their wives, either fleeing into the military or joining the military with the intention of deserting both the war and their wives. Xavier Keefer enlisted with the Twenty-eighth Ohio Regiment but told a friend that as soon as he got paid "I will run off from the company and go to Switzerland." Elizabeth Goudy had to write to the governor to force her husband to send his paychecks to her.[112] War could also strain marriages. In an era with no knowledge of post-traumatic stress disorder, men returning from war could struggle to readjust to civilian life. Historians can look to divorce cases, and postwar spikes in domestic violence, to try to understand the intimate impact of this hidden crisis.[113]

Sometimes the war just provided married people an opportunity to stray, whether it was a wife left at home while her husband was at war or a husband who met a new lover while serving his country. The end of the Civil War also created tremendous strain and turmoil. White southerners had to contend with a dramatic change in the social order, one that threatened the white male patriarchy over the household. Soldiers returned home; freedpeople tried to unite their families and left plantations; northerners moved south to rebuild the region. It was a time of change, and this trickled down into family relationships. The postbellum divorce suits in this book reflect the impact of the Civil War on marriages and households in one southern city.

At the war's end, residents of Wheeling and the surrounding Ohio County found themselves in a different position, in many ways, from the one they held at the start of the war. Early in the conflict, the city had been a part of Virginia, both proud of its links to this storied "Old Dominion" and increasingly frustrated with the pattern of neglect it

---

111. *Long, Lewis v. Long, Rosanna* (1866), Records of the Circuit Court of Ohio County, WVRHC, env. 264 b-3 and 267 b-5.

112. *Goudy, Elizabeth O. by her next friend Milleger, James (her father) v. Goudy, James M.* (1868), Records of the Circuit Court of Ohio County, WVRHC, env. 274 e-9.

113. Recent books on the impact of the war on white southern men include Broomall, *Private Confederacies*; Carroll, *Invisible Wounds*.

perceived from eastern Virginians. Now, Wheeling was the capital of a new state, West Virginia, and could carve out its own postwar path. Because it was a Union state, the end of the war came as less of a blow to West Virginians than it did to Virginians, who had to adjust to their recent loss and, eventually, occupation by federal troops during Congressional Reconstruction. Emancipation in West Virginia, as in other border states, would proceed without the same level of federal intervention.

In February 1865, West Virginia Unionists proposed a "test oath" that would allow any voter to challenge another to prove that he had not "borne arms against the United States, against the Reorganized Government of Virginia, or against West Virginia." A year later, the state passed a constitutional amendment that took away the right to vote for former Confederates. This meant that in the years immediately following the war, former Confederate soldiers could not hold public office, vote, practice law, serve as a juror, teach school, or sue in court. Still, just as so-called redeemers swept into power by the early 1870s in other southern states, so too did former West Virginia Confederates regain authority. By 1871, the state legislature removed all the legal and political restrictions on former Confederates. By 1872, voters called a new constitutional convention, reshaping the wartime constitution to mirror more closely those of other southern states.[114]

With former Confederates gaining power in the state, the state capital shifted back and forth from Wheeling to Charleston (in southern West Virginia) during the decades after the war, before moving permanently to Charleston in 1885.[115] By the late 1860s and 1870s, the era of the last third of this book, Wheeling residents probably felt some of the same frustrations they had in the antebellum era. While antebellum Ohio County residents had to compete with eastern Virginia and Pittsburgh, postwar residents worked to prove that their city, rather than Charleston, could be the economic and political center of the new state.

With its political status uncertain, most city boosters chose to focus on the industrial importance of the community. During the two de-

---

114. Conley and Doherty, *West Virginia History*, 294–98.
115. Williams, *West Virginia*, 109–10. During this time, Wheeling was called "the capital on wheels." Ultimately, the legislature put the capital's location to a vote and gave the voters three choices—none of which was Wheeling. Ambler and Summers, *West Virginia*, 441; Conley and Doherty, *West Virginia History*, 295–97.

cades after the Civil War, Wheeling became a prototypical New South city, tapped into northern and southern industrial networks. During this era, almost two-fifths of the value of West Virginia's entire annual product came from Ohio County.[116] This period also reflected a respite for capital, before the city became the site of numerous strikes and labor organizations in the 1880s and 1890s.[117] Wheeling's divorce cases in this era give historians a glimpse into the rapidly changing and industrializing sections of the postwar South.

Life in the Urban South

In December 1845, John Michael Wehner and Mary Jane Chapman were married in Wheeling's Catholic church. After a year, the couple welcomed their first child—a daughter. Life was busy. John Michael Wehner, known as Michael in the community, ran a local tavern, and Mary Jane spent her time caring for their infant daughter. In the winter of 1847–48, Michael became sick and was confined to his bed for almost nine weeks. Mary Jane, whom he expected to nurse him through his illness, was strangely absent. He felt abandoned "in his lonely sick chamber." He could think of no reason for her estrangement and odd behavior. By September 1848, it was Mary Jane's turn to take to her room—this time preparing to give birth. She soon welcomed another child—a boy. But Michael did not share in her joy. According to his 1849 divorce petition, he was "heartsick and astonished" to learn that his wife "was delivered of a mulato child." He remembered that during his illness, he had employed a local free Black man named Jefferson at the tavern, and he accused Mary Jane of adultery with "said negro Jefferson, or with some other negro."[118] Within months, he and Mary Jane were divorced, and Mary Jane fled to Pennsylvania to raise her son.

The Wehners' story reflects the fluid, multiracial, multiethnic, busy, and intimate nature of the urban South. By 1860, Wheeling, Virginia, was one of the largest cities in the South, with almost fifteen thousand residents. A quarter of its population was foreign born, and a small

---

116. Ambler and Summers, *West Virginia*, 455.
117. Fetherling, *Wheeling*, 53–57; Otis Rice, *West Virginia*, 220–21.
118. *Wehner, John Michael v. Wehner, Mary Jane* (1850), Records of the Circuit Court of Ohio County, WVRHC, env. 186 c-9.

but significant minority of free Black residents lived there as well.[119] As the Wehners' story reveals, these free Black people interacted on a surprisingly intimate level with their white neighbors, were employed in homes and businesses in the city, and made multiple appearances in the divorce records of the county.[120] The Wehners' divorce reveals the possibilities for interracial relationships in the urban South, but it also gives us a broader picture of life in southern cities in this era. When most people think of the antebellum South, they picture plantations and farms—the rural South. True, this was the dominant South, both economically and geographically. However, this was not the only South. In the antebellum era, a number of southern cities grew in size and prominence. Cities such as Richmond, Savannah, and New Orleans became centers of industry and the growing interstate slave trade and a critical link between the agricultural parts of the South and national and international markets.[121]

As nineteenth-century southern cities boomed, they helped create "an increasing diversity in the occupational structure of the antebellum South."[122] Residents of Wheeling reflected this shift. Divorcing men and women and their deponents made a living as tavern keepers, rivermen, engineers, firemen, mechanics, brewers, dockhands, factory workers, carpenters, and merchants selling boots, shoes, tobacco, and other goods. Even the superintendent of the marvelous Wheeling Suspension Bridge made his way into these papers after running away with his mistress and failing to show up for a shift at the bridge.[123] In fact, in these cases, farmers form a distinct and almost undetectable minority.

Even more importantly, studying the urban South reveals the existence of wage-earning women in this region. This would certainly not have been something white southerners would have cheered. The ideology of the elite white southerner revolved around glorifying the region's particular brand of femininity. White southern women did not work; work was for enslaved women. The identity of enslaved women was bound up in their supposed capacity for labor, and the identity of

---

119. United States Federal Census for 1860. Only ninety-seven free Black people lived in Wheeling and 126 in Ohio County. The county had an enslaved population of one hundred people. United States Federal Census for 1860.

120. See also *Brareton v. Brareton* (1862) (chapter 6); *Green v. Green* (1870)(chapter 7).

121. Towers, *Urban South and the Coming of the Civil War*.

122. Delfino, Gillespie, and Kyriakoudes, "Editors' Introduction," 14.

123. *Scatterday, Emeline B. v. Scatterday, Pulaski* (1867), Records of the Circuit Court of Ohio County, WVRHC, env. 273 b-2.

white women defined by its opposition to this stereotype.[124] As abolitionists mounted increasingly pointed attacks on slavery in the nineteenth century, white southerners argued that slavery helped white women. White northern women, they argued, were forced to labor in factories or worse. In the South, white women were shielded from this. In the North, white women had begun to agitate for equality in a very unladylike way, some even speaking to large gatherings of women *and* men. White southern women had no need for such reforms because they were happy with their place.

Like most proslavery rhetoric, this belief was either willfully ignorant or an outright lie. Of course white southern women worked. Yeoman farmers' wives labored in the fields, sometimes alongside their husbands or enslaved people. Certainly, poor white women had to find work, whether agricultural or industrial. Even elite white women worked—managing large plantations with a frighteningly forceful hand.[125] And especially in southern cities, working women formed a crucial part of the economy and a vital form of assistance to families struggling to make ends meet. In fact, Michele Gillespie, Susanna Delfino, and Louis M. Kyriakoudes have argued that "the emergence of women as an important component of the labor force—and, most important, as income-earners—in both urban and industrial occupations modified gender relations within the households."[126] This is a critical and undervalued story in southern history. Most women's historians focus on the role of the war in shifting attitudes toward household roles, but as more and more women found work outside the home, regardless of the pressures of war, they too forced white southerners to reexamine the position of men and women in the home.

Some women used their work to highlight the failures of their husbands. For instance, neighbors grew angry when they saw Margaret Bole working the counter at her husband's shoe store only days after she had given birth. "His manner to her was that of a master to his slave," one woman reported.[127] By forcing his wife to work, William Bole had violated southern norms about white women's freedom from

---

124. Morgan, *Laboring Women*, 24–25.

125. Jones-Rogers, *They Were Her Property*, 57–80; Edwards, *Scarlett Doesn't Live Here Anymore*, 32–47.

126. Delfino, Gillespie, and Kyriakoudes, "Editors' Introduction," 14.

127. *Bole, Margaret—by her next friend Jimeson, William W. v. Bole, William* (1855), Records of the Circuit Court of Ohio County, WVRHC, env. 208 b-4. For language on wives being treated as "slaves," see Sword, *Wives Not Slaves*, 207–40.

work. Many other women filed for divorce on the grounds of abandonment, proving their need for the court's pity by mentioning that they had been forced to support themselves in their husband's absence. By doing so, they upheld prevailing gender roles by suggesting that husbands were the natural breadwinners. Failure to fulfill this duty was enough of a sin to warrant a divorce.

Yet, as working women became more common in the urban South, they deployed their work to their advantage in other ways, using it to highlight their virtue as wives. While some women argued that their husbands had been poor providers, forcing them into work, others had worked before and during their marriages and needed divorces to protect their wages and property. Christina Daugua Wells, for instance, was a successful milliner during her fifteen-year marriage to Levi Wells. By the time he began an affair with Annie O'Brien in 1856, she was almost as concerned with the impact his behavior had on her livelihood as with the impact it had on his reputation and her marriage. As he began to drink, he fell more deeply into debt, and Christina's wages were being garnished to pay his debts.[128] She wanted a divorce to save her money.

Women in Wheeling also found work in a way that women have since time immemorial. They became prostitutes. As urbanization boomed, it created fertile ground for the occupation. With scores of unmarried young men pouring into cities and struggling women looking for work, prostitution became a common feature in most urban places in the nineteenth-century United States.[129] A study of New York's sex workers in the 1850s showed that most were fifteen to twenty years old, native born, and unmarried; had been domestic servants at one point; had a sexually transmitted disease; and had had children. The average life expectancy for a prostitute in New York after entering the trade was four years.[130]

Life for prostitutes in Wheeling was not so different. Catherine Chalk testified that when philandering husband Dorrance McGinnis came to her room he specifically asked if she was "scarce of money." She told him that she was because she had recently been sick. He then offered her a couple of dollars in exchange for an hour of her time. The next evening he returned and gave her five dollars. At the time she was liv-

---

128. *Wells, Christina, by her next friend Alexander, James v. Wells, Levi* (1857), Records of the Circuit Court of Ohio County, WVRHC, env. 206 & 216 b-6.

129. Cohen, *Murder of Helen Jewett*; Stansell, *City of Women*, 171–92.

130. Sanger, *History of Prostitution*, 488–522.

ing at a brothel run by a woman named Mrs. Oldfield.[131] Catherine's testimony is short but powerful. We hear in it her poverty but also no trace of shame at her trade. She testified in court in a frank manner in an era that told her that she was immoral. It is rare to hear testimony directly from nineteenth-century sex workers, and it is one of the treasures of these cases.

Other cases tell the stories of the many immigrants in this urban environment. Elizabeth Milleger, for instance, married James Goudy on December 17, 1860.[132] She was seventeen; he was twenty-one. James's father, Isaac, was a carpenter who owned about $4,000 worth of local real estate and about $250 of personal estate. Elizabeth's father was a laborer who owned no real estate and about forty dollars of personal estate. Elizabeth herself had already started working to support the family; she and her older sister Fredericka were seamstresses.[133] In marrying James, it seemed, Elizabeth had made a promising match.

Elizabeth's hopes were swiftly dashed, however. James Goudy never lived with his wife and refused to recognize her as such. Elizabeth wrote to James repeatedly over the next few years, but he did not answer. During the war, he served as a lieutenant in the West Virginia First Infantry Regiment, and her family was able to force him to send money to Elizabeth by soliciting the governor for help.[134] However, by 1868 Elizabeth had no idea of his whereabouts. With no other means of finding him or of making her marriage work, she filed for divorce in the Ohio County Circuit Court. During the depositions for the case, her lawyer asked her family and friends why James had never lived with his wife. As if in one voice, all of Elizabeth's witnesses said the same thing: "Because she was poor and a german girl."[135]

The Goudys were a small part of a larger movement. During the 1840s, the United States experienced a wave of immigration from northwestern Europe. Between 1840 and 1860, over four million immigrants entered the United States, most of them from Germany and Ireland. Fleeing from poverty, famine, and failed revolutions, most of these immigrants (by some estimates as many as 90 percent) ended up

---

131. *McGinnis, Rachel v. McGinnis, Dorrance* (1855), Records of the Circuit Court of Ohio County, WVRHC, env. 207 & 209 b-3.

132. *Goudy, Elizabeth O. by her next friend Milleger, James (her father) v. Goudy, James M.* (1868), Records of the Circuit Court of Ohio County, WVRHC, env. 274 e-9.

133. United States Federal Census for 1860.

134. U.S. Civil War Soldiers.

135. *Goudy, Elizabeth O. by her next friend Milleger, James (her father) v. Goudy, James M.*

in northern states and in cities such as New York and Boston. Therefore, most historians have focused their analysis of these immigrants and their experiences on these northeastern urban communities. But many others spread out, settling in places such as the Ohio River Valley. The cities of Cincinnati, St. Louis, and Milwaukee were sometimes known as the "German triangle."[136]

Wheeling, although a southern city, fit many of the same criteria for immigrants as northern cities. It had a booming industrial economy and was desperate for labor to fill its factories. German immigrants were especially drawn to the Midwest and Ohio River Valley, and their stories fill the pages of these divorce cases. Their experiences even made their way into the landscape of Wheeling itself, including the aptly named German Street.

This influx of immigrants also created a nativist backlash. From the very first days of the early republic, the United States had struggled to balance its image as a land of opportunity against suspicions of outsiders. In the 1790s, nativist frustrations led to harsh naturalization laws and the passage of the Alien Act under the John Adams administration. By the 1840s, an even larger wave of European immigration led to a renewal of nativist fears. Nativists feared the influx of Irish immigrants especially. Anti-immigrant groups advocated for more stringent citizenship laws, fought against Catholic education, and blamed immigrants for a host of problems: crime, violence, alcohol abuse, and poverty. In 1854, these forces coalesced into the American Party. Commonly known as the Know-Nothings, the party found support throughout New England as well as the Midwest. It proved especially appealing to residents of the Upper South in the wake of the Whig Party's collapse.[137] Isaac Goudy and his wife, Sarah, may have been among the many West Virginians sympathetic to this cause. Elizabeth Milleger Goudy's friends all testified that John's reluctance to live with his "poor, German" wife was because of the disapproval of his parents.[138] Reading Wheeling's divorce cases allows us to understand better the lives of newly arrived immigrants in the urban South, whether it is the mundane experience of love gone wrong or the sting of nativist prejudice.

Studying the urban South and, in this case, urban Appalachia also reveals the interconnectedness of those in this region with the rest of

---

136. Ford, *Bonds of Union*, 38–41; Garrison, *German Americans on the Middle Border*.
137. Daniels, *Coming to America*, 265–75; Lee, *America for Americans*, 43–57.
138. *Goudy, Elizabeth O. by her next friend Milleger, James (her father) v. Goudy, James M.*

the country. Often this region has been stereotyped as particularly isolated.[139] Residents of Ohio County, and Wheeling specifically, were always on the move, however. The river formed the backbone of the community, and people easily moved across it and on it. Riverboats appear in these pages as places of employment, opportunities for escape, and sites of illicit affairs. Although every couple in this book resided in Wheeling, a large number of marriages took place in West Alexander, Pennsylvania.[140] Other people moved almost seamlessly between Ohio and West Virginia, forming relationships, joining military regiments, and finding work. Even traveling far into the North, a daunting prospect in the mid-nineteenth century, was not nearly as uncommon as we would expect. Frederick Conrad, for instance, dragged his young daughter, Nellie, all the way to New York City under the pretext of a work visit. There, he forced her to remain in a small apartment while he conducted an extramarital affair. In another case, after a fight with his wife, Thomas Rogers decided to clear his head by taking a trip to visit his mother—in Plymouth, Massachusetts.[141]

The urban South was also a place with a remarkable lack of privacy. Fights between husbands and wives spilled into the street, where they regularly asked neighbors to intervene. Workplaces served double duty as homes, and customers were privy to the details of shop owners' families. In a community filled with struggling immigrants, few lived in single-family households anyway. These living arrangements meant that deponents often had very specific details, having witnessed sexual encounters firsthand or having stepped in to stop intoxicated husbands from abusing their wives. Especially in the cruelty cases, neighbors gave detailed and incredibly specific testimony. Their decisions to intervene also reflect the ways in which urban environments in the nineteenth century could protect women from violence. Christine Stansell, for example, has shown the ways in which women turned to New York

---

139. Whisnant, *All That Is Native and Fine*, 8–9; Shapiro, *Appalachia on Our Mind*, 3–31; Williams, *Appalachia*, 8–17; Catte, *What You Are Getting Wrong about Appalachia*, 10–15.

140. Over a quarter of the marriages featured in this book took place in West Alexander, Pennsylvania (specifically, nine cases—the McGinnises, Hesters, Sniders, Braretons, Welches, Hamiltons, Goudys, Armstrongs, and Normans). West Alexander is fifteen miles from Wheeling and only a mile over the border into Pennsylvania.

141. *Conrad, Francisca v. Conrad, Frederick* (1868), Records of the Circuit Court of Ohio County, WVRHC, env. 274 b-12; *Rogers, Elizabeth A. v. Rogers, Thomas* (1854), Records of the Circuit Court of Ohio County, WVRHC, env. 206 b-1.

City neighbors to act as a buffer against their violent husbands.[142] This same sort of community protection happened in Wheeling.

Focusing exclusively on the rural South only reinforces myths of Southern "backwardness." The history of the nineteenth-century United States should not be flattened out to compare a purely industrial North and a purely agrarian South. Instead, historians should analyze the ways in which some places stood at the junction between. Wheeling, and Ohio County, is a fruitful and understudied example of this. An industrial city still connected to its rural hinterlands, a southern city on the edge of the North, it tells us much about the complexity of life in the antebellum United States and the places that do not fit the myths we have created.

Although they seem to be a simple thing, a legal testament to one couple's hardest moment, divorce records are so much more. They can allow us to go inside the homes of the past, to see how people loved and hated, to watch child-rearing practices in action, to hear how neighbors helped, supported, and spied on one another, to see how families functioned economically, to chart the impact of war and slavery on everyday southerners, and to see how marriage differed in urban and rural, northern and southern environments. Divorce records are refreshingly revealing, while also deliberately obfuscating. They are enigmatic sources that challenge us as historians and students. By using these records, this book hopes to shed light on Wheeling, its diverse and dysfunctional residents, and divorce practices in the nineteenth-century United States.

Editorial Procedure

Between 1850 and 1873, over 120 citizens of Ohio County were either a plaintiff or defendant in a divorce case. Because of space restrictions, I could not include all of those cases in this book. Therefore, I have chosen the cases that best represent the process of divorce, the environment of Wheeling, the lives of those living in the city, and the impact of the war on Ohio County marriages. The transcriptions of the cases

---

142. Stansell, *City of Women*, 81–83.

not included here can be found with the supplementary material on the book's website (search for the book at www.ugapress.org).[143] One particularly interesting case had to be left out because it was the same length as nearly half the cases in this book, combined. The cases in this book were filed by both men and women, white and Black Wheelingites, spouses in lengthy marriages and spouses who had lived together for only a single day. They provide a thorough and detailed look at divorce and this community.

Within each case, I researched the background and biographies for the husband and wife, as well as their lawyers and the judges. I researched the backgrounds of only those witnesses who appeared in multiple cases or whose background was especially pertinent to the case. As readers will note, the historical records are biased against most of the litigants in these cases. While the judges are easy to research, with their biographies found in numerous volumes with titles such as *Prominent Men of West Virginia*, a working-class milliner who filed for a divorce from her abusive, intoxicated husband left few records for historians to find. In cases like that, I had to mine through census records, death indexes, marriage licenses, city indexes, pension records, and gravestones.

As much as possible, I have left the text unaltered. Since most of these documents were transcribed or prepared by lawyers and notaries, the spelling is fairly good. That being said, the style of nineteenth-century legal documents includes far more run-on sentences than most of us would be comfortable employing. Sometimes a single sentence runs onto multiple pages. When necessary, I have added commas and periods to make the text more readable to the modern eye. In some places I added apostrophes to indicate possessive phrasing. Even through the legal language and through my slight changes, it is still possible for us to hear the language and laments of the divorce petitioners of Ohio County—if we choose to listen.

---

143. These cases do not include the editorial comments found in this book. The cases in this book do not serve as a true representative sample, since I have not attempted to ensure a proportional amount of cases by case, racial/ethnic background, or outcome.

PART 1
Antebellum

View of Wheeling from Chapline Hill, 1854;
New York Public Library Digital Collections.

CHAPTER 1

Adultery

HER SKIN SHOULD NEVER TOUCH HIS

John Michael Wehner v. Mary Jane Wehner, 1850

[Wehner, John Michael v. Wehner, Mary Jane *(1850), Records of the Circuit Court of Ohio County, West Virginia and Regional History Center (WVRHC), env. 186 c-9. John Michael Wehner filed his original bill on August 28, 1849. The court issued a summons for Mary Jane Wehner on the same day. The sheriff, sent to deliver it, reported that she had left the city. In February 1850, Michael, as he was known, filed an amended bill. In the original bill he stated that he would file with the General Assembly, but because of a new law, his amended bill filed his divorce in the courts. Because both bills are the same in all other details, only the amended bill is included in this collection. In May, Michael published notice in local newspapers of his intent to get a divorce and take depositions.*]

Amended Bill for Divorce

To the Honorable Joseph L. Fry,[1] Judge of the Circuit Superior Court of Law and Chancery for Ohio,[2]

Your orator John Michael Wehner[3] for his amended bill to his original bill heretofore filed in this Court, humbly complaining shows unto

---

1. Joseph L. Fry was born in Culpeper County, Virginia, in 1795. He served on the Ohio County Circuit Court from 1831 to 1852, when he lost the first public election the region had held for his position. In 1860, he lived in Wheeling's Second Ward with his wife, Elizabeth, seven children, and one enslaved man. Cranmer, *History of the Upper Ohio Valley*, 1:545; *Journal of the House of Delegates of Virginia, 1850–1851*; United States Federal Census for 1860; West Virginia Wills and Probate Records; 1860 United States Federal Census—Slave Schedules.

2. Chancery courts arose in England as courts with less strict rules than common law courts. Chancery courts had jurisdiction over issues of equity, especially domestic matters such as family law and property law.

3. John Wehner and Michael Wehner are fairly common names for this era. A marriage certificate for Michael "Warhner" and Mary Jane Chapman exists, corroborating their wed-

your honor that he has been a citizen of and resident in the City of Wheeling in the state of Virginia for the thirteen years past and still resides there; that in the month of December in the year 1845 your orator intermarried with Mary Jane Chapman of said city, the marriage ceremony being performed by the priest of, and in conformity with the rites of the Roman Catholic church[4] of said city, lawful license being first granted to said priest to solemnize the rites of matrimony between your orator and the said Mary Jane Chapman. Your orator further shows unto your honor, that in about one year after his said marriage his said wife bore him a female child, which child is still living. That your orator and his said wife lived together with comfort and happiness and without any thing to disturb those near and dear relations which properly attend the conjugal state until in the winter of 1847–8 your orator being then a keeper of an ordinary[5] in said city, was taken down to a bed of sickness when he was prostrated by disease for near nine weeks, and that during his said sickness he first observed that his wife seemed to be estranged from him, neglecting him, and leaving him in his lonely sick chamber many times suffering greatly for want of those little attentions which it is at all times the pleasure as well as the duty of a good wife to administer to her husband when he is prostrated by the strong arm of sickness. Your orator was at a loss to account for her evident estrangement from his affections, for he had always treated her kindly and tenderly and as became a husband. This estrangement of the affectionate conduct of your orators said wife continued until some time in the month of September in the year 1848 your orators said wife was delivered of a mulato male child. Your orator was heartsick and astonished, but when assured by the physician then attending upon the accouchment[6] of his said wife that the said mulato male child the said offspring of his said wife, must have been begotten by a negro, your orator recolected that whilst he was sick as before stated, and also previous to that time he had in his employment, in his said business as a tavern keeper in said city, as a hostler[7] and servant a negro man commonly called Jefferson. Your orator therefore charges that his said wife

---

ding date, December 11, 1845. No information about their birthplaces or ethnicity exists. West Virginia Marriages Index.

4. This would have been the Cathedral of St. James on Eoff and Thirteenth Streets, the only Catholic church in the city.

5. A tavern or inn, specifically one that serves meals.

6. The "laying in" period in which women gave birth.

7. A person charged with caring for horses, often at an inn.

committed adultery in the month of December in the city of Wheeling aforesaid, and at divers other places and times with said negro Jefferson, or with some other negro, without the knowledge, connivance or consent of your orator. Your orator [states] that he has not cohabited with his said wife, since her delivery of said mulato male child, or since your orator has reason to believe that his said wife had been unfaithful to him, but that as soon as his said wife had recovered from her said accouchment and confinement the said wife of your orator left his house and removed from this Commonwealth as your orator is informed and believes into the state of Pennsylvania. Your orator further represents unto your honor that the said female child, born as aforesaid to your orator about one year after his said marriage remained in the custody and house of your orator after his said wife and your orator had parted as aforesaid, until [date left blank] when on the night of said day whilst your orator was attending to his duties in his capacity as keeper of a public house, his said child was abducted from his possession, as he believes & therefore charges as true by his said wife, & carried beyond the jurisdiction of this Commonwealth. In consideration of all which and forasmuch as your orator is without remedy except in this court of chancery, to the end therefore that the said marriage of your orator with his said wife may be the decree of this Honorable Court forever dissolved, and that your orator may be at liberty if he should so desire, to again contract marriage, and that his said wife may be forever barred from any right of dower in his lands or interest in his moneys goods & chattels. And that your orator may have such other or further relief in the premises as the nature & circumstances of his case may require, and to your honor shall seem meet. May it please your honor to grant unto your orator the Commonwealth's writ of subpoena to be directed to the said Mary Jane Wehner, thereby commanding her at a certain day and under a certain pain therein to be limited to personally be and appear before your honor in this Honorable Court and then and there tell true direct and perfect answer make to all and singular the allegations of this bill of complaint, and further to stand to perform and abide, such further order, direction and decree therein as to your honor shall seem meet. And your orator will every pray &c

by Alfred Caldwell, Sol[icitor, or attorney] for Complainant[8]

---

8. Alfred Caldwell was born in Belmont County, Ohio, in 1817 to Congressman James Caldwell Jr. He attended Harvard Law School before moving to Wheeling. Caldwell served as mayor of Wheeling from January 1850 to January 1852, as well as from January 1856 to

Depositions of Witnesses[9]

WILLIAM BAMFORD

I am pretty well acquainted with Michael Wehner and Mary Jane his wife. [I lived] with them at their house in Wheeling from March 1848, unto the time she was delivered of a mulatto child. I saw the negro man called Jefferson twice about Wehner's house during the time I boarded there. Wehner kept a house of private entertainment[10] at that time. I was in the house as a boarder at the time the child was born. I went up to see the mother and child, the third day after it was born, and saw both. She asked me if I thought it would change its colour. I was going away to Philadelphia. She told me that I should not find her in Michael Wehners house when I came back, that a fortune teller told her she would not have three children by Michael; I was absent about one month, and then came back to Wheeling. I found she had gone from her husband. I boarded with Mr Wehner after my return for six or seven week, & untill he sold out to Miche Earnst. I believe he has resided here ever since. I never saw anything improper in her, except that I saw others go into her room and act as I thought too free with her. Mr Wehner provided well for his family. At one of the times Negro Jefferson was there, he was shaving Wehner and making the lather. He, Jefferson, rubbed the lather brush across her face. I thought it was making very free for a Negro to a white woman. Wehner has never lived with her since I returned from Philadelphia. I was jobing at days labour for different persons about the City, when I boarded there.

DIONESIUS WINGERTER

John M. Wehner was married to Mary Jane Chapman on the 11th day of December 1845, by the Rev. W. Commeford of the Roman Catholic Church. I was present at the marriage. It took place at the priest's house in Wheeling. They lived together in wheeling until after she had

---

January 1858. In 1856, he was elected to the Virginia State Senate. While he owned one slave in 1850, he owned none in 1860 and became a prominent Republican and abolitionist. Connie Rice, "Caldwell, Alfred," 504–5.

9. William Bamford, Dionesius Wingerter, and Robert Cummins testified in Wheeling on May 13, 1850, at the mayor's office. Philip Bier, an alderman and justice of the peace, deposed them. All signed their names.

10. The Virginia state assembly definition of a "house of private entertainment" allowed for a person to "furnish, for compensation, lodging or diet to travelers . . . or boarders in his home . . . within five miles of any city, town, or village." They were not allowed to sell alcohol. *Acts and Joint Resolutions*, 203.

the mulato child and it is said, she left her husband as soon as she got well from her confinement. A negro man by the name of Jefferson lived in the employ of Wehner for some well about a year before the birth of her second child, and I think whilst Wehner was sick. I said a year before, it might have been nine months or a year, or more or less. I am not certain of the time, but I saw him there frequently about that time.

DR. ROBERT H. CUMMINS[11]

I was called upon professionally to attend to Mrs. Wehner, the wife of Michael Wehner, at her confinement, in September 1848, when she was delivered of a male child. That at the time of delivery the room was so darkened that it could not be discovered whether it was a white or a mulatto child. Some time after wards I saw the child in her arms, and I saw that it was a mulatto child. I have no doubt but it was the same child of which I delivered her at her confinement. I have not the slightest doubt that it was a Mulatto Child, about this I do not think I could be mistaken. I delivered her on a former occasion about two years ago of her first child, being a female, whose complection was remarkably fair. Mr Wehners complection is a good white skin, and his wifes is very fair. I have no doubt of the father of the child was a black man. I have been a practicing Physician in this City of Wheeling for nine years.

[In September 1850, the court ruled in John Michael Wehner's favor, granting his divorce a vinculo matrimonii.[12] *Mary Jane Wehner was banned from any right of dower in his property. John Michael Wehner had to pay the costs of the suit. J. Michael Wehner died on December 17, 1856, seven months after receiving a license to open a coffeehouse. He was forty-five and survived by his widow, Regina Fredericka Krieg Wehner, a German immigrant with four children.*[13] *Mary Jane Wehner's whereabouts are unknown.]*

---

11. Dr. Cummins also served as a witness in *Leasure v. Leasure* (1871). He was Martha Griffith's doctor in *Griffith v. Griffith* (1868). His brother, James Cummins, served as a witness in *Griffith v. Griffith* (1868). Robert Cummins was born in Pennsylvania in 1817. By the time of this case, he was practicing in the city and living in a local hotel. Ten years later, he had married and had two children. He was quite wealthy by that point, with his real and personal estate valued at over $24,000. His family had four white domestic servants. By 1870, around the time of the other cases, he had six children and was valued at over $100,000. He died three years later. United States Federal Census for 1850, 1860, 1870; U.S. Find a Grave Index.

12. A divorce *a vinculo matrimonii* was an "absolute divorce," or a divorce in which the parties could remarry (unless the court specified otherwise).

13. I cannot be certain that this is the same person as in this case, but his occupation and

Rachel McGinnis v. Dorrance McGinnis, 1855

[McGinnis, Rachel v. McGinnis, Dorrance *(1855), Records of the Circuit Court of Ohio County, WVRHC, env. 207 & 209 b-3. Rachel McGinnis filed her bill in April 1855. Dorrance was born in 1832 in Virginia.*[14]]

Bill of Divorce

To the Hon. George W. Thompson, Judge of the Circuit Court of Ohio County,[15]

Humbly complaining showeth unto your Honor your oratrix Rachel McGinnis,[16] who sues by her next friend Vashtie Dillon,[17] that on the 25th day of November in the year (1853) Eighteen hundred and Fifty three your oratrix, being at that time more than twenty one years of age, and unmarried and residing in the city of Wheeling in the said County of Ohio, did contract matrimony with one Dorance McGinnis . . . and that said marriage was duly consummated by the cohabitation of your oratrix and the said McGinnis, as husband and wife, and that said cohabitation continued for several months in the city of Wheeling. And your oratrix further shews that subsequently to said marriage, the said McGinnis has proved unfaithful to the marriage re-

---

name suggest that he was. *Wheeling Intelligencer*, May 16, 1856.

14. United States Federal Census for 1910.

15. George Thompson was born in Ohio in 1806 and attended college in Pennsylvania, although he eventually studied law in Richmond. In 1850, he was elected to Congress, serving as a Democrat. He resigned that position to serve as judge of the circuit court. He was reelected in 1860. Thompson left office in 1861, objecting to what he viewed as illegal action by the Wheeling convention to create a new state. He died in 1888 outside of Wheeling. Cranmer, *History of the Upper Ohio Valley*, 1:545–46; U.S. Find a Grave Index.

16. Rachel Dillon Hornbrook was a widow when she met and married Dorrance McGinnis. She was born in Ohio on March 7, 1814, making her eighteen years older than Dorrance. Her deceased husband, Frances, had been an English immigrant, and they had two children together before he died in 1852, leaving everything he owned to her. U.S. Find a Grave Index; United States Federal Census for 1850, 1860; West Virginia Wills and Probate Records.

17. In most states in the 1850s, married women could sue in court only if represented by their "next friend." This was a legal device used for those who were considered legally incompetent by the courts—married women, minors, and the mentally disabled. Most women had their fathers, and in rare cases single mothers, bring the suit on their behalf. Vashti Dillon, a Quaker, was born in New Jersey in 1794. She was Rachel's mother. U.S. Find a Grave Index; West Virginia Deaths Index; U.S. Encyclopedia of American Quaker Genealogy, Vol. 1–6, 1607–1943. For more on next friends, see Chused, *Private Acts in Public Places*, 31.

lation, has frequently solicited the chastity of other women, and been guilty of repeated acts of adultery; that he did on or about the days of September or October last (1854) repeatedly visit a house in the North part of the city of Wheeling, known and reputed a house of ill fame,[18] and then and there committed adultery, by having carnal connection with a female of the name of Catherine J Chalk; that also on a day not known to your oratrix in the last week of January or the first week of February last (1855) said McGinnis committed adultery with a female whose name is unknown to your oratrix in the eastern part of the city, that said McGinnis has also committed other acts of adultery with other parties to your oratrix unknown and has also solicited the chastity of other women,[19] among others, of one Mary Culomon in the city of Wheeling—all which acts & doings on the part of the said McGinnis are in fraud of the conjugal rights of your oratrix, & destructive to the peace & happiness of herself & family, although your oratrix has had no children by the said McGinnis, & contrary to equity & good conscience.

And your oratrix further shows that she and the said McGinnis have been since the marriage and are now both residents in the County of Ohio, in the state of Virginia. In tender consideration whereof, and as matters of this kind are exclusively cognizable & relievable in a Court of equity, your oratrix prays that the said McGinnis be made a party defendant to this suit, that your Honor will make a decree dissolving the bonds of marriage between your oratrix and that said McGinnis: dirrecting your oratrix a vinculo matrimonii and annulling forever all the rights & relations growing out of said marriage, as though the same had never been contracted. And that your Honor will grant until your oratrix all such other and further relief as to your Honor shall seem meet, & the circumstances of this case may require. May it please your honor to grant unto your oratrix the Commonwealth writ of subpoena commanding the said McGinnis &c.[20]

Fry and Paull for Plaintiff[21]

---

18. A brothel.

19. This generally meant asking or encouraging another person to commit an "act of unlawful sexual intercourse." Garland and Michie, *American and English Encyclopaedia of Law*, 1152.

20. The court issued a summons for Dorrance on March 24, 1855.

21. It seems likely that Fry was Joseph Fry, judge in the previous case. James Paull was born in Belmont County, Ohio, in 1818. He attended college in Pennsylvania and then studied law at the University of Virginia. Before the Civil War, he was elected to the Virginia

Depositions of Witnesses[22]

JOHN BURTON

QUESTION: Are you acquainted with Dorrance McGinnis, the defendant to this suit?

ANSWER: I am.

QUESTION: State what you know if anything of any act or acts of adultery committed by said McGinnis and the time and place.

ANSWER: I dont know of any acts of adultery that he ever committed. I saw him come out of a house called the Black Horse Tavern in North Wheeling at the corner of Washington and Market Street.

QUESTION: What was the repute of that house and who lived in it at that time?

ANSWER: I believe there was a family lived in it of bad repute, one of the women was a Jane Chalk and a Mrs Oldfield. I have often heard young men speak of going there after them.

QUESTION: Was there any tavern kept there at the time you speak of?

ANSWER: Not at that time, nor had been for several years.

QUESTION: At what time was it you saw Mr. McGinnis come out from there?

ANSWER: It was some time last fall but I cannot state at what precise time I could not say exactly what time of the day it was.

CATHERINE J. CHALK

QUESTION: Are you acquainted with Dorrance McGinnis the defendant in this suit?

ANSWER: I know him when I see him. I have seen him often and know him well

QUESTION: State if you know anything and if so what, in regard to any act or acts of adultery committed by said McGinnis within the last year or 18 months. If so, state the time and place.

ANSWER: He come up to our house sometime last fall, the house for-

---

General Assembly as a Whig and attended the first Wheeling convention, which helped create the state of West Virginia. In 1872, he was elected a judge of the Supreme Court of Appeals of West Virginia. He was married twice, and his first wife was the daughter of Joseph L. Fry. *History of West Virginia, Old and New*, 2:614.

22. John Burton, Catherine Chalk, Dennis White, John Sutherland, Jacob Winesburger, William Wickham, and Mary Calbatrom testified in Wheeling on Friday, May 18, 1855, on behalf of Rachel McGinnis. All signed their names, except Dennis White and Mary Calbatrom, who signed only with their mark.

merly known as the Black Horse Tavern on the corner of Market & Washington Street. He come in and asked me how times was, and if I was scarce of money. I told him I was. I had been sick for some time. He told me to come in the room, and he gave me either a two dollar a half gold piece of a few dollar gold piece I dont mind which. It was the first time & told me he would be back the next evening. The time refered to above I went into the room with him and went to bed with him, and remained with him an hour or hour and a half and had adulterous intercourse with him. He came back the next evening as he had writ he would he then gave me I think a five dollar gold piece. I went alone to bed with him and remained with him as before and the same thing occurred as on the evening before. I was living then with Mrs Oldfield she kept the house he asked me on that evening if I would go with him to his house on the Island[23] the next evening I was not at home next evening nor subsequently on one or two occasions when I understood he was there. I did not see him afterwards.

DENNIS WHITE

QUESTION: Are you acquainted with Dorrance McGinnis the defendant in this suit?

ANSWER: I am acquainted with Mr McGinnis. He was the husband of the widow Hornbrook. Have known him for twenty years.

QUESTION: State what you know if anything of any act or acts of adulterous or lewd character committed by him and at what time and place.

ANSWER: I carried a letter from Mrs Wineburgh to McGinnis. I carried it for about two weeks before I got to see him. I saw him on a saturday morning. I do not recollect the day of the month, but I think it was sometime in last January. I told him I had the letter and if he would wait a few moments I would get it for him. He went in to Goodricks store. I went down street a piece, then come back and gave it to him. Then he came out on the pavement and opened the letter and asked me who gave it to me. I told him I did not know the lady. I told him I wanted an answer. He said he would give me one

---

23. "The Island" refers to Wheeling Island, the largest island in the Ohio River and an extension of the city of Wheeling. In 1849, the Wheeling Suspension Bridge connected the island with the rest of the city and allowed residents to move easily back and forth. Otis Rice, *West Virginia*, 80–89.

in the evening or on Sunday. He then asked me where I lived. I told him he then said he would come down either that evening or sunday and give me an answer. I understood from my wife he was there, but I was not at home and did not see him again till the next Wednesday morning in market. He then came to me and told me he did not want to have anything to say to that woman she wanted to draw him into a fuss and said that he had been at her house, but they were not sharp enough to catch him. This woman Mrs Wineburgh was reputed and known to be a woman of ill fame or loose character.

QUESTION: Did you know the reputation of the house called the Black Horse Tavern?

ANSWER: It was reputed to be a house of ill fame where loose women lived, and where men could be accommodated. The time I refer to was during the last year, and in the last fall and winter.

QUESTION: State if you know of any specific acts of adultery or lewdness committed by the defendant Dorrance McGinnis?

ANSWER: I saw him sometime during last winter just after dark at Hubbards saw mill[24] with a lewd woman. I saw him in the act of carnal connexion with her. Her name was Lucinda Johnson. I lived near the saw mill at the time and could see a man and woman there from my back porch. I went near enough to talk with the woman afterwards.

JOHN SUTHERLAND

QUESTION: State where did you reside on the 24th of November 1853 and what office did you then fill?

ANSWER: I resided in the town of West Alexander, Washington County, Pennsylvania, and held the office of Justice of the Peace for said county & state.

QUESTION: Whom did you marry on that day?

ANSWER: On that day I married at West Alexander, Washington County, Dorrance McGinnis and Mrs Rachel Hornbrook. I had known Dorrance McGinnis was from Wheeling and they both alledged they were from Wheeling.

JACOB WINESBURGER

QUESTION: Are you acquainted with Dorrance McGinnis, the defendant in this suit?

ANSWER: Yes, I am.

---

24. A lumber mill.

QUESTION: State what you know if anything of any act or acts of adultery with lewd women by said McGinnis during the past year or 18 months?

ANSWER: Some time last fall, whether October or November I do not remember, I was in a certain house in East Wheeling. There was a lady and me sitting talking. She went to the door and said Mr. McGinnis is comeing, I would like you to step out a little bit. I want to see him privately. I stepped out far enough so that I could hear the discourse betwixt them. I heard him promise her that he would be back one certain evening, but I forget which evening of the week it was. It was to have been at 9 or 10 o'clock of the evening he was to come, but I cant remember what evening of the week it was to be. Sometime in January last I think between 7 & 8 o'clock in the evening as I was passing by the Baptist Church I had occasion to go into a waste house, and while there a man and woman came in. As they come in they stood between me and a large window without any sash. There [illegible] on the ground so that I could distinguish them easily. The lady had on a tight dress and the man a dark dress. When they came in I heard the man ask the woman to lay down. She said oh no Mr McGinnis let us stand up, she persisted, and she repeated it twice but after that they did lay down and he lay with her and they had their pleasure. They did not see me, there was a large chimney in the house I stood behind that, so that they could not see me. They went out before I did. I would have gone out before but seeing them come in I did not desire to be seen there, and so remained till they went away.

WILLIAM S. WICKHAM

QUESTION: Do you know Dorrance McGinnis and the plaintiff Rachel McGinnis and where does the plaintiff live for many years back, and where did the said Dorrance live in the beginning of this winter, the 24th day of March past?

ANSWER: I am acquainted with both the parties to the suit, the defendant for more than twenty years and Mrs McGinnis from her childhood. Mrs McGinnis lives now in the County of Ohio Virginia and has lived here from her childhood. Mr McGinnis has lived in said County of Ohio ever since I have known him up to the first week of April last, I think about the 3d day, when he left this County with his family for the West but what part of the West I do not know. He went to reside as I understand. By his family I mean his children that were with him of his first wife. He had no children by his marriage with the plaintiff as I understood. Said Dorrance has never returned to this commonwealth since he went away as aforesaid as I know of. I think Mrs. MrGinnis is over thirty years of age, or about that age.[25]

MARY CALBATROM

QUESTION: Are you acquainted with Dorrance McGinnis the defendant to this suit?

ANSWER: I have no personal acquaintance with him, but I know him when I see him.

QUESTION: State what passed between you and Mr. McGinnis sometime during the past year, where, and when it was.

ANSWER: As I was going past the Catholic Church a gentleman stept up to me and asked which way I was going that time of night. I told him I was on my way home. He asked me if I would not go home with him. I thanked him and told him no, thanks, that I had a home of my own. He then asked me if I would not meet him some evening at the bridge. I told him not. He said he would pay me well. It was sometime between 7 Oclock and nine oclock in the evening. The gentleman who had the conversation with me was Mr McGinnis. I knew him by sight but had never spoken to him before. It was either in January or February last. I live in East Wheeling. Mr McGinnis lived on the Island at the time which is reached by the wire bridge from the other parts of the city.

[In a decree issued May 20, 1855, the court granted Rachel McGinnis's divorce, giving her rights to her name, legal independence, and the right to property ownership, as she had before her marriage. Rachel Hornbrook (her name prior to her second marriage) never remarried. She raised her two daughters from her previous marriage, Agnes and Lorilla, and remained in Wheeling for the rest of her life. After they were grown, she lived next door to her aging mother. Rachel died on January 25, 1897, at the age of eighty-four. Dorrance McGinnis was held responsible for the costs of the suit—$27.32. Dorrance remarried on September 16, 1855, in Belmont, Ohio. He and his wife, Elizabeth, moved to Missouri and then Iowa. During the war, he served as a private in Company F of the Seventeenth Regiment of the Iowa Infantry. Over the years, he and Elizabeth had five children. They remained together until her death in 1904. He died in 1920

---

25. I can find no record of Dorrance's first marriage.

at the age of eighty-seven. Rachel Hornbrook, Dorrance McGinnis, and Elizabeth McGinnis are all buried in Peninsula Cemetery in Wheeling.[26]]

James Davis v. Hester Davis, 1857

[Davis, James R. v. Davis, Hester *(1857)*, Records of the Circuit Court of Ohio County, WVRHC, env. 217 c & env. 220 b-2. *James R. Davis filed a bill of divorce against his wife in August 1857. A few days later, he swore an "affidavit of non-residency," stating that Hester no longer lived in Virginia. The court still issued a summons, but it was never delivered. As required by law, he published notice in local newspapers of his intent to file for divorce and take depositions.*]

Bill of Divorce

To the Honourable George W. Thompson, Judge of the Circuit Court of Ohio County, Virginia,

Your orator James R Davis of the City of Wheeling, Ohio County and State of Virginia respectfully complaining sheweth to your Honour that in the month of June 1845 your orator was lawfully married to Hester his present wife, Hester Davis, and lived together as husband and wife from their said marriage until Dec 1854. That during said period, they had two children, [both] are still living, the elder about ten years of age, and the younger, about four years of age. That from the time of their marriage your orator and said Hester, lived together as husband and wife in harmony, until the fall of 1854. When your orator being what is usually termed a river man, an Engineer employed, as his occupation is running Steam Boats, on the Ohio, and other Western Waters, and being therefore necessarily much absent, from his family, on his return, found in the possession of his wife Hester several letters from a gentleman, whose name he is advised is not material or necessary to disclose, to his said wife addressed by a fictitious name, which fully satisfied your orator, of her infidelity to him as a wife, and in consequence

---

26. United States Federal Census for 1870; U.S. City Directories; West Virginia Wills and Probate Records; United States Federal Census for 1850, 1880; *Wheeling Register*, January 30, 1897; Virginia Death Records; West Virginia Deaths Index; U.S. Find a Grave Index; Ohio, U.S., County Marriage Records; U.S. Civil War Soldiers; United States Federal Census for 1860; General Index to Pension Files; Schedules Enumerating Union Veterans and Widows; Veterans Administration Pension Payment Cards.

of said discovery, your orator left her, and with his two children has since Dec. 1854 lived seperate and apart from said Hester. Your Orator further shews that on the 4th day of July 1857 said Hester, and one John Mix[27] of Marshall County Virginia went, from said County of Marshall to the County of Green[28] in the State of PA, and were there formally married to each other and on the same day returned as husband and wife to the residence of one John Jones, in the neighbourhood of Cameron in said county of Marshall, and remained, at said Jones's house, some three days and nights occupying the same bed at night, as husband & wife, and then left Camerone by the Baltimore & Ohio Rail Road for some of the Western States, as your orator was informed for the City of Chicago, State of Michigan. All which facts your orator is advised he will be able to prove. Your orator expressly charges that his said wife Hester was on the 4th of July 1857 and thereafter guilty of the crime of adultery with said John Mix & your orator in tender consideration of the premises, prays the benefit of the commonwealth's writ of Subpoena, and that said Hester Davis may be made Defendant hereto and required to answer this Bill and after the hearing of this case, your Honour Decree a divorce of your orator from the bond of matrimony with said Hester Davis according to the Statute on such cases made and such other relief as may be equitable in the premises, and as in duty bound he will ever pray &c

James R Davis by
M C Goods his Solicitor

Depositions of Witnesses[29]

ROBERT LAUGHLIN

I reside in Wheeling, my occupation is that of a tobaccoist. I am acquainted with the Complainant James Davis and Hester his wife. I

---

27. John Mix had previously been married to Margaret Cox. They married in 1841 in Marshall County. The records are a bit confusing. Their seventh child, John, is listed as having been born in May 1857 in Marshall County, but according to the records, Margaret died in April 1857. Assuming some mistaken dates, it seems likely that Margaret died in childbirth, as many nineteenth-century women did. West Virginia Births Index; West Virginia Marriages Index; West Virginia Deaths Index.

28. Marshall County directly borders Ohio County to the south and is one of four counties in the northern West Virginia panhandle. Greene County is the southwesternmost county in Pennsylvania and borders Marshall County, West Virginia, to the east.

29. Robert Laughlin and John Jones testified on September 8, 1857. Robert signed with his mark.

waited on them when they were married. I saw them married. They were married in West Alexander Washington County Pennsylvania. I think they were married by the Rev. Wm. McCluskey the Presbyterian Minister at West Alexander. As well as I now remember they were married in June 1845. After their marriage they came to Wheeling to reside and staid here in Wheeling until I left and went to Washington Pennsylvania which was fully a year after their marriage. I dont know how much longer they remained together. So far as I know they resided in Wheeling until they were separated and the Complainant still lives here.

JOHN JONES

QUESTION: Where do you reside and what is your vocation?
ANSWER: I have resided in Cameron for the last three years. I am a Carpenter by Vocation.
QUESTION: Are you acquainted [with] James R. Davis and Hester Davis his wife formerly of the City of Wheeling?
ANSWER: I know the parties, have known them for some time. Said Davis is an Engineer.
QUESTION: Do you know any thing of the intermarriage of Hester Davis with another man. If so, when and where and state all you know touching said matter.
ANSWER: I was present at her marriage with John E Mix formerly of the place at the house of the Rev Pitcher of Alleppa Township Green County PA on the evening of the 4th of July 1857.
QUESTION: Did they go together as man and wife?
ANSWER: They came to my house the evening after they were married and went to bed together as man and wife. They remained at my house for three days and nights and slept together as man and wife and left as man and wife.

[*On November 19, 1857, the court granted James Davis a divorce* a vinculo matrimonii. *Regardless of James's assertions about Hester's 1857 marriage to John Mix, on August 2, 1863, Hester Davis and John E. Mix married in Wheeling. It is unclear why they waited that long or, if they had already married, why they remarried. A man named James R. Davis from Wheeling died on August 5, 1860, at the age of thirty-five, but it is impossible to determine if he is the same James R. Davis from this case.*[30]]

---

30. West Virginia Compiled Marriage Records; West Virginia Deaths Index.

Christina Wells v. Levi Wells, 1857

[Wells, Christina, by her next friend Alexander, James v. Wells, Levi *(1857)*, *Records of the Circuit Court of Ohio County, WVRHC*, env. *206 & 216 b-6. Christina Wells filed her petition in April 1857. She stated that both she and Levi were residents of Wheeling and requested a divorce* a vinculo matrimonii. *The court issued and served a summons for Levi on April 4.*]

Bill of Divorce

To the Honl George W Thompson, Judge of the Circuit Court of Ohio County,

Humbly complaining sheweth unto your Honor your oratrix, Christina Wells,[31] who sues by her next friend James Alexander,[32] that on the 24 day of May 1842 your oratrix, being then of [blank] years of age, [blank] and unmarried, and residing in the City of Wheeling in the said county of Ohio, did conduct matrimony with Levi Wells, of lawful age, then also residing in Wheeling, & was duly and lawfully married to the said Levi Wells on the said 24 day of May 1842 and that said marriage was duly consummated by the cohabitation of your oratrix and the said Wells, as husband and wife, and that said cohabitation has continued for several years in the city of Wheeling. And your oratrix shews that subsequently to said marriage, & especially within the last few years, the said Wells has utterly failed to make any provision for the maintenance & support of your oratrix, has been greatly addicted to intemperance, and to cruel & improper treatment of your oratrix; that the earnings of your oratrix being a milliner[33] have been taken to satisfy his debts upon legal executions, and this while your oratrix has been & still is in very feebly & delicate health.[34] And your oratrix further shews

---

31. I am unable to find Christina (or Christiana, as she was listed on her marriage certificate) in the census.

32. I am unable to find James Alexander and therefore cannot say what the relationship is between Christina and James.

33. A milliner is a person who makes women's hats.

34. In the nineteenth century, a married woman had no right to her own earnings. They automatically became the property of her husband and could be confiscated by his creditors to pay his debts. This was one of the motivations behind the 1860 New York State Married Women's Property Act. Howe, "Patient Laborers," 137–38; Hoff, *Law, Gender, and Injustice*, 377.

that the said Wells has been unfaithful to the marriage relation, & has been guilty of repeated acts of adultery—that he did in the month of January last, (1857) in the City of Wheeling, on Hamilton Street, visit a female, by the name of Annie O Brien, and did then and there commit adultery, by having carnal connection with the said Annie O Brien; that the said Wells has committed other acts of adultery with other parties to your oratrix unknown, & has been in the habit of visiting houses of ill fame, inhabited by loose & lewd women, within the past few months, & in the city of Wheeling—all which actings & doings are in violation of his marriage engagements, and destructive to the peace & happiness of your oratrix, & contrary to equity and good conscience. And your oratrix further states that she and the said Levi Wells have been for the last ten or twelve years and are both now residents of the city of Wheeling, Ohio County, State of Virginia. In tender consideration wherof, and as matters of this kind are exclusively adjudicated in a court of equity, your oratrix prays that the said Levi Wells be made a defendant to this suit, that your Honor will make a decree dissolving the bonds of marriage between your oratrix and the said Wells, divorcing your oratrix a vinculo matrimonii, and annulling forever all the rights & relations growing out of said marriage, as though the same had never been contracted; and that your Honor will grant unto your oratrix all such other & further relief as to your Honor shall seem meet, and the circumstances of this case may require. May it please your Honor to grant unto your oratrix the commonwealth's writ of subpoena, directed to said defendant, commanding him &c

 Fry & Paull
 for compl[ainan]t

Marriage Certificate

May 24, 1842
Married by the Rev. C. C. Bert
Mr. Levi Wells and Miss Christiana Daugua[35]
Ohio County

---

35. In other places, her name is listed as Christiana Dangus. West Virginia Marriages Index.

Letter Entered into Evidence

February the 13th 1857
My Dear Anny

It is with pleasure I take a portion of my lonly time in this glacing prison House to adress you feeling as I doe for Being so long form your cind imbraces & arms. did you But Know How I feel for you I know your Heart would Breake you Knowe that I am here for no Crime But jealousy But I will be out the first of the weak I am very anxious to see you or here from you *So my Deer Be of good Cheer* and do not Be discouraged for all that I promise you I will perform you see my love is true it gets Better the more it is tride. I was very sorry you come here to see me and could not some of our folks informed the Jale keeper about you and me But I told the Jaler that you was my wash woman and wated to see you so you can call now and tell him you wash for me But you can write o write soon and send it By Mrs Lowes little girl give it to the jailor for Mr Wells and it will Be Right or Bring it your self all I am staying here for is you Dear my wife would Not let me stay here one day if I would for sake you But I will rot here Before I will for sake you my dear My [illegible] all about you If you can get along till I get out I will go all away with you and get Marrid I will Have a divorce as soon as cort acts Please write soon I Remain your True Hearted Lover untill Death Shall disolve us Nuthing els can.

Depositions of Witnesses[36]

EMILY JANE ROSE

QUESTION: Where do you reside?
ANSWER: In the City of Wheeling.
QUESTION: Are you acquainted with the parties to this suit?
ANSWER: Yes, I am somewhat acquainted with Levi Wells.
QUESTION: State what you know of any act or acts of adultery or lewdness committed by the said Levi Wells, with whom, when, and where?
ANSWER: I went to the house in Wheeling where Annie O'brien lived, on Monroe Street sometime in the last January one Monday night, I was slightly acquainted with her and went to call, and found the said Levi Wells was there, I stayed there about an hour, and then Wells

---

36. Emily Jane Rose, Annie O'Brien, A. M. Adams, Samuel Smith, and James Herriott testified on April 30, 1857, at the cost of $23.81. Emily and Annie signed with their marks.

pulled off his clothes and got into bed and said come to bed Annie dear, and then the said Annie O Brien took off her clothes and got into bed with him then I got up and come away.

QUESTION: Who owned the house spoken of above?
ANSWER: Mr. A. M. Adams.

ANNIE O'BRIEN[37]

QUESTION: Are you acquainted with Levi Wells?
ANSWER: Yes sir, I was acquainted with him one week.
QUESTION: State what you know of any act or acts of adultery or lewdness committed by him said Levi Wells and when and where and with whom.
ANSWER: During the last winter I think in [January] or [February] I boarded for a week at the house of a woman named as I understood Jane Street who lived on Monroe Street in the city of Wheeling while I was there I saw Wells there often, saw him give this woman money several times, saw him bring her victuals and provisions, he told me that he had been keeper of her and her baby, he came there in the evening after night, I believe she was a woman of bad character.

A. M. ADAMS

QUESTION: Are you acquainted with Levi Wells the defendant?
ANSWER: Yes, I am.
QUESTION: State whether during the past winter you rented a house to the said Wells? If so, state the facts & circumstances connected with the renting and occupation of said house.
ANSWER: Wells came to me sometime during the winter and asked me whether I had a house to suit. I told him I had. He said there was a widdow woman wanted to rent a house. I asked him how many children she had, he said four. I asked him then as to the moral character of the woman. He said it was good. I then asked him if he knew she was a decent woman. He said he did. I asked him then if she belonged to any branch of the christian church. He said she belonged to the Roman Catholic. I asked her name, & I think he said her name was Donelly. I told him I would not rent it to any woman of loose character, I would rather the house should be idle. He still told me she was a decent woman. I then rented it to him for her, I put a lock on the house and put glass in the windows where bro-

---

37. It is unclear if this is the same Annie O'Brien with whom Levi was having an affair. It was a common name in the Irish community.

ken. The first day after they were in, or I believe the first night, one of my journey men come down to the store in quite a rage saying this woman was one who was with a woman I had a short time before turned out of the house for having kept a house of bad repute. The next day I went up to see if such was the fact and found it was so. I ordered her out immediately she said she would go out as soon as she saw Mr Wells, and would give him the key to give to me. She did not go however, I sent a boy up the next day to see if she had gone out, and to order her out, she had not gone, I did not get them out for about two weeks, and never got any cent for the time they had it.

SAMUEL SMITH[38]

QUESTION: Are you the jailor of Ohio County?

ANSWER: I am.

QUESTION: Are you acquainted with the defendant Levi Wells, and state whether he has been recently confined in the jail of Ohio County.

ANSWER: I am acquainted with Wells, he has been confined in the jail under my charge.

QUESTION: Look at the paper now shown you marked (A) and state who is its creator as far as you know and what is its history?

ANSWER: The first I saw of the above paper was in the hands of Levi Wells. He handed it out of the door of his cell in the jail to James Herriot one of the City Constables, and asked him to give it Annie O'Brien. He said she lived on Clay Street. After I closed Wells' door I told Herriot I must see that letter before it went out of the jail. He gave it to me I opened & read it then handed it back to Herriot. After keeping it some time he returned it to me.

JAMES HERRIOTT

QUESTION: Look at the paper marked (A) and state whether you have had it in your possession from when you received it and what you did with it.

ANSWER: This letter or paper I received from Levi Wells. I dont recollect just how long ago but it was on a Sunday while he was in jail. He gave it to me and said he wanted me to take it and give it to Annie. I told him I would, and before I went out of the jail Mr Smith and I opened the letter and looked at it. I then put the letter in my packet and went home I then come down street again and stopped in at Mr Wickham with the letter and showed it to him. As near as

---

38. Samuel Smith was the jailer of Ohio County.

I can recollect I had this letter in my possession about three weeks. Mr Smith and I were standing on the corner by the Court house & I pulled the letter out to read it. Mr Smith asked me for the letter and said if I would give it to him he would have it published. I gave it to Mr Smith and that is the last I have seen of it till I saw it here. On the evening of the day on which I got the letter I was going past where Annie O'Brien lives, and I went in and read the letter to her and brought it away with me. She knew who Wells was.

[*On May 23, 1857, the court issued its decree, granting Christina Wells a divorce* a vinculo matrimonii. *She was granted permission to return to her unmarried name and given all the property she requested in the suit. Specifically, she asked for and received mirrors, a picture of Henry Clay, twelve chairs, one cupboard, one bed and its bedding, one bureau, one trunk, one rocking chair, one settee, twenty-three yards of carpeting, one parlor stove, one cooking stove, one dining table, one center table, one stand, one rocking chair, and one dozen bonnets and band boxes.*]

John Boyer v. Christina Boyer, 1859

[Boyer, John v. Boyer, Christina *(1859), Records of the Circuit Court of Ohio County, WVRHC, env. 217 b-12. John Boyer filed his bill in April 1859.*]

Bill for Divorce

To the Honorable George W. Thompson, Judge of the Circuit Court for Ohio County.

Your orator John Boyer,[39] humbly complaining sheweth unto your Honor, that your orator was on the 27th day of November 1857, married to Christina Hoefer,[40] by the Reverend George F. Gartner, pastor of the German Lutheran Church at Trenton in the State of New Jersey, said marriage being at said town of Trenton lawfully solemnized, according to the law of said state. That your orator & his said wife, duly consummated said marriage in said town of Trenton where they lived together as man & wife for about the space of three weeks, when your orator, be-

---

39. I am unable to find John Boyer in the census, but evidence in this case makes it clear that both he and his wife were German immigrants.

40. I am unable to find Christina Hoefer or Christina Boyer in the census records.

ing a mechanic by trade, & being unable to procure employment removed from Trenton & came to Wheeling Virginia where he obtained unemployment, leaving his wife temporarily in said town of Trenton, intending to send for her as soon as his business arrangements could enable him so to do. In the meantime rumors had reached your orator, that during the absence of your orator form his said wife, that she had been unfaithful to him & had committed adultery during said absence: In the month of July 1858, your orator received from his said wife, a letter signed by her maiden name of Christina Hoefer, & dated at Baltimore in the state of Maryland, July 2 1858, wherein she informed your orator that she had again got married to a certain brewer, which said letter written in the German Language, (your orator & his said wife both being Germans by birth) together with a translation of the same into the English language, your orator here files marked "A" & prays to be taken as part of this bill of complaint.[41] Soon after the receipt of this letter, your orator's said wife came to Wheeling Virginia, but in consequence of said letter & said report concerning her your orator refused to co-habit with her, & she went to reside in consequence thereof with her father in said city of Wheeling. Since then she has had illicit carnal connection, & committed adultery with divers men in the city of Wheeling, & especially often times with one George Anderson, during the Summer and fall of the year 1858. Your orator further charges, that he is a resident of the City of Wheeling in the State of Virginia, and that he has not cohabited with his said wife after his knowledge of her infidelity towards him as aforesaid. To the end therefore, that a divorce from the bonds of matrimony may be decreed between your orator and the said Christina and that your orator may have such other & further relief in the premises, as the nature & circumstances of this case may require. May it please you to grant unto your orator the commonwealth's writ of summons, to be directed to the said Christina Boyer, summoning her to be and appear before your Honor, on a day therein named, required her to answer all singular allegations of this bill upon her oath, & further to stand to, abide by & perform such orders & decrees as may be made herein, as to your Honor shall seem meet. And your orator will ever pray &c.

    Caldwell & Fisher[42]
    Sols for complainant[43]

---

41. These letters are missing from the court file.

42. This is the only mention of "Fisher" in these records, so I am unable to discover more about him.

43. Christina received a summons to appear on March 14, 1859. She signed and accepted it.

Depositions of Witnesses[44]

GEORGE ANDERSON

QUESTION: Are you acquainted with John Boyer & his wife?
ANSWER: Yes sir.
QUESTION: Where does John Boyer reside?
ANSWER: He has lived for the last year in Wheeling.
QUESTION: Do you know of any acts of infidelity on the part of his wife towards him; if so state fully.
ANSWER: Yes; some time last summer John Boyer went down to Cincinnati and I visited her, and she wanted me to and I had connexion with her, this happened about twice a week for four weeks.
QUESTION: State whether or not Boyer has lived with his wife since he found out that she was unfaithful to him?
ANSWER: Not that I know of.

WILLIAM KLINSORGE

QUESTION: State whether or not you are acquainted with John Boyer and Christina his wife.
ANSWER: Yes I am acquainted with them.
QUESTION: State whether or not you know anything about her being unfaithful to him—and state fully.
ANSWER: About two months ago I was a dock hand on the steam boat Liberty and I saw the engineer of that Boat (who was not John Boyer) have carnal connexion with Christina Boyer on the guards of the boat. He was doing it standing up, and it was about 12 o'clock at night and I was about 3 or 4 feet from him.

PHILIP MACK

QUESTION: State whether or not you are acquainted of John Boyer & his wife.
ANSWER: Yes sir.
QUESTION: State whether or not you know of John Boyer having been married to Christina Heber, and if so when, where & by whom.
ANSWER: I was present when they were married. It was at Trenton in New Jersey about two years ago. The name of the pastor who married them was Goertner—I do not know his first name—he was the pastor of the German Lutheran Church at Trenton.

---

44. These depositions were taken on April 20, 1859. All three witnesses signed with their mark.

Letters Entered into Evidence

Because you have thus written to me, my hope on You is lost. I had not served long, when I got an opportunity to enter into matrimony again and have married, but You can not do any thing against me. I and my husband went to the Squire office and consulted there. I told every thing You have done to me and the magistrate answered, that I can marry again, but if You should come they would put You in the jail.

You must not say, that You know meanness of me, no! I know more of You, which I can prove. You have given Your ring to the prostitutes. You have bought clothing in Trenton and have not paid for it. Somebody from Wheeling has written to me, that you Keep a prostitute, wherewith You spend all Your time and that You have every day a festive day. You must be made asunder yet, before you get the appearance like he is. He is a very man, his business is a brewer, he has told to me: "let that man fellow run". I and my husband are going to Germany the next fall, then I myself seek Your father. Do not write to me any more, now I have got a right good husband. I would not have again such a wild fellow like You. I have played your sweetheart long enough, this is not meanness; but just I wrote to You, because I have seen in Your letters, that I could marry again. You are the greatest fool.

Christina Hoefer

Baltimore, the 2d July 1858
I attest by my own hand and name, that I have been married with John Boyer by George F. Gaertner, on the 24th November 1857 and that now we both have agreed to separate us again and therefore I set John Boyer free and loose from me and promise, that he may marry again at any time.

Christina Hoefer
on the 14th Decr 1857

Being requested by You to write, I write my last letter to You. You say, as I have seen in Your last letter, that I may agree with You. O no! that happens never and not more, You must agree with that one, whose sweetheart You have been, those just now I have experiences that meanness, You have done in Trenton, You must go back again to Trenton, where you can play lasterie with Caspar, than it is not any use more, that You always write to me I will not know any more from You, neither from Your father nor from Your brothers and sisters, they are exactly so dear to me as You and I wish to hear nothing from You, I think, You are a fool. This is my fourth letter, I have written to You, that I wish to know nothing from You. You write, that I have made a mean name to You in Wheeling. You have been already a longwhile mean in Wheeling and I have heard of plenty meanness, You have done on the ship I have sworn on my life and soul to accept You not any more. I give you the right to marry at any time, if it pleases to You, I have nothing against it, I remaine for all my life—time, as I am at present, Your hope on me is in vain.

John Boyer

[*The court issued a decree in May 1859 declaring that because of Christina's adultery, it would grant John Boyer his divorce a vinculo matrimonii. Christina was told to pay the costs. There are no records for either Christina or John after their divorce.*]

Mary Snider v. Isaac Snider, 1858

[Snider, Mary L.—by her next friend Sargent, Andrew J. v. Snider, Isaac *(1858), Records of the Circuit Court of Ohio County, WVRHC, env. 221 b-9. Mary filed her divorce petition in June 1858. On June 5, the court issued a summons for Isaac and determined that he was not a resident of Virginia. She then published notice of her divorce petition in the local papers.*]

Bill of Divorce

To the Honl George W. Thompson, Judge of the Circuit Court of Ohio County,

Bill of the Complainant Mary L. Snider, by her next friend, Andrew Sargent, against Isaac Snider, Defendant.

Your oratrix shews to your Honor that she was lawfully married to the said defendant Isaac Snider on the 10th of January 1856, in the town of West Alexander, Washington County Pa—that after being so married they lived together in the said County of Washington for part of some six months—about that time the said Isaac committed some felony, for which he was arrested & committed to the jail of Washington County, from which he was bailed, and on being so bailed obsconded, and never appeared to answer to an indictment against him & lurked abroad in other places unknown to your oratrix. That after his arrest, bailment, and disappearance as aforesaid, your oratrix removed to the County of Ohio state of Virginia, where she has resided for about the last two years; your oratrix further sheweth that she has supported herself by her own industry & labor for about the last two years, and ever since the said Isaac was arrested & imprisoned for the criminal offense in Pennsylvania. And that she has never lived with the said Isaac since his said imprisonment, nor has the said Isaac in any way contributed to her support since his said arrest & imprisonment. The said Isaac after absconding, on being bailed as aforesaid, lurked abroad in different places, to your oratrix unknown; but he was frequently seen in the County of Ohio, and on Steam boats on the Ohio River, & frequently seen in the city of Wheeling during the last two years. He has not now, nor hath had, so far as your oratrix knows, any fixed residence, since his said escape on bail. Your oratrix further saith that she has understood that he has been recently accused of another felony, or other crime, committed in the city of Wheeling, & that he has fled to parts unknown. She further saith that the said Isaac Snider during this visits or sojournings in the city of Wheeling, and between the 1st of March 1858, and the last of May of the same year, has had frequently criminal connection & committed adultery with various loose women & prostitutes, and especially with two women of bad character, to wit, Lizzie Carr & Mary Long; the precise days their adulteries may have been committed, she cannot undertake to state, but she charges that they were committed within the time before mentioned; she further charges, that he has within the said period, been very often in the company of the said Carr especially & lavished upon her, all the wages & moneys, he could earn by running upon the said Steamboats, or otherwise. Your oratrix further saith that she is not aware of any estate the said Snider possesseth.[45]

In tender consideration of the premises, she prays that the said Isaac Snider should be made defendant & brought before the Court by due process of law, that he answer the Bill, and in the end, that a decree that she be divorced a vinculo matrimonii from the said Isaac by made by the Court. That the property which she has herself accumulated be returned to her; that a suitable provision out of any estate, which the said Isaac may have, may be made for herself, that he pay the costs of this suit, & finally that your Honor may grant such other & further relief as may be agreeable to equity & good conscience.

Fry & Paull for Complt.

---

45. Mary requested a full divorce, alimony, and costs.

Depositions of Witnesses[46]

JAMES BENNETT

QUESTION: State whether you are acquainted with the defendant, Isaac Snider, & how long have you known him?
ANSWER: I have been acquainted with Mr Isaac Snider since the first of March last.
QUESTION: State what you know of any acts of lewdness or adultery committed by the said Snider here or elsewhere.
ANSWER: About the latter part of April last, I was on my way home and at the corner of Quincy and Water Street I met Isaac Snider. This was 6 or 6 ½ o'clock in the evening. We walked up to the corner of Quincy & Main Streets where we met Liz Caton and Mary Long, both lewd women. We continued with said women until we arrived at the alley near the Melodeon buildings. Snider took Mary Long in the board pile. I left him there and did not see him again until the next morning. The next morning he came up into my room before I was out of bed. I then asked him how he made it last night. He replied that he had made it all right, that he had had the woman all night. This was the only time I ever went with Snider on such business. I have seen him in Cincinnati in the company of lewd women—he once told me that he was keeping a woman in Wheeling and invited me to go with him to see her, but I did not go. He told me that Liza Carr was the name of the woman he was keeping. This Liza Carr used to come down to the boat (the Steamboat Liberty, said Snider was a fireman on said boat) when she arrived in port—he always went away with her as soon as he got his money for his wages. The following day he seemed always to be out of money and would ask me to treat him. Mr Snider left the "Liberty," two trips before I did. Sometime about the first of May 1858. I did not see him again until I went on the Steamboat "R. F. Sass" sometime about the last of May 1858. He then told me he was going to St. Louis on the Steamboat "Hickman." I have not seen him since.

SUSAN ALLEN

QUESTION: Are you acquainted with Mary S. Snider the plaintiff in this cause, and where does she reside?
ANSWER: I am acquainted with her. She is my sister-in-law. She resides

---

46. James Bennett and Susan Allen signed their names.

in Wheeling. She has lived here for the last two years. She moved here from Washington County, Penna.

QUESTION: State what you know of her marriage to Isaac Snider the defendant.

ANSWER: She was married to him on the 10th day of January 1857 at West Alexander, Washington County, Penna. I was present at the time they were married. They were married by Esq. Sutherland in the presence of myself and some of the members of Esq. Sutherland's family. The paper hereto annexed marked "A" is the marriage certificate furnished by Esq. Sutherland.[47] It was written by the daughter of Esq. Sutherland in his presence, at his request and handed to Mrs. Snider.

[*On October 19, 1858, the court awarded Mary a divorce* a vinculo matrimonii. *It is unclear what happened to Mary and Isaac after the divorce. Their names are too common to track.*]

---

47. This record no longer exists.

CHAPTER 2

Abandonment

I WOULD NOT GIVE UP MY WIFE FOR THE WORLD

Elizabeth Rogers v. Thomas Rogers, 1854

[Rogers, Elizabeth A. v. Rogers, Thomas *(1854), Records of the Circuit Court of Ohio County, WVRHC, env. 206 b-1. Elizabeth Rogers filed her divorce petition in February 1854. Beginning on March 7, 1854, she advertised her decision in the* Wheeling Argus *for four weeks, stating that she did not believe he was a resident of Virginia anymore. Later that spring, the court accepted a demurrer, giving Elizabeth time to amend her petition and Thomas time to file his own response. Their marriage certificate states that the pastor of the Associate Reformed church in Wheeling married them on June 15, 1853.*]

Bill of Divorce

In the Circuit Court for Ohio County
In chancery,
To the Honorable George W. Thompson Judge of said Court, Your oratrix Elizabeth A. Rogers[1] of the town of South Wheeling in Ohio County Virginia humbly complaining, sheweth unto your Honor that your oratrix whose maiden name was Elizabeth A. Marriott, was married on the 15th day of June 1853 to Thomas Rogers[2] of said county of Ohio, a certificate of which said marriage signed by the Revd. J. T. McClure[3] the duly licensed clergyman who performed said marriage ceremony, your oratrix herewith files and prays that the same may be taken

---

1. Elizabeth Marriott was born on December 13, 1822, in Nottinghamshire, England. U.S. Find a Grave Index.

2. Thomas Rogers was born on December 22, 1822, in Plymouth, Massachusetts. U.S. Find a Grave Index.

3. Rev. James Thomas McClure was a minister at the local Presbyterian church. He was about thirty at the time he conducted this marriage and had moved to Wheeling from Pennsylvania. United States Federal Census for 1870.

as a part of this bill of complaint. Your oratrix further shews unto your Honor that your oratrix and her said husband lived and cohabited together from said 15th June 1853 in the County of Ohio until on or about the 5th day of December 1853 her husband deserted her & left the state of Virginia for parts unknown to your oratrix declaring that he would never again live with your oratrix, and leaving your oratrix in the family way or pregnant with a child by her said husband & without money or means for her support. Your oratrix alledges that the said desertion of her upon the part of her said husband was without any cause whatever, and that she was ever to him a true loving and obedient wife. Forasmuch therefore as her husband has then cruelly and wantonly deserted her & left her without means of support, and to the end that your oratrix may be enabled by a decree made by this honorable Court divorcing her from the bed & board[4] and future control of her husband, to protect any property which she may hereafter acquire from any disposition or control upon the part of her husband, and that your oratrix by such a decree may be enabled to contract as a feme sole,[5] & that your oratrix may have such other & further relief in the premises as may seem agreeable to equity and good conscience, may it please your Honor to grant unto your oratrix the Commonwealths writ of subpoena to be directed to the said Thomas Rogers thereby commanding him at a certain day to appear before your Honor in this Honorable Court and then & there to answer all & singular this premises & further to stand to abide & perform such order & decree as your Honor shall appear agreeable to Equity & good conscience. And your oratrix will ever pray &c.

Alfred Caldwell
Sol for Complainant

---

4. Petitioners could choose between two types of divorces in this era: absolute divorce (or divorce *a vinculo matrimonii*) and divorce from bed and board (or divorce *a mensa et thoro*). Absolute divorces were rarer and were given only for certain causes (such as adultery). In Virginia, petitioners could not get an absolute divorce for abandonment alone. Therefore, Elizabeth would have had to file for divorce from bed and board, which amounted to a legal separation. Neither party could remarry. *Code of Virginia* (1849), chap. 109, sec. 7.

5. A feme sole was a single woman. Married women, or femes covert, lost many legal rights upon marriage. They could not own property independently of their husbands (unless their state was one of the few that had a married women's property law by 1854), they could not write a will, they could not sue or be sued, etc. Reclaiming one's status as feme sole, and therefore one's ability to own and transfer property or earn and keep one's wages, was a major driving factor in many women's divorce cases. Basch, "Relief in the Premises."

Demurrer

The demurrer of Thomas Rogers to the Bill of complaint of Elizabeth Rogers complainant. This defendant by protestation not confessing or acknowledging all or any of the matters and things in the said complainants bill to be true, in such manner and form as the same are herein set forth and alleged doth demur thereto, and for cause of demurer sheweth, that the said complainant, who appears by said Bill to be a feme covert hath exhibited her said Bill without any person being therein named as her next friend,[6] wherefore and for divers other errors and imperfections, this defendant humbly demands the judgment of this Honorable Court whether he shall be compelled to make any further or other answer to the said bill, or any of the matters and things therein contained, and prays to be hence dismissed, with his reasonable costs in his behalf sustained.[7]

M. Nelson[8] for Deft.

Answer[9]

To the Hon. Geo. W. Thompson, Judge of the Circuit Court for Ohio County:

The answer of Thomas Rogers to the bill of complaint of Elizabeth Rogers (who sues by Thomas Omen[10] her next friend) complainant. The said Thomas Rogers, with the usual reservations answering says that he admits that he was married to complainant, and that he lived & cohabited with her for about the period of time in the bill stated: but he denies that he deserted complainant, "without any cause whatever" or that he "left the state of Virginia for parts unknown," as in said bill is alleged.

---

6. Married women in many places (including Virginia) could not sue in their own name because of the practice of coverture. Thomas is pointing out that Elizabeth Rogers tried to sue in her own name.

7. In other words, according to Virginia law, Elizabeth was a married woman, and married women could not sue in court under their own names. She needed to sue for divorce with the help of a "next friend," or a legal representative. Because she had not done that in her first petition, Thomas argued that it should be thrown out.

8. I am unable to locate anyone of this name or alternate spellings.

9. Defendants were allowed to file their own response to the accusations of their spouses. This is Thomas Rogers's answer to Elizabeth's charges. He filed the answer on June 29, 1854.

10. I am unable to find any records for Thomas Omen or determine his relationship with Elizabeth.

He admits that about the 5th day of December 1853, some differences arose between him & complainant, which he will briefly state—

This defendant, who is a mechanic employed at one of the Iron Factories in South Wheeling, Virginia, at the time referred to, spoke to complainant of her neglecting to rise from her bed in the morning to prepare his breakfast [and] to enable him to go to his daily work at the proper house. To this defendant's complaint, which on a review of the whole matter he conceives to have been just & reasonable, complainant replied in an angry and unbecoming manner: not only refusing to respect this defendants request, but using towards defendant language which was disrespectful [and] offensive. At that time defendant & complainant were living in the same house with Henry Marriott, the father of complainant, but separate & apart from said Marriotts family, in a room which defendant & complainant rented from said Marriott & held at a certain rent. That on the occurrence of the difference aforesaid between complainant & defendant, which was in said rented room, complainant left the room, & in a few moments returned with her mother. Mrs Elizabeth Marriott, who, instead of using any means to restore harmony between complainant & defendant; or even to ascertain the cause of the [dispute] or which party was in fault, immediately assailed this defendant with offensive & abusive language & in an angry tone, and in words too foul to be fit here to repeat, ordered this defendant to leave the house, and never to return to it again—and even so far forgetting what became her & her relation to this defendant as to threaten to take the life of this defendant, should he ever enter her house again.

This defendant admits that under the excitement produced by such provocation and insult, he left the house—telling complainant that, if they could not live together peaceably, he thought they had better separate. But denies going to parts unknown to complainant. On the contrary he avers that he informed complainant that the defendant was going to visit his mother & relatives who reside at Plymouth in the state of Massachusetts;[11] and that his intention was to return to Wheeling again in about a month. And this defendant avers that he did thereupon visit his friends at Plymouth & return again to South Wheeling on the 27th December 1853 having been absent but a little more than three weeks: that on his return he sent word to complainant, who without affording

---

11. As previously stated, Thomas Rogers was born in Plymouth, although I am unable to track him or his family in the Plymouth records. U.S. Find a Grave Index.

to defendant any opportunity to see her, sent him word that she was sick. This defendant thereupon called at the house of complainants father enquired for complainant & stated he wished to see her. On which occasion defendant was met by complainants father, who told defendant he could not be permitted to see complainant, and in a very insolent manner ordered defendant to leave his house; and was even guilty of the affront of taking defendant by the collar for the purpose of ejecting him from his house, at the same time ordering this defendant, in very rude & offensive language never to visit his house again.

And this defendant further answering denies that he left complainant destitute of means of support. On the contrary he avers that on the day previous to his leaving her, he had purchased & sent home half a barrel of flour: and that as he was leaving her, he offered her ten dollars in gold, which she declined to receive.

And this defendant further answering says that ever since said 27th December 1853, he has been residing in South Wheeling, where he still resides; and that with a view to a reconciliation with complainant he has sought an interview with her, on several different occasions, which he expects to prove by one Samuel Slater, Robert Haslett, & others. But so far as this defendant can learn, complainant, as well as her father and mother have deliberately slighted & rejected defendant's overtures & advances, in the most insolent & offensive manner. Under such circumstances and in the face of such treatment this defendant denies that complainant is or can be entitled to any relief or decree whatever from or against this defendant. On the contrary he avers that complainant has been herself the party in fault.[12] And this defendant having fully answered prays to be here dismissed with his costs in this behalf wrongfully sustained.

Thomas Rogers

Depositions of Witnesses[13]

HENRY MARRIOTT

QUESTION: Are you acquainted with the parties to this suit?
ANSWER: Yes sir.

---

12. According to contemporary understandings of divorce, a couple could get divorced only if *one* of them was at fault and the other was "innocent."

13. Charles Marshall, a chancery commissioner, supervised these depositions on April 22, 1854. Henry Marriott signed his name; his wife, Elizabeth, signed with her mark.

QUESTION: When were they married & where?
ANSWER: On the 15th of June 1853, in South Wheeling at my house.
QUESTION: How long did they cohabit together, and when and where and how was that cohabitation broken off?
ANSWER: It was about five months that they cohabited together, living in South Wheeling till about the month of November last, then he went away and left her and said he would not trouble me nor her nor her family any more. He left her without money or anything to provide for her. They still live apart and he has never since up to this day spoken to her and has not contributed in any way to her support. I am her Father.
QUESTION: How long last past has the complainant resided in Ohio County?
ANSWER: Since April 1853.
QUESTION: Do you know the cause of the Defendants deserting the Plaintiff? If so please state it.
ANSWER: The only cause I know is words which they had between themselves about matters connected with themselves. All that I know about it is that he is of a very jealous disposition. He accused her of having a correspondence with a young man who has been for several years and still is in California.
QUESTION: Has there been any issue of this marriage? If so state the age and sex of the child.
ANSWER: Yes: there has been a son born the 9th of this month and still living.
QUESTION: What is the occupation and pecuniary circumstances of the defendant?
ANSWER: He is working in the rolling mill, and when he is in full work makes fifteen or twenty dollars a week.[14] He has no property that I know of.

ELIZABETH MARRIOTT

QUESTION: Are you acquainted with the parties to this suit?
ANSWER: Yes sir, I am the mother of the Complainant.
QUESTION: When were they married and where?
ANSWER: On the 15th of June 1853 at our House in South Wheeling.

---

14. A rolling mill flattened and produced iron early in the nineteenth century and steel later in the century.

QUESTION: How long did they cohabit together and when & where & how was that cohabitation broken off?
ANSWER: They lived together five months. It was broken off at our house growing out of some words about his breakfast was the first thing. She had been sick and did not get up to get it early, and he told her that he could not live with her any longer. He said he should be a dead man if he lived with her two weeks longer. He said he would go east and live with his mother the rest of his days. He said that she was jealous of the Scotch girl, and he was jealous of the California man. That troubled his mind and always would do. This occurred about November.
QUESTION: How long last past has the complainant resided in Ohio County?
ANSWER: Since April 1853.
QUESTION: Has there been any issue of this marriage? If so, state the age and sex of the child.
ANSWER: There has been one child—a boy, born on the 9th of this month.
QUESTION: What is the occupation and pecuniary circumstances of the Defendant?
ANSWER: He works in the rolling mill, and when in steady work he gets from fifteen to twenty dollars a week. He has no property that I know of.

HENRY MARRIOTT, CROSS EXAMINATION[15]

QUESTION: In whose house were the Defendant and Complainant living when the separation of which you have spoken took place?
ANSWER: They were living in my house as I stated in the Deposition.
QUESTION: Did you or your wife at or about the time when the Defendant left your house at the time of said separation request or command said Defendant to leave your house, and not return to it again, or to words to that effect?
ANSWER: When Mr Rogers left our house and separated from his wife in the room, I helped him to carry his trunk down stairs by his request. He left there to seek conveyance to take his trunk from the

---

15. Marshall noted that Thomas Rogers arrived at the commissioner's before the closing time for depositions, but Henry had already left. The commissioner recalled Henry for May 2 and allowed Thomas to cross-examine him.

house, while we were in conversation at the door, Mr Rogers told me that he would never trouble me nor the family no mor[e]. I told him then that I did not request any more from him than that. I can make no further answer than I have made. I told him I would never quarrel with any man and he said that I had always treated him as a gentleman and a father and those were the last words he said to me at parting. I told him that if he went away under the present circumstances not to return any more.

QUESTION: Did you hear your wife tell the defendant previous to his leaving your house on the occasion refered to in the former question that if he ever entered it again, she would blow his brains out or words to that effect?

ANSWER: I never did, I was not present at the time if anything of the kind was said.

QUESTION: Did not the Defendant about three weeks after said separation call at your house again and request an opportunity of seeing his wife, & if so how did you treat him on that occasion?

ANSWER: Previous to his calling at my house he sent a message to request an interview with his wife at another House. She sent him word she would not see him at all. After that he came to my House. I asked him what he wanted. He told me he wanted to see his wife, I told him she would not see him. I requested him to leave the house. He told me he would not do it. I kept a tavern, a public house and he had a right in it. I told him he had no right with me. I opened the doors of the bar room. He sat down on the settee. He told me I could not put him out. I told him I would soon let him see that I could. I took him by the collar. He requested me for his goods. I told him I had nothing to do with them, if he could get them by law he could get them, as the suit was then in the hands of an attorney. This happened three or four weeks after the separation. I then forbid him to enter my house any more.

QUESTION: Did the Defendant call at your house more than once, about the time referred to in your preceding answer?

ANSWER: No.

QUESTION: Did you employ Mr Caldwell to institute the present suit?

ANSWER: I did by his wifes request as her Father.

QUESTION: During the time, the parties lived together did not the Defendant rent a part of your House from you for the accommodation of himself and wife?

ANSWER: I accommodated him and his wife with a room in the house. If he can find the receipt of the payment of rent that will prove it.
QUESTION: Do you mean to be understood as denying that he rented a room from you?
ANSWER: I never rented him a room during the whole time he was there with his wife. All the dealings I had about the room was with his wife.
QUESTION: Did his wife pay you rent for the room, during the time they lived together?
ANSWER: Yes, and gave it up the day he left her, and never slept in the room since.
QUESTION: Was said room furnished by the Defendant?
ANSWER: That I know nothing about. I had nothing to do with it.
QUESTION: Did you provide the furniture for the said room?
ANSWER: I had nothing to do with how it was provided. I will answer no further questions with regard to it, without my lawyer is present.

ELIZABETH MARRIOTT, CROSS EXAMINATION

QUESTION: Were you present when the separation between the parties took place?
ANSWER: Yes sir
QUESTION: Did you previous to the Defendant leaving your house request or command him to leave and not to return to it again?
ANSWER: When he got all his money in his pocket and had made up his mind to go, he told her that she had better send up for her Mother as he wished to go quietly, he did not wish to have any disturbance at this time. When I got into the room, I said what is the matter, and he said Lizzy and me has had a quarrel and I said you began very soon again after the first quarrel and he said yes Elizabeth was jealous of the scotch girl and he was jealous of the California man, & he said it always troubled him and always would do so & if he had to live with her two weeks longer he would be a dead man. Then I said the sooner they parted the better if they could not agree to live together, and he said he was going to go home & spend the remainder of his days with his mother as he had been a bad boy he would try and pay his Mother back for what he had done in his younger days. When he said Good bye I said good shoot, I told him not to come any more for if he did and I had anything in my hands I would break his head.

QUESTION: Did you not threaten him that if he ever returned to your house again, you would blow his brains out or words to that effect?
ANSWER: I never mentioned blowing brains out at all.
QUESTION: Did he not return to your house and say that he wished to see his wife again, about three weeks after the separation took place?
ANSWER: I heard he was there but I was sick in bed at the time and neither saw nor spoke to him.
QUESTION: Do you know whether the defendant offered the complt any money at the time he was leaving?
ANSWER: I dont know that he did, but he told her that she might have five dollars that was coming to him at the works if she would go and draw it. And when her Father went for it, he had drawn it himself.[16]

[*In this case, the court never ruled on the petition. After Elizabeth filed her depositions, no other documents appear from this case. In 1870, the couple still lived together in South Wheeling with their sons, William (sixteen) and Albert (thirteen), as well as Elizabeth's mother.[17] Thomas worked in the local rolling mill.[18] Sometime between then and Thomas's death in 1879, the family moved to Louisville, Kentucky. Thomas died there on Christmas Day, 1879; Elizabeth's mother died four months later. Elizabeth Rogers died on September 11, 1888, at the age of fifty-five, in Wheeling.[19]*]

Mary Jane Work v. Alexander Work, 1858

[Work, Mary Jane—by her next friend Goudy, Isaac v. Work, Alexander *(1858), Records of the Circuit Court of Ohio County, WVRHC, env. 221 b-2. Mary Jane Work filed her divorce petition in March 1858. The court issued a summons for Alexander on April 16, 1858, and a summons for witnesses on May 11, 1858. Court officials noted that Alexander no longer lived in Virginia.*]

---

16. Thomas Rogers's lawyer objected to this answer.

17. Elizabeth would have been pregnant with William at the time of her divorce petition. By 1870, he was a teenager working in a local nail factory. Henry Marriott died in late 1868. United States Federal Census for 1870; U.S. Find a Grave Index.

18. The couple was also found living together in 1860 in South Wheeling, although without Elizabeth's parents. United States Federal Census for 1860, 1870.

19. U.S. Find a Grave Index.

Bill of Divorce

To the Hon. Geo. W. Thompson, Judge of the Circuit Court for the County of Ohio:

Humbly complaining sheweth unto your Honor, your oratrix Mary Jane Work[20] of said County, who sues by Isaac Goudy[21] her next friend, that on the 5th day of May 1856, your oratrix then being a feme sole, was lawfully married to Alexander Work,[22] who was then a citizen of said County at the City of Wheeling. That after cohabiting with your oratrix as her husband until about the first day of June 1856 at said County, the said Alexander Work, without any legal or reasonable cause whatever, deserted your oratrix, and went hence to foreign parts and places; and that ever since that time, the said Alexander has without any legal or reasonable cause whatever, remained apart from your oratrix and has wholly neglected to contribute anything to your oratrix towards her maintenance. And your oratrix has been informed and verily believes that said Alexander has declared, and given it out in speeches, that he never would contribute or allow to your oratrix anything whatever for her future maintenance. And your oratrix verily believes, and charges it to be true that said Alexander Work has deserted your oratrix and still is dwelling or sojourning out of this Commonwealth, in parts and places to your oratrix unknown, to evade the fulfilment of his legal and conjugal duties & providing for or contributing to the just and suitable maintenance and support of your oratrix. And your oratrix further sheweth that said Alexander Work in repeated conversations with your oratrix and before her marriage to him, as well as in divers other conversations since that time, declared that he owned,

---

20. Mary Goudy married William Hill in Ohio County, Virginia, on August 19, 1841. William died sometime before her marriage to Isaac Goudy. Using the date of her marriage, we can surmise that she was probably born around the early 1820s. West Virginia Marriages Index.

21. Isaac Goudy was born in Virginia (eventually West Virginia) in 1818; his parents were from Pennsylvania. Because of his age, I suspect that he was Mary's brother, but I cannot prove this. By the time of the divorce case, he was married to Sarah Ann Goudy and living in Wheeling with his growing family. His son, James, would be involved in his own divorce case after the war, which is also featured in this book (*Goudy, Elizabeth v. Goudy, James* [1868]). Isaac worked as a carpenter. By 1870, he had moved south to Moundsville, West Virginia, and become a farmer. United States Federal Census for 1850, 1870, 1880; U.S. Find a Grave Index.

22. Alexander Work is not an uncommon name, and since he appears to have lived in Wheeling only a short time (and in between federal censuses), he is very hard to track.

and had title to suntry valuable parcels of land situated in the state of Iowa, and containing in all as much as three hundred and sixty acres or more. And although your oratrix does not certainly know the present value of said lands, she has understood from various sources that the same has been estimated by competent judges to be worth some twenty dollars per acre or more.

Your oratrix is advised that by reason of the matters above stated and set forth, she is entitled to a divorce from said Alexander Work "a mensa et thoro," and to have a just and reasonable allowance decreed to her, to be paid to her by said Alexander Work, in quarterly, or semi-annual payments, for her alimony. Your oratrix, therefore, prays that said Alexander Work be made a defendant to this suit with proper words to charge him, and that he be required to answer upon oath all and singular the premises and allegations aforesaid, as fully and explicitly, to all intents and purposes, as if the same were here again repeated, and that your oratrix be allowed by the decree of this Honorable Court a divorce from said Alexander Work "a mensa et thoro" in due and proper form, and that said Alexander be decreed to allow and to pay to your oratrix, in quarterly or half yearly payments, as to your Honor shall seem fit, just and reasonable sum or sums of money, so and for her alimony, and that the same be made a charge upon the real estate of the said Alexander Work; and that your oratrix may have such further and general relief in the premises as to equity may appertain and to your Honor shall deem just and right, may it please your Honor to grant unto your oratrix the commonwealth's most gracious writ or writs of subpoena.

M. Nelson[23] for Complt.

Depositions of Witnesses[24]

MARY ANN COUGHMAN

QUESTION: Are you acquainted with the parties to this suit?
ANSWER: Yes, sir.
QUESTION: State if you know when the complainant was married to the

---

23. Without a clear first name, I cannot track this lawyer.

24. Charles Marshall, the commissioner in chancery, took these depositions on May 18, 1858, at the office of Morgan Nelson, Esq., in Wheeling. All deponents signed their names.

defendant, and where, and whether or not you were present at said marriage.

ANSWER: It was about May 1856, that they were married in Wheeling & I was present at the marriage.

QUESTION: State if you had any conversation with the Defendant respecting his intention to marry the Complainant previous to their marriage. If so, state what you heard him say about it.

ANSWER: I had a conversation with him on the subject. He said when he married her he intended to take her & her family and do for them as if they were his own, & that he intended to take her sons and keep them at his house until they were old enough to go to trades; the two girls he would keep at home and support them as long as they lived at home, and be a father to them.

QUESTION: State if you know what opportunity he had had of becoming acquainted with Complainant and her family previous to their marriage.

ANSWER: He boarded with her for a year or more; she kept some few boarders.

QUESTION: Did you hear him speak of his intention to marry her more than once before his marriage?

ANSWER: Yes sir, a number of times.

QUESTION: State if you understood from the conversations how long before their marriage he had addressed complainant or signified his desire to marry her.

ANSWER: About a year.

QUESTION: State if you know about how long he lived with complainant after their marriage.

ANSWER: About four weeks.

QUESTION: Do you know whether he remained in Wheeling after that, or if not, where he went to?

ANSWER: He went to Steubenville, Ohio.[25]

QUESTION: Do you know where he is now and whether since he left complainant he has done anything towards her support?

ANSWER: I do not know where he is and I know he has not done anything for her.

QUESTION: Do you know of any cause that the Defendant had for leaving the Complainant?

---

25. Steubenville, Ohio, is about thirty miles north of Wheeling, up the Ohio River.

ANSWER: I heard him say before he left that he would not support her family, and that is what took him away.

QUESTION: What number of children has the Complainant?

ANSWER: Five: Three boys & Two girls.

QUESTION: State if you know from conversation with the Defendant what property he had at the time of their marriage.

ANSWER: I heard him say that he has land in Iowa, I am not positive how much; I do not recollect of hearing him speak of any other property.

DANIEL H. BIRD

QUESTION: Are you acquainted with the parties to this suit?

ANSWER: Yes sir.

QUESTION: State if you know how long the Defendant had been acquainted with the complainant & her family before their marriage.

ANSWER: I am not able to say how long they were acquainted, but he boarded some considerable length of time with her before they were married.

QUESTION: Do you know how long he lived with her after their marriage?

ANSWER: I can not be positive, but I suppose about four weeks.

QUESTION: What was his business or employment?

ANSWER: He was a laboring man. He worked around our shop. He had no trade that I know of, I was working at the Baltimore & Ohio Rail Road machine shop.[26]

QUESTION: Do you know where the Defendant moved & where he has been since he left the complainant?

ANSWER: I do not. I understood he went to Ohio. I do not think he has lived here since. I have not seen him lately.

QUESTION: Do you know from any conversation that you had with the Defendant why he left the complainant?

ANSWER: On account of having to maintain her children was the reason he gave me. He always spoke in the highest terms of her to me and as far as I could learn he gave her the same character to others.

JOHN T. STEVENS

QUESTION: Are you acquainted with the parties to this suit?

ANSWER: Yes sir.

---

26. A railroad machine shop was responsible for all of the repairs necessary to keep the railroad and its cars running. "National Register of Historic Places Nomination."

QUESTION: Do you know how long the parties were acquainted before their marriage?
ANSWER: The Defendant boarded in her family very nearly a whole summer. I lived two doors from them.
QUESTION: Do you know how long they lived together after their marriage?
ANSWER: A very short time—three or four weeks.
QUESTION: State if you know where the Defendant now is and where he has been since he left the complainant.
ANSWER: I can not say: the last time I heard of him he was in Ohio.
QUESTION: Do you know why he left the complainant?
ANSWER: On account of her children, he said he would not support them.
QUESTION: Did you hear him say what property he has?
ANSWER: Before he married. (I did not know he was going to be married at the time.) He was sitting on my porch at the time. He said he was going to sell his property in Iowa, which he said was worth $7000 and buy improved property here.

JOHN GOUDY

QUESTION: Are you acquainted with the parties to this suit?
ANSWER: Yes sir—the complainant is my sister.
QUESTION: How long had you been acquainted with the Defendant previous to their marriage?
ANSWER: About 18 months I believe, it may have been more or less.
QUESTION: What opportunity had the Defendant of becoming acquainted with the Complainant & her family before their marriage?
ANSWER: He boarded with her, over a year at different times. He was there, twice or thrice within 18 months as a boarder.
QUESTION: What was the complainants name before her marriage with the defendant and what family had she?
ANSWER: She was the widow of Wm Hill. She had five children 3 boys & 2 girls. Her oldest son at the time of her marriage was about 13 years old, & her youngest daughter 3 or 4 years old; they were all living at home at the time he was boarding there.
QUESTION: State what conversation if any you had with the Defendant respecting his desire to marry your sister previous to their marriage.
ANSWER: Some three or four weeks before they were married, he came to me and told me that he had proposed marriage with Mary, and that she refused him on account of her children. She did not want them seperated; he stated that he had told her frequently that he

would not separate the children that he would maintain them as his own; he wished me to intercede for him. I told him I could not under the circumstance she was old enough to choose for herself, not that I had anything against him & that if she did marry I wanted her to marry a man that would take care of her children; for she had brothers enough to help her to take care of her children: He said he had pledged himself to her and he would do the same to me, if she would marry him, to take care of the children & do a fathers part by them (those were his words). He said that his reasons for speaking to me was that I was her oldest brother and he wanted to make my advice on the subject. He said "I want her and will have her if I can get her" I then stated, "if you will have her, it is not worth my while to say anything more to you about it only one thing I will advise you, I want you to weigh the matter well before you say anything more to her about it, you have never had a family to maintain and know nothing about the expence of supporting a family; if you think you can do a fathers part by the children I have got nothing more to say about it, I will not dictate to you or to her." I told him that there was one thing more I wanted to say to him, that he must not expect her to go to the west with him as long as her mother lived. He said he was glad that I had mentioned that for that was one of her principal objections to marrying him. He said he had told her and he would tell me the same thing, that he would sell his land in Iowa and that he would never ask her to go there, for he had come to the conclusion to sell his land in Iowa and buy an improved farm here, either in Virginia or Ohio, he thought Virginia would suit him best. I told him I did not wish to dictate to him what he should do, only I knew she would go neither with him or any other man to the west as long as her mother lived. He said he knew that, he had learned that from herself, that he had agreed to all those things.

QUESTION: State when they were married and whether you were present at their marriage.

ANSWER: They were married about the first week in May 1856. I was present.

QUESTION: About how long did they live together after their marriage?

ANSWER: About four weeks.

QUESTION: State if you know where the Defendant has been since, and where he now is.

ANSWER: From the letters I received from him, I know that a part of the time he has been in Ohio and a part of the time in Iowa. I do not know where he is now. He has been in Virginia once or twice but I do not know that he stayed overnight, it was for a very short time.

QUESTION: Has the Defendant so far as you know or have reason to believe contributed anything toward the support of the complainant since he left her?

ANSWER: Nothing at all.

QUESTION: State if you know why he left the complainant?

ANSWER: He said he would not support the children. He told me that the day before he left.

QUESTION: Did he give any other reason besides his unwillingness to support her children?

ANSWER: None at all.

QUESTION: Did he say anything to you on that occasion respect[ing] the complainant, and if so what?

ANSWER: He said he had nothing to say against her.

QUESTION: Did you ever hear the Defendant say what property he had and what he considered it worth?

ANSWER: He told me he had two tracts of land in Clayton County, Iowa. One he was told was worth $25 per acre and the other $15. He supposed his land would bring him between $5 and $7000 and he thought that would get him a good improved farm here: to the best of my recollection one tract was 320 acres and the other was 80 acres.

[On May 14, 1858, the court granted a divorce from bed and board to Mary Jane Work, as well as alimony and costs. She would receive fifty dollars for the case and an annuity of $120, payable semiannually. There is no record of whether she obtained this money. Alexander Work appears to have returned to Iowa and his farm. Mary Work took her former name, Mary Hill, and continued to live in Wheeling. She lived in the Fifth Ward of Wheeling, near her brother, Isaac. In 1860, she lived with all five of her children. Her older sons, Hamilton and Wellington, were working as a boiler and a nailer, respectively. Her household looked much the same by 1870. After that, I can find no record of her.[27]]

---

27. United States Federal Census for 1860, 1870.

CHAPTER 3

Cruelty

ENCOURAGING THE DISOBEDIENCE OF HIS WIFE

Margaret Bole v. William Bole, 1855

[Bole, Margaret—by her next friend Jimeson, William W. v. Bole, William *(1855), Records of the Circuit Court of Ohio County, WVRHC, env. 208 b-4. Margaret filed her divorce petition in May 1854. The court then issued a summons for William Bole and confirmed that he no longer lived in Virginia. In October and December, she published notice of her divorce case in the local papers.*]

Bill for Divorce

To the Honorable George W. Thompson, Judge of the Circuit Court of Ohio County, Virginia:

Humbly complaining showeth unto your Honor your Oratrix Margaret Bole[1] of the City of Wheeling in the said state of Virginia, who sues in this behalf by William W. Jimeson[2] her next friend, that she was married to William Bole[3] on or about the [blank] day of [blank] in the City of New York in the State of New York. That she came to the City of Wheeling with her husband the said William Bole in the year 1848, and that your Oratrix and the said William Bole resided in the said City of Wheeling and County of Ohio, and cohabited as husband and wife thereon from the year last named until about the 15th of October 1853. That since the said William Bole and your Oratrix were married, they

---

1. The only record I can find of a Margaret Bole is of a marriage to a man named Basil Kingessner in 1869. I cannot determine if this is the same Margaret Bole. West Virginia Marriages Index.

2. Wm. W. Jemison lived in Wheeling's Second Ward in 1840. I cannot determine his relationship with Margaret. This name also differs slightly from the "William W. Jimeson" listed in the document, although misspellings were common in court and census records. United States Federal Census for 1840.

3. I have found no record for William Bole in Wheeling or New York.

have had ten children six of which are now living—the oldest child will be fourteen years of age on the 28th day of July 1854 and the youngest three years of age on the 12th day of April 1854. That when the said William Bole came to Wheeling to reside in the year 1848 he had about seven thousand Dollars and with that capital opened a Boot and Shoe Store on the West side of Main Street between Madison and Union Streets in the City of Wheeling—and resided with his family in the same building that contained his store room.

Your Oratrix further shews unto your Honor that for years previous to the 14th day of October 1853, she has been treated with great cruelty by the said William Bole, that he has often struck her, and spit in her face, and frequently threatened to shoot her, and once drew a knife upon her threatening to rip her up. That for several months previous to the 14th day of October 1853 she lived in such continued dread of the said William Bole and entertained such apprehensions of bodily hurt, that your Oratrix was compelled every night to lock herself up, in an open unfinished apartment in the upper story of the said building in which they dwelt to protect herself against him. That said William Bole, compelled your Oratrix to perform all the menial offices about their household and never permitted her to hire a Servant but compelled her to do all of the house work and attend to the store in addition, and abused her with the most approbrious epithets in the presence of their children for not doing enough often accompanying such language with blows.

Your Oratrix further shews unto your Honor that she patiently submitted to the ill treatment to which she was subjected—she made no complaint—and endeavored to obey every command, and yielded to every caprice of the said William Bole her husband—that she continued to live with the said William Bole until about the 14th of October 1853. At that time the said Bole left the City of Wheeling avowedly for the purpose of going to Zanesville to collect money. That he took all the money there was in the house, amounting to about One Hundred Dollars. That he drew from the Merchants & Mechanics Bank of Wheeling all the money he had in deposit there and took it with him. That he was expected to be gone a few days only. Your Orator has never since heard from [him] directly. She is informed and believes that the said William Bole about four weeks after he left Wheeling as above mentioned wrote a letter to William W Jimeson of the City of Wheeling in which he stated he was on board of a ship, in the City of New York just about leaving for Australia. Your Oratrix has never heard from him and does not know what has since become of him

Your Oratrix further states that at the time the said William Bole left Wheeling as aforesaid, she is informed he was indebted to a large extent to various individuals and firms in Baltimore, Philadelphia, and elsewhere. That they or some of them have since attached the effects of the said William Bole and they have since been sold by order of Court.[4] Your Oratrix is informed and believes and so charges, that the proceeds of said sale are insufficient to pay off the debts of the said Bole—so that a large amount still remains in arrear and unpaid. That in consequence of this indebtedness of the said William Bole any property which your Oratrix by her own labor and industry may acquire, she is advised, will be liable to be taken by the creditors of said Bole in discharge of his said debts.[5] That while your Oratrix admits that said debts ought to be paid, and if she had the means to do so she would willingly pay them all yet as she had been deserted and abandoned by her husband the said William Bole, and as he has taken with him all the ready money at his command and as some of the creditors have attached and sold all the other property he possessed, and your Oratrix is left alone and without means to carry on business she submits to your Honor, that the proceeds of her own labor ought in justice to be appropriate to the support and maintenance of herself and her six children, who are entirely dependant upon your Oratrix for a livelihood.

Wherefore in as much as your Oratrix is remediless in the premises except in a Court of Chancery where by virtue of an Act of the General Assembly, such matters are properly cognizable, your Oratrix prays that the said William Bole be made a party defendant to the Bill of complaint with apt and fit words to charge him as such—that he be required fully to answer this Bill of complaint—that in consequence of the aggravated cruelty of said William Bole towards your Oratrix continued during a series of years, and the abandonment and desertion of your Oratrix by the said William Bole, leaving her without means or resources other than her own labor to support herself and children and subjected her to his heavy indebtedness, your Oratrix prays that by the order and decree of this Honorable Court your Oratrix and said Wil-

---

4. A writ of attachment allows the court to freeze or seize someone's assets while legal action is ongoing.

5. Avoiding liability for their husband's debts was a major reason why married women filed for divorce. See the introduction for a discussion of the evolution of married women's property laws in the United States.

liam Bole may be divorced; and perpetually separated and that your Oratrix may be protected in her person and in any property she may thereafter acquire in such manner and to such extend as the law in such cases will permit.[6]

And your Oratrix prays further for such other relief in the premises as the nature and circumstances of the case may require and to your Honor may seem meet. And that one or more writs of Subpoena directed to the said William Bole commanding him to appear may be awarded to your Oratrix. And your Oratrix will every pray &c.

Russell[7] & Fitzhugh[8]

Letter Entered into Evidence

New York City Oct. 24th 1853
My Dear Friend Jamison

It would be [crossed out] imposible for me to leave this Country without giving you some clew to my whereabouts. After the consultation with you and Friend Warner, I left Wheeling by the 2 oclock stage for the West. I cannot tell how it happened that I made no preparation to be absent more than one week not further, although I intended to be absent about three weeks. So here I am in the City of New York and arrived here with out much knowledge of the fact. Money short and distracted mind I applied to an old acquaintance and opened my mind to him on the subject of my domestic grievances (*which you but partially understand*). After one days consultation and his advice I agreed to Ship

---

6. The language here suggests that Margaret would like a divorce *a vinculo matrimonii*. Yet, for her to qualify for a divorce *a vinculo matrimonii* from William, he would have had to have abandoned her more than three years before she filed or have committed adultery. Hence, she may have hoped more for the "perpetual separation" than for the divorce.

7. Charles Wells Russell was born in Sistersville, Virginia, in July 1818. As a young man, he came to Wheeling to attend the Linsly Institute and then graduated from Jefferson College in Pennsylvania. He then went into practice with Edward Fitzhugh. When Virginia seceded, he went with it, serving multiple terms in the Virginia legislature during the war. He also served as a member of the Confederate Congress. Atkinson, *Bench and Bar of West Virginia*, 13; Lawson, *Downwardly Mobile*, 54.

8. Edward Henry Fitzhugh was born on September 21, 1816, in Caroline County, Virginia. He attended Warrenton Academy in Fauquier County, Virginia. By the 1850s, he was practicing law in Wheeling. In a city with only one hundred enslaved people, Edward owned three of them. Like Russell, he left the city at the outbreak of war and moved to Richmond. During the war, he served as acting quartermaster general for the state of Virginia. *Representative Men of the South*; 1860 United States Federal Census—Slave Schedules.

for Australia, with a side promise that I should be appointed an overseer of the mines.[9] Before this reaches you I will be many miles away on the mighty deep, before me a Long Voyage and an unknown land. Among my greatest regrets is the parting with my adopted Country for whose people Institutions and soil I could lay down my Life any time, but you know I have been go[a]ded on to madness and this is the results. One thing in the consultation with my friend came up which for Guarded me against the destructive power of Popery, viz change my name as I am no longer Wm. Bole, but have a name I cannot let you know for this reason—you may recollect a conversation with me at the time Crawlys daughters came to chastise me that I would remove to the West. You advised me not to move that she would hunt me down there with as much certainty as at Wheeling. I inquired if there were any popists[10] established in Australia. The answer was yes, hence of the change of names. If this comes to anything I shall never forget my children, I do not think it necessary to show the letter to the madam (*who is the cause of all this trouble*), simply say I have gone a good ways from home. Perhaps She will rejoice for she too often told me to so.

Should I be so fortunate or unfortunate as to arrive at Melbourne Australia I will communicate to you over a certain [illegible] mark with key to it.

William Bole

P.S. If I chance to be successfull in that far off Land I may return at the end of two years, but I do not positively promise. If you do not do as I told you about my store you may have reason to regret that property will be conveyed to the hands of the priests, before long who will become Guardians as is Customary.

---

9. By the 1850s, Europeans had discovered and begun mining a number of valuable minerals in Australia, including lead, copper, and silver, but the gold rushes of the 1850s really drew people to the continent. We do not know which of these industries drew William Bole. Davy, *Gold Rush Societies*.

10. William Bole appears to be anti-Catholic, or at least worried about the influence of the Catholic Church. Disputes between Protestants and Catholics were heated in the Ohio River Valley during the 1850s, and Wheeling would have been a prime spot for such tensions. Home to many Catholic immigrants, as well as Protestant refugees, it would have been fertile ground for debate. See Ford, *Bonds of Union*.

Depositions of Witnesses[11]

MARY BOLE

QUESTION: Are you the daughter of William Bole and Margaret Bole, parties to this suit?
ANSWER: Yes sir.
QUESTION: What is your age?
ANSWER: I was fourteen on the 28th of July last.
QUESTION: State whether your father & mother have lived together in this city and how long.
ANSWER: It has been about seven years since they first came here to live, and from that time they lived together until about the fourteenth of October 1853 when he left here and I have not seen him since. When he was leaving here at that time he said he was going to Zanesville Ohio to collect money from the Rail Road, and I do not know what has become of him. My mother has had no letter or word from him since, as far as I know.
QUESTION: State how many children your father and mother have living.
ANSWER: They have six and I am the oldest.
QUESTION: What is the age of the youngest?
ANSWER: The youngest will be four years old next April, and they are all living with my Mother.
QUESTION: State how your father was accustomed to treat your mother when he was with her.
ANSWER: He threatened once that he would kill her by blowing her brains out with a pistol and he threatened a great many times that he would kill, in my presence.
QUESTION: Did you ever see him draw a knife on her?
ANSWER: I did see him once a good while ago draw a knife on her in a threatening manner.
QUESTION: State what more you remember if any thing as to his treatment of her.
ANSWER: He threatened a great many times that he would have the ocean between them & I saw him kick her and strike her in the face.

---

11. Charles Marshall, a commissioner in chancery, took the following depositions at the office of Russell and Fitzhugh in Wheeling. All witnesses signed their names.

He said he would reduce her to such poverty that she would have to go the washtub[12] for her living or beg.

QUESTION: State how long according to your remembrance he continued to beat her in the manner you describe.

ANSWER: It has been about three years since he first began to treat her so badly. He was not so bad before. I saw him when he ordered her out of the room about a week after the birth of his youngest child, at that time she was confined to her bed.

QUESTION: Where was your mother accustomed to stay at night during the last year or two before your father left her?

ANSWER: She had to go in the garret. It was a room with bare walls, no furniture except the beds, the children slept there with her. The first night my mother had to go up there, my father cursed and swore all of the time and took the dishes off of the table and threw them at the door. He came up to the garret door and tried to get in, but it was fastened.

QUESTION: State what labour if any your father required your mother to perform in the house or store.

ANSWER: To do all the house work and to attend to the store, too. He kept no clerk in the store and no servant in the house. One morning when he was eating his breakfast he was summoned to serve on the Jury and he threw a cup of boiling tea in her face. Also he used to spit tobacco in her face. It was not long before he went away that he threw the tea in her face. He told the children if their Mother did not give them every thing they wanted to pull her hair out and if that did not do to take her eyes out. This was a short time before he went away. He used to tell them not to mind any thing she told them to do.

WILLIAM S. WICKHAM

QUESTION: Are you the sheriff of Ohio County and if so how long have you been sheriff?

ANSWER: I am & have held that office since the first monday in July 1852.

QUESTION: State whether any process against William Bole ever came into your hands as such sheriff, & if so state the result of your proceedings under said process.

---

12. The phrase "go to the washtub" means that she would have to become a washerwoman, or a woman who took in other people's laundry to make a living.

ANSWER: Shortly before the first of December 1853 several attachments were placed in my hands, which were levied on a stock of boots shoes & other articles, found in the store room previously occupied by Wm Bole, who was reputed to have left the country. Which property was sold in February 1854 in pursuance of an order of court and was insufficient to pay the claims in my hands. The property levied on and sold by me was all the property real or personal which I know of that Wm Bole had. I knew him for several years in this City, & I have not seen him since the levy of that process.
QUESTION: State if you know anything of said Boles habits as to sobriety, or as to his treatment of his wife.
ANSWER: He was in the habit of getting drunk. I was not acquainted with his wife, but occasionally saw her attending to the business in the store, when he was there and idle. On one occasion I had some business with him and while I was in the store, his manner towards her and his son was harsh and dictational and unkind in great degree.

WILLIAM S. GOSHOM[13]

QUESTION: Are you acquainted with Wm Bole the defendant to this suit, and if so, state how long you have known him.
ANSWER: I am acquainted with Wm Bole and have been acquainted with him ever since he moved into the city, I do not recollect how long—certainly several years. My fathers office where I usually stayed was up stairs and adjoining the house of Mr Bole.
QUESTION: State when he left her[e] and under what circumstances so far as you know.
ANSWER: He left here in the summer or fall of 1853 as I understood (though not from him) to go over to the Central Ohio Rail Road to collect some debts—near Zanesville. He never returned.
QUESTION: State what occurred after his departure, in relation to his property.
ANSWER: After his departure, his property was seized under several attachments. I acted as clerk at sale made by the sheriff.
QUESTION: State whether you are acquainted with said Boles handwriting.
ANSWER: I have seen him write frequently.
QUESTION: Look at the letter now shown to you (the witness is here

---

13. This deposition was taken on February 12, 1855.

shewn the paper marked (A) and say whether or not in your opinion it is in the handwriting of said Bole.[14]

ANSWER: It is my opinion that it is in his handwriting.

QUESTION: State in what circumstances Bole's wife is left & how many children she has.

ANSWER: She is left without any visible means and has 5 or 6 children, six I believe.

QUESTION: State if you have observed any thing as to the said Bole's treatment of his wife while he resided here.

ANSWER: I never was in the part of the House where the family resided. I was very frequently in the Store. If Bole was in the store alone & idle, and a customer or customers came in, he would knock on the counter for his wife—to come down and wait on the customer or customers. He hardly ever, unless they were *very* busy, would wait on them himself.

QUESTION: What [were] Bole's habits as to sobriety?

ANSWER: He was very dissipated & when under the influence of liquor was very cross and illtempered.

ANNE ELIZABETH MOORE[15]

QUESTION: Are you acquainted with Wm Bole and his wife, parties to this suit?

ANSWER: Yes sir.

QUESTION: State if you know anything in regard to the said Wm Bole's treatment of his wife while they lived together in Wheeling.

ANSWER: I went in the store and found Mrs Bole behind the counter, and knew she was not well, and told her she had better go to her chamber. She made the reply, that her baby was nearly a week old, and I asked her why she did not go upstairs. Her reply was, she could not, that she had to stay there. Mr Bole came in the store and I told him I thought Mrs Bole ought to be in her chamber. He made reply that that was his business. I told him i would make it my business to see if she was not taken care of. He said if I was a man, I should not talk to him in that way. I told him if I was a man I would not use no word. I told him I would go down street and if she was not in her room when I got back I would see if she could not be put there. When I returned I looked in the store and did not see Mrs

---

14. This is the letter entered into evidence above.
15. This deposition was taken on February 13, 1855.

Bole. This was when the youngest living child was born. At another time before that I went in the store and Mr Bole called Mrs Bole down stairs to wait on me. I just told him I wanted a pair of shoes & he called her down & I saw she had been crying. I asked her what was the matter and she said she thought her baby was dying. I called in two or three days after that and asked her how the child was. She told me it was buried. I think it died the evening of the day when I first called or early the next morning.

MARTHA J. KEATING

QUESTION: Are you acquainted with Wm Bole and his wife, the parties to this suit?

ANSWER: I have known them for the last three or four years, since 1851. I believe, they lived together as husband and wife until he left here, a year ago last fall & she still resides in Wheeling.

QUESTION: State what opportunities, if any, you had of knowing how he treated his wife while he lived with her.

ANSWER: I have frequently been in the store to purchase shoes and he would be setting reading—mostly reading a book and he would call for his wife to leave her domestic work up stairs. Once or twice he said to her "wife," come and wait on Mrs Keating, but mostly he would say "Madam." His manner to her was that of a master to his slave, and she was very submissive and obedient to him, and when he spoke to his children it was with the most abusive language, calling them dogs & every thing that was bad. They were afraid as death of him. The only time I was in his private dwelling before he went away, was when his wife was confined with her youngest child. It was two or three days after the birth of the child. I asked permission of him to go & see her & he gave me permission and I was very much surprised to find her in a large room with a bed and a few chairs, no carpet & no furniture. There was also a stuffed quilt for a carpet laid down before the bed. She was without a nurse, except her own little girl.

ELIZA ELLIOTT[16]

QUESTION: Are you acquainted with Wm Bole and his wife, parties to this suit?

---

16. The following depositions were taken on February 15, 1855.

ANSWER: I am acquainted with them. I have known them for the last 5 or 6 years.

QUESTION: State if you know anything in regard to the said Wm Bole's treatment of his wife while they lived together in Wheeling.

ANSWER: I was with her when she was confined, and I requested him to go for the doctor. He said he did not know where the doctor lived. I asked him to go to one of the stores and any boy could tell him where the doctor lived. He answered me very short, and I dont know whether he went or not, but the doctor came. She had no one to attend on her. Her little daughter came over and requested me to come to see her mother and I went with her, and he seemed so queer and cross that I did not know what to do. I went backwards & forwards for a few days to dress the baby and during that time she had no one to wait on her. I never saw him in the room with her while she was sick. At other times in the store I have heard him speaking crossly to her. I think it was four or five years ago that I attended on her in her sickness. It was towards morning that I asked him to go for the doctor. Her daughter had come for me about midnight and I remained with her.

ANN HIGGINS

QUESTION: Are you acquainted with Wm Bole and his wife, parties to this suit?

ANSWER: I have been acquainted with them since they first came to the neighborhood. I think it has been seven years ago. I lived a near neighbour to them all the time since they came to Wheeling.

QUESTION: State if you know anything as to his treatment of his wife while they lived together in Wheeling.

ANSWER: I saw a great many actions of Mr Bole which I thought were unkind, but nothing very definite until the birth of the youngest child. At that time Mrs Bole sent for me in the morning, by her little daughter, I found her very ill and no person there. I went to the store to see Mr Bole to see if he had gone for a physician and he was not there, but on returning to Mrs Bole's room I found that he had been told to go, and the doctor came, another neighbour came in, and who it was I dont recollect. It was not Mrs Elliott, it was after she had removed from the neighbourhood. The doctor asked for some brandy. I went to the store, to see Mr Bole, but he was not there. I asked one of the little boys for his father and he said that he was at the Monroe House. I went back to Mrs Bole's room without any. I saw nothing of Mr Bole during my going in and out during the day. I did not continue my visits after that day. I left Town on a visit on the next Wednesday. The day before I left I went into the store to get a pair of shoes. He seemed to be in a very bad humour and told me that he could not find the shoes I wanted. I remarked "Mrs Bole never has any difficulty to fit me." He put the shoes away and in a very gruff manner said "I will have her down tomorrow." I replied "I would be very sorry to see Mrs Bole in the store tomorrow." He said "she will be well enough" and he said something else which I did not understand, and I left, for I was disgusted. Her child had been born on the saturday Before and this was on tuesday. The child referred to by Mrs Elliott in her deposition died some time before the birth of the child of which I have spoken and while the child was very ill and on the very day that it died its mother was made to stay in the store and wait on the customers and I saw her there in passing. The same evening I was sent for and found the child dead. I told Mr Bole at the time, that the child had died from neglect. Mrs Bole was compelled to stand in the store, instead of attending to her children, and he made no answer.

[*In May 1855, the court issued a decree, granting Margaret Bole a divorce from William Bole but only a divorce from bed and board. She was awarded custody of her children, and he was given the costs of the case. A woman named Margaret Bole married a man named Basil Kingessner in Wheeling in 1869, but I cannot determine if it is the same Margaret Bole.*[17] *Either using his already common name or having changed his name, William Bole disappeared from view after this case.*]

---

17. West Virginia Marriages Index.

CHAPTER 4

Jail

IMPRISONED FOR CRIMINAL OFFENSE

Mary Williams v. William George Williams, 1859

[Williams, Mary, by Sissons, George, her next friend v. Williams, William George *(1859)*, *Records of the Circuit Court of Ohio County*, WVRHC, env. *224 b-7. Mary Williams filed her divorce petition in September 1858. On September 27, the court issued a summons for William Williams, which was then delivered. She nonetheless published notice of her divorce in the* Wheeling Daily Times and Gazette *for four weeks starting March 18, 1859.*]

Bill of Divorce

To the Hon. Geo. W. Thompson, Judge of the Circuit Court for Ohio County,

The Bill of Complaint of Mary Williams, who being a minor under the age of twenty one years, files this bill by George Sissons,[1] her father and next friend.

Humbly complaining sheweth under your Honor, your Oratrix, Mary Williams, that on the 29th day of September in the year 1857 in the City of Wheeling and County of Ohio aforesaid, she (being then and now a lawful citizen of said City and County) was lawfully married to William George Williams, then of said county, who was of the lawful age of twenty one years.

Your oratrix further shews unto your honor that on the same 29th day of September 1857, and within an hour after the solemnization of the said marriage, the said William George Williams was arrested under a warrant issued against him for a violation of the laws of the United States for the regulation of the Post Office Department, and duly committed to the Jail of the County Court and having been indicted for

---

1. I have been unable to track either Mary or her father in the records.

said offence in the District Court of the United States for the Western District of Virginia, was arraigned, and on the 8th day of September 1858, was tried in the said Court and convicted and on the 11th day of September in the year 1858 he the said William George Williams was duly sentenced by the said District Court to be confined at hard labour in the penitentiary of the United States in the District of Columbia for the period of two years from the 1st day of October in the year 1858: All of which will more fully and at large appear by reference to the transcript of the proceedings against the said William George Williams.[2]

Your Oratrix further shews unto your Honor that said marriage was never consummated, she never having cohabited with the said William George Williams. Your Oratrix prays that the said William George Williams may be made a defendant to this bill with apt words to charge him &c. And forasmuch as under the statute for such case made and provided, as the said defendant Williams has been sentenced to confinement in the penitentiary, your Oratrix is entitled to a divorce from the bond of matrimony, she, your Oratrix, prays that by the decree of this Court, the said marriage between her and said defendant may be dissolved and that a divorce from the bond of matrimony, uniting your Oratrix with said defendant, may be decreed for the cause aforesaid.

May it please your Honor to grant unto your Oratrix all such other and future relief in the premises, as to your Honor may seem meet and to make all and every other order or orders, as much become necessary in relation to the premises and to award one or more writs of subpoena, directed to the said defendant, commanding him to appear, &c &c.

James S. Wheat[3] for Complainant

---

2. William Williams may have been convicted of mail theft. Stealing mail was a very serious offense in this era. William Blackstone recommended a severe punishment due to the "great malice and mischief of the theft" and ranked the crime alongside killing someone else's farm animals and plundering ships in distress. It is, of course, possible that Williams committed a different offense. During the antebellum era, Congress passed a number of laws ensuring a monopoly on services for the post office. Known as the Private Express Statutes, these laws prevented private companies from delivering letters. No transcript of Williams's trial appears in the existing divorce records. Blackstone, *Commentaries on the Laws of England*, 451; *Federal Cases Comprising Cases Argued*, 1080; *United States Postal Service*, 11, 13.

3. James Sanders Wheat was born to a wealthy slaveholding family in Prince George's County, Maryland, in 1810. By 1850, he lived in Wheeling, representing Ohio County in the Virginia House of Delegates. He served as a delegate to the first and second Wheeling conventions and was eventually chosen as the attorney general for the Restored State of Virginia. Lewis, *History and Government of West Virginia*, 183; Atkinson, *Bench and Bar of West Virginia*, 23–24.

Consent for Divorce

The State of Virginia, Ohio County: *To all whom* it may concern:

Greetings, Know ye that I W. G. Williams do hereby give my full and free consent to have the marriage compact dissolved and rendered void, which now exists between myself and wife Mary Williams, whose maiden name before marriage was Mary Sisson and do hereby release her from all conjugal obligation whatever so far as related to me.

Given under my hand and seal this twenty fifth day of September AD 1858 at the City of Wheeling Va

Marriage Certificate

To the Clerk of the Clerk [*sic*] of the Court of Ohio County in the State of Virginia[4]

> Date of Marriage: Sept. 29th
> Place of Marriage: Wheeling Va
> Full Names of Parties married: William Williams & Mary Sisson
> Age of Husband: 21
> Age of Wife: 18
> Condition of Husband: widower
> Condition of Wife: single
> Place of Husband's Birth: [blank]
> Place of Wife's Birth: Wheeling Va
> Place of Husband's Residence: Wheeling Va
> Place of Wife's Residence: Wheeling Va
> Names of Husband's Parents: Wm Williams
> Names of Wife's Parents: George & Elizabeth Sisson
> Occupation of Husband: [blank]

Depositions of Witnesses[5]

JAMES A. HILLER

QUESTION: Are you acquainted with the parties to this suit?
ANSWER: I am.

---

4. A. A. Roger, minister of the Methodist Episcopal church, authorized this document on November 26, 1857.

5. Charles Marshall, county commissioner, took these depositions on April 29, 1859. All deponents signed their names.

QUESTION: Were you present at the marriage of Wm George Williams & Mary Sisson on the 29th of September 1857?
ANSWER: Yes sir I was. They were married by the Rev. A A Roger pastor of the north street Methodist Episcopal Church. She was married at her fathers house in the city of Wheeling between 7 & 8 o'clock in the morning.
QUESTION: When was Wm George Williams arrested under a prosecution at the suit of the United States?
ANSWER: He was arrested on the same day that they were married, about an hour after they were married. I was present when he was committed to the jail of Ohio County, by the U.S. Commissioner to answer the charge for which he was arrested.
QUESTION: Were you present at his trial?
ANSWER: Yes sir, he was tried some time in September 1858 before the District Court of the United States for the Western District of Virginia at Wheeling. He was convicted and sent to the penitentiary.

A. A. ROGER

QUESTION: State your residence [and] profession.
ANSWER: I am a minister of the gospel in Wheeling, Virginia.
QUESTION: Were you licensed to solemnize marriage on the 29th of September 1857 by the laws of Virginia in Ohio County?
ANSWER: Yes sir, I was licensed for the state.
QUESTION: State whether or not you did solemnize marriage between the complainant Mary Williams, then Mary Sisson and the Defendant Wm George Williams, & if so when.
ANSWER: I did, on the 29th day of September 1857 at the house of George Sisson her father in Wheeling Virginia. I made a return according to the law of the marriage and the Exhibit marked (1) and filed with the complainants bill is a copy [of] my return.
QUESTION: State all that you know in regard to the arrest and trial of the Defendant.
ANSWER: He was arrested on the same day that he was married. I was present and a witness when he was examined by the United States commissioner and also when he was tried by the United States Court.

[*On May 31, 1859, the court granted Mary Williams an annulment. I do not know what became of either Mary or William after the annulment. With such common names, Mary and William are impossible to track.*]

PART 2
Wartime

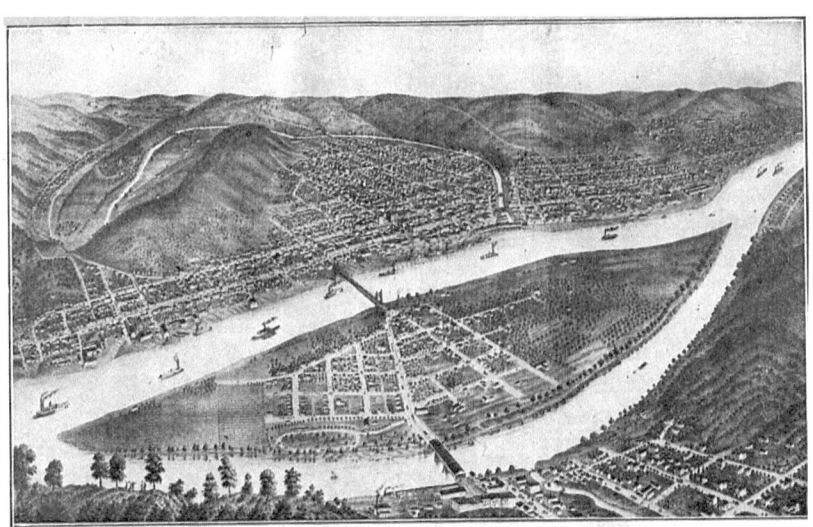

Bird's Eye View of Wheeling, West Virginia, 1861;
West Virginia and Regional History Center.

CHAPTER 5

Wartime Cases

CATHARINE SHALL NOT MARRY HER SAID PARAMOUR

Enoch Brareton v. Caroline Brareton, 1862

[Brareton, Enoch v. Brareton, Caroline *(1862), Records of the Circuit Court of Ohio County, WVRHC, env. 233 b-6. Enoch Brareton formally filed his divorce petition in April 1862. The court issued a summons for Caroline Brareton on March 17, 1862, before the formal filing. She accepted it.*]

Bill of Divorce

To the Hon. R. L. Berkshire,[1] judge of said Court,

Your orator Enoch Brareton humbly complaining sheweth unto your honor that on or about the [blank] day of March 1859 he married Caroline[2] his present wife at West Alexander in the state of Pennsylvania. That from the date of said marriage untill the said Caroline left the said Enoch Brareton they cohabited in said county of Ohio. That your orator and said Caroline are now and were at the time of the institution of this suit residents of said county of Ohio and state of Virginia. That your orator has always been a consistent faithfull and appropriate husband to the said Caroline. Said Caroline on the other hand has been an inconsistent unfaithfull and undutifull wife. Said Caroline has been

---

1. Ralph Lazier Berkshire was born in 1816 in Pennsylvania, although his grandfather had been one of the first settlers in Monongalia County, West Virginia. He became the prosecuting attorney of Morgantown, West Virginia, in the late 1840s, married, and had five children. He ran for circuit court judge in 1861 but lost to George W. Thompson. Berkshire was a leading voice against secession in western Virginia and served as a delegate to the second Wheeling convention in 1861. When Thompson refused to take the oath of office, believing the creation of the new state to be illegal, Berkshire became circuit court judge in his place. He resigned in 1863 to become the first chief justice of the Supreme Court of Appeals of West Virginia. *Biographical and Portrait Cyclopedia of Monongalia*, 42–44; Atkinson and Gibbens, *Prominent Men of West Virginia*, 253–54.

2. I cannot find a record for Caroline Brareton.

guilty of the crime of adultery with Charles Dennis[3] and various other persons since your orator married said Caroline and also said Caroline did willfully desert and abandon your orator on the [blank] day of [blank][4] and cohabited with said Charles Dennis.

Your orator further shews to your Honor that there has been no child or children born to them that your orator is poor and dependent on his daily labor for his support. In tender consideration and inasmuch as your orator is remidyless in the premises except in a court of chancery where such matters are properly heard, therefore that the said Caroline may if she can show why your orator should not have the relief hereby prayed your orator prays that the said Caroline may be made a defendant to this bill and required to render a full true and perfect answer to the same upon her oath that your orator may be entirely divorced from her the said Caroline and the marriage be dissolved and for such other and further relief as his case may require and to equity may seem necessary.[5]

Depositions of Witnesses[6]

JOSEPH FOWLER

QUESTION 1: State where you reside and what is your age and occupation?
ANSWER: I reside in the City of Wheeling. My age is about forty four and I work in the rolling mill.
QUESTION 2: Are you acquainted with the parties to this suit?
ANSWER: Yes sir, I am well acquainted with both the parties.

---

3. I can find no record of a man named Charles Dennis in Ohio County. In 1910, a man named Charles Dennis lived with his wife, Caroline, in Troy, Ohio. The couple told the census taker they had been married for fifty-three years (which would mean they wed in 1857). They lived with their three adult children—William, Cora, and Ezra. William Dennis, forty-nine in 1910, had been born in 1861, which would make him the same age as the child born to Caroline Brareton in late 1860 or early 1861. Witnesses in the Brareton case claimed that Charles Dennis recognized that child as his own. However, this Charles Dennis is listed as "white," although he would not have been the first person to "pass" in this period. United States Federal Census for 1910.

4. In the document, Enoch stated that Caroline had left him in "186" with a space after the "6." Although this leaves it unclear when she left, we know it was between 1860 and 1862. Joseph Fowler's testimony suggests that Caroline moved out in the spring of 1861.

5. The lawyer in this case is not listed.

6. Gibson L. Cranmer, commissioner in chancery, recorded this deposition on April 16, 1862, at the office of Nathaniel Richardson. The witness signed his name.

QUESTION 3: Where have they resided since you knew them?
ANSWER: Principally in Wheeling.
QUESTION 4: How long have you known them?
ANSWER: I have known the plaintiff about seven years and the defendant five years.
QUESTION 5: When were they married?
ANSWER: Over three years since.
QUESTION 6: Do you know how long they resided together?
ANSWER: I do not. I know they were not together very long.
QUESTION 7: Did she leave him?
ANSWER: I dont recollect that.
QUESTION 8: Where has the defendant been residing since they separated?
ANSWER: She has been in Louisville and Wheeling.
QUESTION 9: When she resided in Wheeling where did she live?
ANSWER: I had a house to let in Ritchietown[7] and her brother from Ohio rented the house from me, expecting to move into it, himself and family. He didn't come but his sister Caroline the defendant did.
QUESTION 10: How long did she remain in that house?
ANSWER: I believe she went into it in the Spring of the year 1861 and remained in it about six weeks or two months.
QUESTION 11: How far is that house from the one in which you resided at that time?
ANSWER: It was next door.
QUESTION 12: How many rooms were in the house at that time?
ANSWER: Three rooms.
QUESTION 13: Did any one reside there except herself?
ANSWER: No, Sir.
QUESTION 14: Do you know of her receiving any visits from any persons there at night. State all you know about it.
ANSWER: I knew perfectly well that of nights about eight or nine oclock a gentleman came there and staid sometimes until five oclock in the morning because I have seen him at that hour of the morning leaving the house. I supposed he had been there all night. His visits were about two or three times a week. I one morning got up pretty early and I saw him standing in the room where she was. She was in her night dress and he was dressing. They appeared to have just gotten out of bed.

---

7. Ritchietown was another name for South Wheeling.

QUESTION 15: Was that man her husband?
ANSWER: No Sir.
QUESTION 16: Was he white or black?
ANSWER: I cannot say.
QUESTION 17: Do you know whether or not she has ever had a child since she has been married?
ANSWER: Yes sir, she had.
QUESTION 18: State when she had that child as near as you can remember?
ANSWER: When she lived in my house the child was some three or four months old.
QUESTION 19: Do you think that a white man begot the child?
ANSWER: No sir I do not.[8]
QUESTION 20: How many beds were there in the house she occupied?
ANSWER: Only one.

MALINDA WATSON[9]

QUESTION 1: Where do you reside?
ANSWER: In Wheeling.
QUESTION 2: Do you know the parties to this suit?
ANSWER: Yes Sir.
QUESTION 3: Do you remember when they were married and if so, state when?
ANSWER: I think they were married about three years ago last march or in the winter.
QUESTION 4: State where the defendant lived last Spring and Summer?
ANSWER: She lived in Ritchietown in this County.
QUESTION 5: Where did you reside during that time?
ANSWER: I resided in Ritchietown during the spring in the same house with the defendant. I also resided there during the month of August and part of September.
QUESTION 6: Do you know when Enoch Brareton and his wife Caroline separated?
ANSWER: I cant tell.

---

8. For information on interracial relationships, see Hodes, *White Women, Black Men*; Rothman, *Notorious in the Neighborhood*; Pascoe, *What Comes Naturally*; Molloy, "'An Illicit and Criminal Intercourse.'"

9. Malinda Watson's deposition was recorded on April 18, 1862. She signed her name.

QUESTION 7: Was he living with her during last spring and summer?
ANSWER: No he was not.
QUESTION 8: Do you know of any man visiting her during last Spring and Summer and if so state all you know about it?
ANSWER: Yes sir I do. Charles Dennis was his name. He was there two or three times a week over night and was there from Sunday night until Monday morning. He was there every week two and three times all the time I was there. I have seen them in bed together several times, in the morning, and on Sundays. I lived there in the same house with them steady, three weeks in August. They had a child, Dennis, and he recognized it as their child. At that time I think the child was four months old. The plaintiff and defendant have not been living together since then.

[*During the court's spring term in 1862, the court ruled that Enoch Brareton receive his divorce* a vinculo matrimonii *from Caroline Brareton. She was told to pay the costs of the suit. A woman named Caroline was married to a man named Charles Dennis and living in Troy, Ohio, with him and their three children in 1910. However, Charles was listed as "white," and the couple told the census taker that they had been married since 1857. Although I am not certain it is the same person, a man with a similar name (Enoch Brereton) was listed as serving in the Thirteenth Ohio Cavalry during the Civil War.*[10]]

Frederick Altpeter v. Catharine Altpeter, 1863

[Altpeter, Frederick v. Altpeter, Catharine *(1863)*, *Records of the Circuit Court of Ohio County, WVRHC, env. 235 b-7. Frederick Altpeter filed his divorce petition in March 1863. On March 19, 1863, the court issued and served Catharine with a summons.*]

Bill of Divorce

To the Hon Ralph L. Berkshire, Judge of the Circuit Court for Ohio County, Virginia,

---

10. U.S. Civil War Soldiers; 1910 United States Federal Census. See footnote 3 in this chapter for more on this relationship.

Humbly complaining sheweth unto you Honor, your orator Frederick Altpeter[11] that your orator on the [blank] day of February AD 1850 was married to Catherine Beshor[12] in Allegheny County in the State of Pennsylvania where your orator and the said Catherine then resided. Subsequently to the said marriage, to wit on the [blank] day of August 1851, your orator with his said wife Catherine removed to Ritchietown in the county of Ohio and State of Virginia where he has since resided and still does reside and where your Orator and the said Catherine lived together as man and wife until the [blank] day of August A.D. 1860, when the said Catherine left the bed and board of your said Orator and went to live with one Peter Coleman[13] with whom she has ever since been living and still lives and by whom she has had one child now about two years of age and is now enceinte[14] with another by the said Peter Coleman.

Your orator further shews unto your Honor that during the time your Orator and said Catherine lived together as man and wife your orator had by the said Catherine four children, all girls, two of which said children are dead and two of whom are living, to wit Mary aged 13 years and Elizabeth aged 11 years, both of which said children are now in the custody and possession of the said Catherine and her paramour the said Peter Coleman and whom they refuse to give unto the care and keeping of your said Orator.

Your Orator further shews that always ever since their said marriage, down to the desertion of your said Orator by the said Catherine he has always acted and conducted himself towards the said Catherine as a chaste, faithful, and affectionate husband, and towards the said children as a kind and indulgent father, providing everything necessary for the support and maintenance of the said Catherine and his said chil-

---

11. A man named Frederick Peter Altpeter was born in December 1830 in Völklingen in what is now Germany. Saarland, Germany, Births, Marriages, and Deaths.

12. I cannot track Catherine by this name or the alternate spelling in the marriage certificate. A comparison with women of the same name in Pennsylvania strongly suggests that the Catherine in our case, like Frederick Altpeter, had German ancestry. United States Federal Census for 1850.

13. Peter Coleman is also a very common name. An Irish immigrant named Peter Coleman lived in Wheeling's Fifth Ward in 1870 with his Swiss-born wife, Terrissa, and three children, all under five. A more promising Peter Coleman registered for the draft in Wheeling in 1863. He was thirty-four and had been born in Germany. His address was located in Centre Wheeling, which is where witnesses in this case said that Peter Coleman lived. United States Federal Census for 1870; U.S. Civil War Draft Registrations Records.

14. Another word for "pregnant."

dren. Yet your Orator charges that the said Catherine is now openly and criminally living with the said Peter Coleman and has so continued to live with him in adultery since the month of August 1860.

In tender consideration whereof and inasmuch as your orator is without remedy in the premises, except in a Court of Equity. To the end therefore that the said Catherine be made a defendant to this bill, that she answer the same upon oath, that your Orator may be divorced from the bond of matrimony, and that an order may be made giving the said children Mary and Elizabeth into his care and custody and that he may have such other and further relief as the circumstances of this case may require and to your Honor shall see[m] just and equitable. May it please your Honor to grant to your Orator proper process against the said Catherine Altpeter, commanding her to appear and answer this bill &c.

G. L. Cranmer[15] Sol.

And your orator asks that it may be decreed by your Honor that the said Catherine shall not marry her said paramour Peter Coleman which she expects to do if the said decree for divorce should be obtained.[16]

Marriage Certificate

Birmingham, Alleghany County, Pennsylvania[17]

I the undersigned pastor of the german united evangelical Church of Birmingham do certify, that according to the Church Register of the above named congregation pro 1849. No 131. on the twenty second day of March in the year of our Lord one thousand eight hundred and forty nine (March 22, 1849), Frederick Altpeter and Katherine Boeshaar

---

15. Gibson Lamb Cranmer was born in Cincinnati in 1826. He moved to Wheeling to study law under his relative Daniel Lamb. He served as a member of the General Assembly of Virginia from 1855 to 1856 and was a delegate to the first Wheeling convention, which helped form the state of West Virginia. He was clerk of the House of Delegates for the Restored State of Virginia. Cranmer, *History of Wheeling City*, 460–1; Atkinson and Gibbens, *Prominent Men of West Virginia*, 339.

16. In the antebellum era, it was common for courts to argue that spouses "at fault" in divorce cases had forfeited their right to remarry. Of course, in a day before consistent record keeping and computers, this ruling often held only as far as the county line. Many spouses just moved to another community and remarried without a fuss. Schwartzberg, "'Lots of Them Did That,'" 574.

17. Birmingham was an industrial community just to the south of Pittsburgh in the early 1850s. In 1872, it officially became part of Pittsburgh. Negley, *Allegheny County*, 2–4.

were joined in the holy estate of matrimony by the minister of the same church. Witness to the marriage ceremony was Henry Dietzberger.

That the above certificate of marriage is a true copy from the Church Records I certify.

Birmingham, April the 13th 1863

C. H. Herman

pastor of the german united evangelical church

Depositions of Witnesses[18]

CATHERINE HEIL

QUESTION: State if you are acquainted with the parties to this suit.
ANSWER: Yes sir.
QUESTION: State if you know them to be married.
ANSWER: Yes they are husband and wife.
QUESTION: State if the defendant left and deserted the plaintiff, and if so state all the facts you know connected with it.
ANSWER: Yes the defendant left the plaintiff about (3) three years ago this spring. She has been living with Peter Coleman since she left her husband Frederick Altpeter and has had by Coleman three (3) children since said desertion. She had previous to her said desertion of her said husband two (2) children by her husband Altpeter Mary aged (13) thirteen and Elizabeth aged (11) eleven.
QUESTION: State whether the defendant has any property & if so state where it is situated.
ANSWER: Yes she has property in Ritchietown.

JOHN HAZLET

QUESTION: State if you are acquainted with the parties to this suit.
ANSWER: Yes sir.
QUESTION: State if you know with whom Mrs Catherine Altpeter is now living and has been for the last 2 or 3 years.
ANSWER: She is living with Coleman now.
QUESTION: State how many children she has had by Coleman.
ANSWER: I know she has had two (2) from what she herself said, and I believe she had another last Easter.

---

18. George Dulty, a justice of the peace, recorded these depositions on April 25, 1863, at the law office of Gibson L. Cranmer. All deponents signed their names.

HENRY MORRIS

QUESTION: State if you are acquainted with the parties to this suit.
ANSWER: Yes I am.
QUESTION: State what you know about the defendant leaving this plaintiff and who she is now living with.
ANSWER: I know she left her husband and is now living with Peter Coleman.
QUESTION: State if Altpeter treated her well.
ANSWER: Yes he treated her kindly.
QUESTION: State if Catherine Altpeter has some property in Ritchietown.
ANSWER: Yes she has.
QUESTION: State how many children she has by Altpeter now living.
ANSWER: She has two, aged about 13 years and 11 years.
QUESTION: State where Altpeter's children are now living.
ANSWER: They are living with her, the defendant, in Centre Wheeling.

[*On May 23, 1863, the court issued its ruling, granting a divorce* a vinculo matrionii *to Frederick Altpeter. The court also issued a decree restraining Catharine Altpeter from marrying again. The court ordered Catharine to relinquish custody of Mary and Elizabeth Altpeter to her former husband and to pay the costs of his suit. I can find no record of Frederick or Catharine after this case.*]

PART 3
Postbellum

Steamboat City of Wheeling *on Ohio River*, 1902;
West Virginia and Regional History Center.

CHAPTER 6

Adultery

SINCE HIS DISCHARGE, SHE HAS BEEN
LIVING A LEWD AND ADULTEROUS LIFE

Jacob Stroble v. Ellen Stroble, 1865

[Stroble, Jacob v. Stroble, Ellen *(1865), Records of the Circuit Court of Ohio County, WVRHC, env. 259 b-5. The court issued a summons for Ellen on August 23, 1865, and she accepted it. Similarly, the court issued a summons on November 14, 1866, which she also accepted.*]

Bill of Divorce

Circuit Court September Rules,[1] 1865
To Hon. E. H. Caldwell Judge of said Court, in Chancery sitting.[2]
Your Orator Jacob Stroble,[3] humbly complaining shews unto your Honor, that he has been (and still is) a citizen of the State of West Virginia ever since its formation and before the formation of the said State of WV was for many years a resident of the State of Virginia living in the City of Wheeling in said State. That for more than three years he was a soldier in the Army of the United States engaged in fighting rebels.[4] That in April 1858 or 1859 at West Alexander in the State of PA

---

1. "Rules" was just another way of referring to the court's session.

2. Elbert Halsted Caldwell lived in Moundsville, West Virginia. He was born in 1809 and was originally from Brooke County, north of Wheeling. He attended college in New England. He served as a delegate to the first Wheeling convention and as a member of the first West Virginia constitutional convention. He was elevated to the court in 1863, under the new state government. He served as circuit court judge until his death in 1869. Cranmer, *History of the Upper Ohio Valley,* 1:546.

3. Jacob Stroble was a German immigrant, born in 1841, who had come to the United States by the time he was eight or nine. His father, Conrad, was a tavern keeper in Wheeling. United States Federal Census for 1850.

4. Jacob Stroble was a private in the First Regiment of the West Virginia Light Artillery, Company G. The regiment was organized on June 28, 1861, in Wheeling. U.S. Civil War Soldier Records and Profiles; "Battle Unit Details."

he was legally married to Ellen Watkins[5] then a resident citizen of the State of Ohio by one J. L. Mayes a Justice of the State of Pennsylvania and that they lived together as man and wife in Wheeling and have had no child by their marriage.

That the laws of the State of PA requiring no record of any marriage which is solemnized in said State, he is unable to procure record proof of the same but will have to rely on oral proof for the same.

That during the absence of your Orator in the service of the United States as a soldier and since his return from the service she the said Ellen his wife has committed adultery with John Hunter and with divers other men whose names are now to your orator unknown and that ever since July 1865 at which time your Orator left her and since which time your Orator has not lived with her, she has been lewdly cohabiting and living with the said John Hunter in the State of Ohio and in other places. That she and the said John Hunter have travelled together as man and wife and did stop at the Scott House a Hotel in the City of Pittsburgh Penn as man & wife and occupied the same room as man & wife.

All of which is contrary to Equity and inasmuch as your Orator is remediless by the strict rules of the Common law and is only relievable in this Honorable Court he prays the said Ellen his wife be made defendant hereto and that she answer the same according to law.

He prays that upon the hearing of this case the Court would decree that he be divorced from the bond of matrimony between him and his said wife for the causes aforesaid and that such other and further relief as the Court may deem proper for his case be granted and he will ever pray &c.

G. L. Cranmer Solr for Plaintiff

Depositions of Witnesses[6]

WILLIAM S. ALEXANDER

QUESTION: Please state where you resided in April 1859 and on what occasion you met the parties Jacob Stroble and Ellen Stroble his wife.
ANSWER: I resided in West Alexander Washington County PA at that

---

5. If we assume that Ellen Watkins Stroble and Ellen Hunter, who was listed in the 1870 census as the wife of John Hunter, are the same person, we can establish that Ellen was born in 1843 in Virginia. United States Federal Census for 1870.

6. These depositions were recorded on November 23, 1865. All deponents signed their names.

time. The occasion on which I met these parties on the 10th day of April 1859 was their marriage. They called upon me to unite them in marriage on that day and I performed the ceremony and united them in marriage according to the laws of PA.

QUESTION: In what capacity did you act at that marriage?

ANSWER: In the capacity of a Justice of the Peace.

QUESTION: What if any minute[7] did you make of their marriage at that time?

ANSWER: I made a minute of their marriage upon my record of marriages at that time a copy of which record I herewith file and marked Exhibit A.[8]

QUESTION: State if at that time the laws of PA required any record of marriages solemnized by you to be kept of such marriages.

ANSWER: No Sir, they did not.

JOHN WEIGGERBER

QUESTION: State where you reside and what was your occupation in the winter of the year 1863?

ANSWER: I resided on Market Street near Union Street in the City of Wheeling and I lived there then. I kept a saloon at that time.

QUESTION: State if Ellen Stroble the wife of the complainant visited there and under what circumstances.

ANSWER: John Hunter and a young woman who I did not know at first, used to come in to my place there generally on market days. I afterwards found out that the young woman was the complainaints wife. They generally came in there with their marketing—if she came in first she asked for him—if he came in first he asked for her—when they met they would set in the back room some times for a half hour and would have a drink together—they would sometimes drink hot whiskey punches and always they drank strong liquors. After drinking he would say "let us go home now" and he would take up the market baskets and go away together.

QUESTION: How often would that occur in a week?

ANSWER: It occurred twice a week during the whole winter. It may not have occurred twice in every week during the whole winter but I know they were there frequently during the whole winter.

---

7. In this sense, the term "minute" refers to a memorandum.
8. This record no longer exists.

QUESTION: At that time was Jacob Stroble the complainant in the service of the United States as a soldier or not?

ANSWER: Yes Sir, he was a soldier in the service.

QUESTION: State if you know long he so continued in the service subsequent to that time.

ANSWER: I think about two years.

QUESTION: Was he in the service before that time and if so for how long a time?

ANSWER: Yes Sir, he was in the service for about one year before that time.

QUESTION: Do you recollect about what time in the year 1865 the Complainant came home.

ANSWER: It was in the fall of that year.

QUESTION: From the conduct of the said John Hunter and Ellen Stroble while in your house what was your opinion concerning them and on what was that opinion based?

ANSWER: I took them to be man and wife; because they bought marketing together and took it home together and generally they acted like man and wife.

JOSEPH KRAMER

QUESTION: State if you are acquainted with the parties to this suit and if so how did you become acquainted with them.

ANSWER: I have seen both of them and know them. At the time we were keeping Kramers Hotel on Main Street next to the Grant House. In 1863 Ellen Stroble frequently came to the house in company with John Hunter and they would take dinner together. Sometimes she would come over an hour before he would and go up into the parlor. I would go up to call them to dinner and find the door locked. There was no one in the room on these occasions but John Hunter and this complainants wife Ellen Stroble.

QUESTION: Who would pay the bill when at your house?

ANSWER: John Hunter would pay for both.

QUESTION: How long were they in the habit of visiting at your Hotel together?

ANSWER: For six or seven months.

QUESTION: State if you know whether John Hunter was in the habit of buying goods for Ellen Stroble.

ANSWER: He was in the habit of bringing packages of goods to the house and leaving them there for her she would call and get the packages.

QUESTION: During the time that John Hunter and Mrs Stroble were in the habit of visiting at your Hotel where was Jacob Stroble?

ANSWER: He was in the army of the United States.

QUESTION: When was he discharged from the army?

ANSWER: July 1865 and he has not lived with her since then.

F. FALLOUR

QUESTION: Please state where you reside and what is your business?

ANSWER: I reside on Monroe Street in Wheeling, and I am a confectioner.[9] I have been in my present stand for three years past or it will be 3 years next May. Previous to that kept an eating saloon in Main Street near Monroe.

QUESTION: Are you acquainted with the parties to this suit?

ANSWER: I know the complainant Jacob Stroble but I do not know the Defendant. I have had a person pointed out to me as the wife of complainant but that was some time ago and I do not think I would recognize her now.

QUESTION: Did you ever see the Defendant Ellen Stroble and if so when and where and what was her conduct and who was in company with her at the time? State fully all the circumstances.

ANSWER: Yes Sir. She was pointed out to me. John Hunter and Ellen Stroble, it was as I understood afterwards, and another couple came into my eating saloon about dusk in the evening—this was four years ago I think. They called for Oysters[10] and I went to the kitchen to prepare the oysters and when I came into the dining room out of the kitchen I saw Hunter with his arm around Strobles waist with his hand in an improper place. It was outside of her clothes and not under her clothes. As soon as Hunter saw me he picked away his hand and straightened up immediately. Not knowing the woman at the time I wished to find out who she was and enquired who she was. I ascertained it was complainant's wife.

---

9. A confectioner is a person who makes sweets, such as candy, cakes, and other treats.

10. Oysters were incredibly popular in the nineteenth century. Some historians have even said that there was a "great oyster craze." Because oysters were so abundant and Wheeling was on the Baltimore and Ohio Railroad line, city residents would have been able to get inexpensive oysters from the Chesapeake Bay. Kurlansky, *Big Oyster*.

JACOB MASER

QUESTION: State if you are acquainted with the parties to this suit.
ANSWER: Yes Sir I know both of them.
QUESTION: State how long it is since they lived together as man & wife.
ANSWER: They lived together for about one week or two after the complainant came back from the army—that was last July one year ago—in July 1865. Prior to that time the complainant was away in the army for three years.
QUESTION: Are you acquainted with John Hunter?
ANSWER: Yes Sir I am.
QUESTION: Have you ever seen John Hunter and Ellen Stroble in company together if so state when where and under what circumstances. State fully all you know about it.
ANSWER: The first I noticed of their being together was when they lived close neighbors to me in West Wheeling Ohio. I saw Hunter going in and out of her house and I often saw him carrying marketing into her house. I met them coming from market together frequently before day light. Since they (Ellen Strobles fathers folks) moved from my neighborhood to a house back of Wagners paper mill I saw him at different times setting at the table eating with the family. I saw them buggy riding together at different times. Hunter stays at her house regularly from what I can see I think. He has been there all summer and fall. I saw Hunter going to her house and going with her abroad during the whole time this complainant was in the army. She Ellen Stroble I mean does not bear a very good character among the people in our town [of] West Wheeling. She has the general reputation of being a prostitute.

ARTHUR HIGGINS

QUESTION: Please state your age residence and occupation and whether you are acquainted with the parties to this suit.
ANSWER: I am 49 years of age. I reside in Bridgeport Belmont County Ohio. I am a Pilot by occupation.[11] I am well acquainted with the Defendant Ellen Stroble and I know the complainant but not well.
QUESTION: State if you know John Hunter and do you know any thing of his being intimate with the Defendant and if so state all you know about it.

---

11. Most likely he was a steamboat pilot.

ANSWER: I know John Hunter and I know that he and Ellen Stroble were very intimate. I travelled once with them on the cars to Pittsburg from Bridgeport and I saw them together frequently at other times. After we arrived in Pittsburg on the occasion referred to above I met him and her on the street in Pittsburg. I asked him where he stopped. He said we are stopping at the Scott House and she laughed.

QUESTION: State if at any other time you saw her and John Hunter together and if so where and when.

ANSWER: I saw them together in Columbus. John Hunter was in my Regiment. I was Liet. Col of the 170 Ohio Regiment NG [National Guard]. They put up at the American Hotel together. I met them there. I went to register and saw their names registered John Hunter & Lady or wife, it was one or the other. I will not be certain which. They were registered as being in the same room and I was satisfied they were rooming together there. I have frequently seen them start from Bridgeport to go away together on the cars.[12]

QUESTION: What is the general reputation of the Defendant for chastity so far as you know?

ANSWER: It is very bad. She is known by reputation as a prostitute.

[*In December 1866, the court issued a ruling, divorcing Jacob and Ellen Stroble forever. Jacob Stroble remarried the following year. He and his new wife, Caroline Seabright, had six children. Like her husband, she was a German immigrant. He died in April 1892, at the age of fifty-one. Caroline lived until 1925 and was eventually buried alongside her husband in Martins Ferry, Ohio, across the river from Wheeling. Although Hunter is a common name, the 1870 census lists a couple named John and Ellen Hunter living together in the Seventh Ward of Wheeling. He was a brick manufacturer, and she, like most women, was listed as "keeping house."[13]*]

---

12. This would suggest that they frequently took the train from Bridgeport to Pittsburgh.

13. West Virginia Marriages Index; United States Federal Census for 1870, 1880; U.S. Find a Grave Index.

Lewis Long v. Rosanna Long, 1866

[Long, Lewis v. Long, Rosanna *(1866)*, *Records of the Circuit Court of Ohio County, WVRHC, env. 264 b-3 and 267 b-5. The court issued a summons for Rosanna on March 21, 1866; she accepted it.*]

Bill of Divorce

To the Hon. E. H. Caldwell Judge of the Circuit Court of Ohio County, West Virginia. In chancery sitting.

March Rules A.D. 1866

Humbly complaining sheweth unto your Honor your Orator Lewis Long that on or about the 7th day of August AD 1859 your orator at the time being a resident of Ritchietown in the said County and State intermarried with the defendant Rosanna Long, her name being at that time and prior to her marriage with your orator Rosanna Reininger, the said Rosanna at the time also being a resident of Ritchietown in said County and State.[14]

Your orator further shews unto your Honor that said defendant and your Orator were married in Ritchietown in said County and State by one Rev Helfer, a Lutheran Minister, all of which will more fully appear by the certificate of said marriage a copy of which is herewith filed marked "1" and prayed to be taken as part of this Bill.[15]

Your Orator further shews that on or about the 23d day of September AD 1861 he enlisted as a private soldier in the Service of the United States for three years or during the war and that during the absence of your Orator as aforesaid in the service of his Country, and since his discharge, she the said Rosanna defendant has been living a lewd and adulterous life and your orator avers that said defendant has for at least one year last past lived in an adulterous intercourse with one James B. Hays and is now so living and he charges that she is now obtaining groceries on the credit of the said James L. Hays and that said James L. Hays pays the rent to the house in which she now lives.[16]

---

14. I can find no record under these names, but there is a marriage certificate for Lewis Long and Rose Lekner on August 6, 1859. This is the same year that Lewis Long, twenty-two and born in Bavaria, was naturalized in Ohio County. West Virginia Marriages Index; West Virginia Naturalization Records.

15. This record no longer exists.

16. Lewis Long enlisted as a private in an Ohio regiment in September 1861. He transferred to the Ohio Twenty-fifth Light Artillery Battery on February 17, 1863, and mustered

Your Orator further shews unto your Honor that ever since August 12 1863, he has lived separate and apart from said defendant by reason of her lewd and improper practices. Your Orator further shews that prior to and up to the time of the separation of your orator from said defendant he was faithful, kind and attentive to her as a husband and amply provided for the support and maintenance of said defendant fully providing her with all the comports and necessaries of life which one in her state in life and society demanded.

Your Orator further shows that he is a Citizen of the State of WV and that said defendant is a resident in Ritchietown County of Ohio and State of WV, that since the said separation and since the said act of adultery of said defendant, he has at no time cohabited with said defendant, and that said act of adultery occurred within five years from the commencement of this suit.

In consideration whereof and to the end that justice may be done your Orator prays that said Rosanna Long may be made defendant to this bill and be required to render a full true and perfect answer to the same upon her oath, that your Orator may be entirely divorced from her and the marriage dissolved and your Orator released a vinculo matrimonii, and for such other and further relief as his cause may require and as to equity may seem meet, and your orator will ever pray &c.

G. L. Cranmer, Solicitor for Complt.

[*On November 1, 1869, the court dismissed the case after years of inactivity. I can find no record of either Lewis or Rosanna after this.*]

Emeline Scatterday v. Pulaski Scatterday, 1867

[Scatterday, Emeline B. v. Scatterday, Pulaski *(1867), Records of the Circuit Court of Ohio County, WVRHC, env. 273 b-2. A marriage certificate states that Emeline's unmarried name was Benjamin and that she and Pulaski were married in the Methodist Episcopal church. Emeline filed her divorce petition in August 1866. The court issued a summons for Pulaski on August 16, 1866, and determined that he no longer lived in Virginia. Emeline published notice of her petition in the* Wheeling Intelli-

---

out on December 12, 1865, at Camp Chase, Ohio. U.S. Civil War Soldier Records and Profiles.

gencer *for four weeks beginning on August 31, 1866, and again on August 3, 1867.*]

Bill of Divorce

To the Hon. E. H. Caldwell, judge of the said court, in chancery now sitting,

Humbly complaining, shews unto your honor, your oratrix, Emeline B. Scatterday, who sues by her next friend, Levi Benjamin, that on the 6th day of December 1838, she was married to Pulaski Scatterday at Wheeling then in the State of Virginia, the said Pulaski Scatterday then being a widower, with four children.[17] That your oratrix cared for and raised the child[ren] of the said Pulaski Scatterday until they, arriving at the age of maturity, removed from their fathers home, as they have all done, but that your oratrix has had no children of her own.

That your oratrix has always since her said marriage lived in Wheeling with her said husband, until his abandonment of her as herinafter shown, that her conduct was always proper, discreet and irreproachable, never giving any cause of complaint to her said husband, nor was any such complaint ever made by him.

That on the 4th day of October 1865, without any just cause or reason, the said Pulaski Scatterday, her husband, totally abandoned your oratrix, and since that time has not returned to her nor contributed anything to her support.

That the only property left in Wheeling by the said Pulaski Scatterday was the East half of lot number 175 One hundred and seventy five, situated on Zane street in East part of the City of Wheeling known as East Wheeling upon which are erected two dwelling houses, in one of which houses was some household furniture.

That under the direction of the said Pulaski Scatterday, her husband, your oratrix has sold the greater part of the said household furniture for the purposes of paying some debts owing in Wheeling by the said Pulaski Scatterday, which she has done out of the proceeds of such sale.

---

17. I can find no record of Levi Benjamin, but since Emeline's unmarried name was Benjamin, we can assume he was a male relative. Emeline was born in 1818 in Pennsylvania. In 1840, the couple lived in the Fourth Ward of Wheeling with eight people in their household. Pulaski Scatterday was born in Virginia in 1806. In the antebellum era, he was a street commissioner and city collector. Emeline volunteered as a nurse for the Union army during the Civil War. West Virginia Marriages Index; United States Federal Census for 1840, 1850. Civil War Pension Index.

That the said half lot and houses thereon erected are worth about Two Thousand Dollars but are subject to an attachment for about the sum of Seventy Dollars.

That one of the said houses yields ten dollars a month rent and that for the rent of the other she obtains her board, but that the taxes on the said property now delinquent, are sufficient to exhaust and take up all the rents which the two houses can yield between the present time and the first of April next.

That previous to abandoning your oratrix, the said Pulaski sold and converted into cash other property; and that at the time of his said abandonment of her, he had in his possession two or three thousand dollars, and that he still has such sum or the greater part thereof, which as your oratrix is informed and believes is deposited in a bank in the State of Pennsylvania.

That the said Pulaski Scatterday is now in Allegheny, Pennsylvania working at his trade, which is that of a carpenter.

That your oratrix has no means whatever of subsistence except such as may be derived from the aforesaid real estate.

All of which actings and doings of the said Pulaski Scatterday being contrary to equity, your oratrix being remediless by the strict rules of the common law and only relievable in this court, therefore prays that the said Pulaski Scatterday may be made defendant hereto; that he may be enjoined from conveying or in any way disposing of the said real estate situated in the City of Wheeling, until the final order or decree of the court in this case; that he may be required to pay to your oratrix an amount sufficient for her present maintenance and for the prosecution of this suit; that your oratrix may be divorced from the bed and board of her said husband, Pulaski Scatterday; that she may be allowed by the decree of this court the real estate aforesaid with such other and further property or sum of money as may seem to the court just and proper, as alimony; and that such other and further order or decree may be made as your orator's case may require, or to the court shall seem just and proper.

And your oratrix will ever pray &c

Peck & Hubbard for Complt.[18]

---

18. Daniel Peck was one of the oldest lawyers in these cases. He was born in 1799 in Vermont. By the 1860s, he was practicing law in Wheeling, first with William Hubbard and then with Robert Cochran. His wife, Olivia, was twenty-two years younger and had been born in Ohio. When he died in 1886, he named her as executrix of his will. United States

Amended Bill of Divorce[19]

To the Hon. E. H. Caldwell, Judge of the said court now in session:

Your oratrix Emeline B. Scatterday, by her next friend Levi Benjamin, humbly farther complaining, in addition & amendment to her original bill filed in this case, here farther shows to the court, that her said husband, while he was her husband, to wit, on the first day of September 1865, & at divers time, before & since that time, committed adultery with one Anne M. Mitchell in the city of Wheeling & elsewhere:

That her said husband, the said Pulaski Scatterday, while he was the husband of your oratrix, to wit, on the first day of April 1862, & at divers times before & after that day, committed adultery with one Louisa Rippets in this county.[20]

Your oratrix is informed that these acts of adultery entitles her [to] be divorced fully & entirely from her said husband, Pulaski Scatterday, & she therefore farther prays that for the cause aforesaid, she may be divorced from her said husband, fully & entirely, & that the said Pulaski Scatterday for his said adultery be by the decree of this court prohibited from ever marrying again, & she again prays as she has before prayed, of as such & farther relief as this court may deem proper & right.

Peck & Hubbard
Atto. for Complt.

Depositions of Witnesses[21]

SARAH GROVE

QUESTION: State if you are acquainted with the parties to this suit and if so state how long you have known them also state where you have resided for the last five years.

ANSWER: I have known Mr and Mrs Scatterday for about 5 years past. I

Federal Census for 1880; U.S. City Directories; West Virginia Wills and Probate Records. William Hubbard was the son of Chester D. Hubbard, who served as a member of Virginia's secession convention and played a pivotal role in the creation of the state of West Virginia. William was born in Wheeling in 1843. He was educated locally and in Connecticut. He served as a lieutenant in the Third West Virginia Cavalry. After the war, he served as clerk of the West Virginia House of Delegates, before eventually being elected to Congress. *History of West Virginia, Old and New,* 2:621–22.

19. Emeline filed her amended bill in February 1867. She also requested that Pulaski be prohibited from remarrying.

20. This should likely read "Louisa Rickards."

21. These depositions were taken on February 25, 1867, at the law office of Peck and

lived for 2 years of last 5 beside them and for 3 years I have lived on Lane Street near Sixth in Wheeling.

QUESTION: State what if any thing you have heard pass between Mr Pulaski Scatterday the defendant and Mrs Ann Mitchell of an improper nature and what it was. State fully all you know about it.

ANSWER: I called at Mrs Mitchells house on one Sunday afternoon about one year ago—it was just before Mr Scatterday and Mrs Mitchell went away. I knocked at the door when Mr Scatterday came to the door. He would not let me in for about ten minutes. I asked for Mrs Mitchell when he told me she was up stairs dressing. She came down in a few minutes after I was admitted into the house. They acted as if they had been guilty of improprieties I thought. After this occurred and before they started away together Mrs Mitchell called at my house and in a conversation between her and myself she stated to me that she could part Mr and Mrs Scatterday if she wished to. Shortly after this Mr Pulaski Scatterday and Mrs Ann Mitchell went away.

QUESTION: State whether Mrs Mitchel was married or a widow woman.

ANSWER: She was a widow woman.

QUESTION: About what time did they leave here?

ANSWER: They left here in the fall of 1865 in the month of October.

QUESTION: Where was this house of Mrs Mitchell of which you speak?

ANSWER: It was next door to Mr Scatterday on the Island.

QUESTION: State if you have seen Mrs Mitchell and Pulaski Scatterday since they left her[e]. If so state where and when.

ANSWER: I saw Mrs Mitchell since they left here but I have not seen him. I called at Mrs Mitchells house in Manchester opposite Pittsburg Pa in July last to see them. I saw her and enquired for Mr Scatterday. She told [me] he was not in then but that he would be there to see me—that he wanted to see me but when I went there they were out walking.

QUESTION: Did you ever see him at any other time at Mrs Mitchells house on the Island?

ANSWER: No Sir, I did not.

QUESTION: How has Mrs Emiline Scatterday the complainant conducted herself during all this time well or otherwise?

Hubbard on Fourth Street in Wheeling. John Ewing's deposition was on February 28, 1867. All deponents signed their names.

ANSWER: Well as far as I know. I have been with her a great deal during that time.

EMILY MIRABEN

QUESTION: State if you are acquainted with the parties to this suit and if so state how long you have known them.
ANSWER: I have known Mrs Scatterday ever since she was a little girl—I do not know Mr Scatterday at all except by sight.
QUESTION: State how Mrs Scatterday has conducted herself for the last two or three years past.
ANSWER: As far as I know with the greatest of propriety as a lady should. I have been intimate with her for 30 years.

BERTRAND J. MIRABEN

QUESTION: State if you are acquainted with the parties to this suit. If so state how long you have known them.
ANSWER: I have known Mrs Scatterday for a great many years. I have known her for 3 or 4 years.
QUESTION: How has Mrs Scatterday conducted herself during the time you have known her?
ANSWER: She has always conducted herself with propriety.
QUESTION: State if you were acquainted with Mrs Ann Mitchell when she lived on the Island and how near her did you live then?
ANSWER: I knew her when I saw her but I had no acquaintance with her.
QUESTION: State if you ever saw Pulaski Scatterday going to her house.
ANSWER: No Sir, I did not.

FRITZ TARHLING

QUESTION: State if you are acquainted with the parties to this suit and Mrs Ann Mitchell and how long you have known them.
ANSWER: I know them all and have known them for some time.
QUESTION: State how near you lived to Ann Mitchell when you lived on the Island.
ANSWER: I lived next door in the same house.
QUESTION: State if ever you have seen Pulaski Scatterday go into her house. If so how often and under what circumstances?
ANSWER: I have seen him go there frequently. I could not tell how often. I did not know what he went there for.

QUESTION: How long would he stay when he went there if you took any notice to that?
ANSWER: I could not say—when they went away Scatterday went first and she went very soon afterwards.

LOUISA RICKARDS[22]

QUESTION: State if you are acquainted with Mr and Mrs Scatterday and if so how long you have known them.
ANSWER: I have known both of them for six years.
QUESTION: State if you know of Pulaski Scatterday having connection with any other woman than his wife if so state where and when.
ANSWER: No Sir, I do not of any but with myself.
QUESTION: State who is the father of your child Edward?
ANSWER: Pulaski Scatterday is—He never did [illegible] towards supporting it. He gave me some money.

JOHN EWING

QUESTION: State if you are acquainted with the parties to this suit and if so how long you have known them, also where you reside and your occupation.
ANSWER: I know both of them—have known him for 4 or 5 years and have known her about the same length of time. I board on the Island in the 7th ward and am in the employ of the Wheeling & Belmont Bridge Co at the toll house and office. Mr Scatterday was in the office also for 3 or 4 years while I was there.[23]
QUESTION: How has Mrs Scatterday conducted herself during the time you have known her?
ANSWER: She has always conducted herself like a lady so far as I know.
QUESTION: State if you know the time Scatterday left here and if so when was it and under what circumstances did he leave, also how you came to know it.
ANSWER: Scatterday went away on the 4th day of October 1865. He was at his office as usual on that day and went to his supper at his usual

---

22. Louisa Rickards lived with the Scatterdays in 1850. Pulaski was fifty-four, Emaline forty-two, and Louisa twenty-two. She was listed as a "domestic." United States Federal Census for 1850.

23. Pulaski Scatterday served as the superintendent of the Wheeling Bridge. *Williams' Wheeling Directory City Guide.*

time in the evening returning about dusk with something bulky under his left arm. He was then going towards the Island. He passed by without speaking and I jokingly asked him for his tote to let him know that I saw him. He said something which I could not understand. The next morning he sent the key of the safe by William Mitchell a son of Mrs Ann Mitchell who remembered to me that Scatterday had requested him to give me the key of the safe. I then asked him where Scatterday had gone and he said to Steubenville. I then said to him that I thought it very strange that he had not said something to me about going away as he had always given me the key of the safe in person when he was going away. I asked when he was coming back and he said he did not know. I have not seen Scatterday since then. On that day or the next day after that Mrs Mitchell came to the office. She told me to come into the office that she had something to tell me. She stated that Scatterday had left. I asked her where she had gone and she said she could not tell me. I then said to her that it could be possible that he had left in the manner in which he did that he had his own private money in the safe in the office and she Mrs Mitchell remarked that he had taken all with him.

QUESTION: State if he had any reason or cause to leave in the manner in which he did on business of the Company or for any reason you know.

ANSWER: He had no reason or cause to leave that I know of. He had no business of the company to leave for he was not embarrassed with the company that I ever heard of.

QUESTION: State if you ever saw Mrs Mitchell and Scatterday together in the office of the Bridge Co or elsewhere.

ANSWER: Mrs Mitchell called at the office of the Bridge Company frequently. Often times would remain in his office with Mr Scatterday for an hour or more.

QUESTION: On what terms did they appear to be?

ANSWER: On very friendly terms. He always seemed to me to be on more friendly terms with Mrs Mitchell than he was with his wife when she called there.

QUESTION: State if you ever saw him going towards Mrs Mitchells house and if so at what time of the day?

ANSWER: I have seen him going towards her house on the Island frequently in the evening about dark or after dark a while. It would almost always be after dark.

QUESTION: State if you ever knew of Scatterday going security for Mrs Mitchell.
ANSWER: I heard her ask him to go security for her.

[*On October 2, 1867, the court issued a decree stating that Emeline and Pulaski Scatterday be forever divorced. The court awarded Emeline alimony and ordered Pulaski to pay the costs of the suit. Pulaski Scatterday died on June 20, 1870. Strikingly, Emeline was listed as his widow in his death record, as she would be in city directories for years to come. When Emeline died on February 5, 1902, the* Wheeling Daily Register *described her as "the wife of the late Pulaski Scatterday."*[24]]

Francisca Conrad v. Frederick Conrad, 1868

[Conrad, Francisca v. Conrad, Frederick *(1868)*, *Records of the Circuit Court of Ohio County, WVRHC, env. 274 b-12. The case cost $30.16. Francisca filed her divorce petition in March 1868. The court issued a summons for Frederick on March 28, 1868; it was delivered to a man named August Frederick who lived at that residence.*]

Bill of Divorce

To the Honorable E. H. Caldwell, Judge of the Circuit Court of Ohio County, West Virginia,

Your oratrix Francisca Conrad of Ohio County, respectfully represents that she has been for the last ten years a resident of Ohio County and State of West Virginia.[25]

That, to wit, on the 12th day of August 1855 at the City of Wheeling in Ohio County WVa, she was married to Frederick Conrad of the City of Wheeling, Ohio County WVa, as will more fully appear by reference to the duly certified copy of the marriage certificate herewith filed marked Exhibit "A" and prayed to be read and received as part of this bill, and that she had while living with the said Frederick Conrad the following

---

24. U.S. Find a Grave Index; Wheeling, West Virginia City Directory, 1898; West Virginia Deaths Index; *Wheeling Daily Register*, February 8, 1902.

25. Francisca Conrad appears to have gone by "Fanny" and "Frances" in some census records. She was born around 1832 in Germany. United States Federal Census for 1860.

children Mary N. [known as "Nellie" or "Nelly"] Conrad, born August 2nd 1857, and Frederick Conrad born October 5th 1859.[26]

Your Oratrix further shows that the said Frederick Conrad, regardless of his marital duties towards your oratrix, did to wit on the 15th day of March 1865 at the City of New York in the State of New York, commit adultery with one Lizzette Bauman, and that the said Frederick Conrad did, to wit on the 15th day of May, 1865 to wit at the City of Wheeling Ohio County, commit adultery with the said Lizzette Bauman, and the said Frederick Conrad has since that time, left your Oratrix and has lived and cohabited with the said Lizzette Bauman, in open and notorious adultery, to wit in Ohio County and State of West Virginia.

Your Oratrix further shows that she last lived and cohabited with the said Frederick Conrad at Ohio County West Virginia and further shows that since the adultery of said Frederick Conrad as aforesaid, she has never cohabited with him, to the end therefore that the said Frederick Conrad may upon his corporal oath, full true direct and perfect answer make to all and singular the matters herein contained and set forth as fully as if the same were herinafter repeated and she thereunto particularly interrogated and that your Oratrix may be divorced from the bond of matrimony, and that your Oratrix may have such other and further relief, as the nature of the case may require and to your Honor seem meet. May it please this Honorable Court to grant unto your oratrix, that proper process may be directed to the said Frederick Conrad and that he may be made defendant to this bill. And your Oratrix will ever pray &c

Chandler & Davenport[27]
Solicitors for Complt.

---

26. Frederick Conrad was born in Byrne, Germany, in 1831 and naturalized in 1855. West Virginia Naturalization Records. I can find no naturalization record for Francisca Conrad. The 1860 census finds the Conrads living in the Fifth Ward of Wheeling with their children: "Nelly" and "Fred," who was only one. Frederick listed his personal estate as fifty dollars. United States Federal Census for 1860.

27. George O. Davenport was a prominent lawyer in Wheeling, who later served as a member of the House of Delegates. Atkinson and Gibbens, *Prominent Men of West Virginia*, 56, 68; West Virginia Wills and Probate Records; U.S. City Directories. John G. Chandler was born in 1838 and served as a captain in the Union Army during the Civil War. Francis H. Pierpont Civil War Telegrams, WVRHC, box 9, folder 20; U.S. Civil War Draft Registrations Records.

Marriage Certificate

Age of Husband—Born the 7th of January 1831
Age of Wife—Born on the 7th of February 1837
Condition of Husband & Wife—single
Place of Husband's birth—Bavaria, Germany, Europe
Place of Wife's birth—Prussia, Germany, Europe

Depositions of Witnesses[28]

CHARLES CONRAD

QUESTION: What is your age, residence, and occupation, and are you related to any of the parties to this suit?
ANSWER: I am twenty nine years of age. I reside on Main Street in the city of Wheeling. I am a confectioner. I am a brother to the defendant.
QUESTION: State if you know that Frederick Conrad and Francisca Conrad were married and if so when and where and whether or not you were present at the marriage?
ANSWER: They were married by Rev Helfer in this city about twelve or thirteen years ago. I was present and saw them married.
QUESTION: How many children did they have?
ANSWER: Four. Two are living and two are dead. Nellie and Frederick living.
QUESTION: State if you know where Mrs Conrad the complainant and her husband the defendant last lived and cohabited together.
ANSWER: In Ohio County.
QUESTION: State if you are acquainted with Lizette Bowman?
ANSWER: Yes Sir, I know her.
QUESTION: Please state if you are acquainted with her reputation for chastity and if so state what it is.
ANSWER: I am acquainted with her reputation for chastity. It is bad, that is what I heard.
QUESTION: State any facts or circumstances within your knowledge going to show improper intercourse between your brother the defendant and Mrs Bowman.
ANSWER: One evening this summer four years ago I was sitting in

---

28. J. F. Jones, a notary public, took these depositions on April 20, 1868. All deponents signed their names.

front of Mr Bassetts store with Mr Charles Thisch and Frederick Molder between eight and nine oclock. I saw Mrs Bowman coming up Main Street towards Roemers Corner and there she waited until my brother came up. They went down Biddle Street to the first alley. They stopped a few minutes and then went on down to the Baltimore Ohio Rail Road House. The woman that kept the house said they asked her for a room. They stayed there about five minutes then came out and went up street. We watched them all the time excepting while they were in the house. Mrs Bowman was a married woman at the time.

QUESTION: When did you last hear from your brother?
ANSWER: Last March a year ago I was up at Wellsburg at my brother-in-laws and he (my brother-in-law) showed me some letters from my brother. I knew they were from him, for I knew his hand writing. I dont remember now much that was in the letters. My brother-in-law would not let me see the whole of any of them. I saw the signature it was Frederick and Lizette as if from husband and wife.
QUESTION: State what kind of a woman Mrs Conrad the complainant is.
ANSWER: She is a very nice woman. I never heard anything against her.

NELLIE CONRAD[29]

QUESTION: How old are you and whose daughter are you?
ANSWER: I will be eleven years old the third of August. I am the daughter of Frederick Conrad and Francisca Conrad.
QUESTION: Do you know Mrs Bowman?
ANSWER: Yes sir.
QUESTION: Where did you see her?
ANSWER: I saw her in Wheeling and in New York.
QUESTION: When did you see her in New York and state all the circumstances.
ANSWER: On the fourth of July three years ago I went to New York. I started from here with my father. He told my mother that he was going to take me to my grandmothers up in Wellsburg. We didnt go there we went to New York. We went to a large Hotel it was painted yellow. I dont know the name of it. My father locked me up in a room from eleven o'clock in the morning until eleven o'clock at

---

29. Nellie married Peter H. Gensen in 1883. She died in 1928 in Monroe, Pennsylvania, at the age of sixty-nine. Her father's name was listed as "Louis Conrad" and her mother's name as "Frances Pfiester." Pennsylvania Death Certificates.

night. He then brought Mrs Bowman in the room. We all slept in the same bed. I next the wall Mrs Bowman in the middle and my father in front. In the morning father waked me up and told me to wash myself and dress myself and go into the room until he waked Mrs Bowman up. We slept that way four nights. Mrs Bowman told my father that he should take me home and should come again. She took all her clothes off but left her chemise on. She took her drawers off. I saw her setting on my fathers lap. He had his arms around her and he kissed her. My father told me not to tell my mother where we was.

QUESTION: Have you ever seen Mrs Bowman and your father together in Wheeling?

ANSWER: Yes sir. One Sunday we went to church up at the cathedral. Then we went down to where her husband had a photograph gallery on Main Street. After we went in the house he told Mrs Bowman to come and sit on his lap. She sat on his lap and they whispered. Another Sunday when she lived at Lafayette Hall [we] went to see her and drank coffee with her.

QUESTION: State whether or not you told your mother anything about what you saw in Wheeling until after he went to live with Mrs Bowman.

ANSWER: I did not.

AUGUST FREDERICK

QUESTION: What is your age and do you reside at Mr Conrad's?

ANSWER: I am twenty five years of age and have lived and made my home there since July 1863.

QUESTION: Are you acquainted with Mrs Lizette Bowman?

ANSWER: I am.

QUESTION: Are you acquainted with her general reputation for chastity?

ANSWER: I am.

QUESTION: Is that reputation good or not?

ANSWER: It is very bad. In Grafton she was known to be a whore. I heard this from Railroad men and soldiers who knew her.

QUESTION: State whether or not Mr Conrad was in the habit of being out late at nights and whether he gave true statements as to where he had been when he came home. State all you know about it.

ANSWER: He was in the habit of being out late at nights. One night he came home about three oclock and rapped at the door he had left his key in his sunday pants pocket. I went down stairs and opened the door I asked him what time it was. He said it is about two o'clock. I said it is pretty late. He said then well it was a man's birth day and we had to go singing. He then went up stairs to his room and I went to mine. The second day after some men came in and asked where Fred Conrad had been that evening why he had not been a long with them singing. His wife said was not he along? He told me he was and that he had been singing that night. I was in the store at the same time. The same week he came home at three o'clock one night and wanted to tell me where he had been. I told him I didnt want to know and it was none of my business.

ELIZA JANE RIDER

QUESTION: Where do you reside and where have you resided for the last four years and what is your occupation?
ANSWER: I have been keeping the Baltimore & Ohio Rail Road House in centre Wheeling for the last seven years.
QUESTION: Are you acquainted with Frederick Conrad and if so state what your acquaintance was?
ANSWER: I have no acquaintance with him only knew him when I saw him. I have dealt with him in Mr Bassetts store. One evening about eight oclock he came to my house with a woman and asked me for a room to stay in all night. I told him I did not keep ladies and gentlemen. I asked him if the lady was his wife. He refused to answer the question and walked out the door. I think it was the second or third day after that I heard he had run off with this same woman.
QUESTION: Why did you refuse to give them a room?
ANSWER: I did not believe them to be husband [and] wife. I know Mrs Conrad. It was not her.

[*On May 21, 1868, the court ruled that Francisca Conrad be divorced forever from her husband, Frederick. She was given custody of Frederick Conrad Jr. and Nellie Conrad. He was told to pay the costs of the suit. By 1880, Francisca Conrad had remarried. She and her husband, H. C. F. Fredrich, also a German immigrant, lived with Nellie, who was twenty-one, and three other children, ranging in age from three to nine. Sometime between 1880 and Nellie's death in 1928, Francisca likely married again. Her name was listed as "Frances Pfiester" on Nellie's death certificate.*[30] *There is no further record of Frederick Conrad.*]

---

30. United States Federal Census for 1880; Pennsylvania Death Certificates.

Elizabeth Welch v. Connor Welch, 1871

[Welch, Elizabeth v. Welch, Connor *(1871)*, *Records of the Circuit Court of Ohio County, WVRHC, env. 288 b-3. The case cost $29.78. Elizabeth (Elisabeth) Welch filed her petition in December 1870. The court issued a summons for Connor on December 26, 1870, serving it the same day.*]

Bill of Divorce

State of West Virginia, Ohio County Circuit Court

To the Hon. T. Melvin, Judge of the said court, in Chancery now sitting:[31]

Your oratrix, Elisabeth Welch, of the said county, humbly complaining, here shows to the court, that on the [blank] day of August 1869 she was lawfully married in said county, to Connor Welch, both then & ever since residents of the City of Wheeling, a certificate of which marriage is here exhibited & marked A.[32]

That she has always conducted herself properly & kindly towards her said husband, & has endeavoured to do her part & has been a faithful wife to her said husband, but that he has abused her in fits of drunkenness, & has left her without any support whatever, & has lately declared that he could do nothing for her.

That before she & her said husband were married, in about June 1869, at the county aforesaid, without her knowledge, her said husband had been notoriously a licentious person, in this, that he cohabited with a married woman, by the name of Mary Riddle,[33] & kept her at a tav-

---

31. Thayer Melvin was born in 1835 and was originally from Hancock County, the northernmost county in West Virginia. He was a prosecutor before the war. During the Civil War, Melvin volunteered for the Union Army as a private. After the war, he was twice elected attorney general for West Virginia before resigning to become a judge in Wheeling. Cranmer, *History of the Upper Ohio Valley*, 546–47; West Virginia Deaths Index.

32. Although his marriage certificate suggests he was born in 1836, Connor Welch listed his birth year as 1831 in the 1870 census. In both, he states that he was born in Arkansas. By 1870, he was working in a box factory. He and Elizabeth lived together with her daughter, Virginia, who was fifteen. He is not listed as having any real estate or personal wealth. United States Federal Census for 1870.

33. Mary Riddle lived with her husband, Clark, in Wellsburg, West Virginia, in 1870. She was born in 1844 in Virginia. Her husband was a butcher, and she was a milliner. While her husband listed no personal wealth, she had real estate valued at $1,200 and a personal estate valued at $400. United States Federal Census for 1870.

ern or boarding house in Wheeling; that since their said marriage, her said husband has kept up his improper connection with the said Mary Riddle, & has brought her to his own house under the false pretense that she was his sister, when in fact there was no relationship whatever between them, & that he has at divers times & in divers places, in the said City, committed adultery with the said Mary Riddle & she here avers, that she has not cohabited [with] her said husband, since she so learned that she became aware that he was such [a] licentious person, or that he had as aforesaid mentioned committed the said adultery.

She here shows, that neither she or her said husband have any property, of consequence, nor is there any issue of the said marriage.

She prays a divorce from the bonds of matrimony from her said husband for the causes aforesaid, & the costs & reasonable alimony; & she will ever pray &c.

Peck & Cochran Solrs. for Compt.[34]

Marriage Certificate

CERTIFICATE TO OBTAIN A MARRIAGE LICENSE

To be annexed to the License, required by the Act passed 15th March, 1861.

Time of Marriage: [blank][35]
Place of Marriage: [blank]
Full names of Parties Marriage: Conner Welch & Elizabeth Hanna
Age of Husband: Thirty three years
Age of Wife: Thirty years
Condition of Husband (widowed or single): Widower
Condition of Wife (widowed or single): Widow
Place of Husband's Birth: Helena, Ark.
Place of Wife's Birth: Benwood, WVa
Place of Husband's Residence: Ohio County WVa
Place of Wife's Residence: Ohio County WVa
Names of Husband's parents: [blank]
Names of Wife's parents: [blank]
Occupation of Husband: Printer

---

34. Robert H. Cochran was born in Ohio in 1837. He moved to Wheeling in 1869 and joined Peck's practice. United States Federal Census for 1880; Cranmer, *History of Wheeling City*, 245.

35. The marriage license was signed by R. B. Woods on July 7, 1869.

MINISTER'S RETURN OF MARRIAGE

I Certify, that on the 31st day of August 1869, at my residence on John St. Wheeling W.Va., I united in Marriage the above named and described parties, under authority of the annexed License.

John P. Farmer

Notes from Attorney

It is almost impossible to prove adultery by an eye witness, but the whole course of the short married life of this couple, the husband was showing this woman Mrs. Riddle around as his sister, & even taking her to his own house as such & imposing her on his wife as his sister.

By the testimony of Benter, he had last fall a woman in his room after night, & by Brown the conductor, we find last fall, he went to West Alexander with a woman, the same no doubt, & went to the justices for the purpose of marrying her. He did not in so many words tell Brown on his return the next day, but introduced the woman as his wife. It is passed all doubt, he passed the night with her at Hard Scramble, & think past all doubt the adultery is made out.

Daniel Peck

Depositions of Witnesses[36]

MARIAH JANE MARSHALL

QUESTION: Are you acquainted with Mr. and Mrs. Welch, and if so how long have you known them?

ANSWER: Well, I have known Mrs Welch for about two years. As for Mr. Welch I only know him by sight.

QUESTION: State whether you were at the wedding when they were married or not?

ANSWER: Yes sir.

QUESTION: What do you know about Mr. Welch bringing a strange lady to his house and keeping her there as his sister, since they were married?

---

36. These depositions were taken at the offices of Peck and Cochran on December 31, 1870. Both Elizabeth and Connor Welch were present. All deponents on December 31, 1870, signed their names, except for Elizabeth Brown, who signed her mark. Virginia Hanna's and John Boring's depositions were taken on January 2, 1871. William Brown's and Joseph Benter's depositions were taken on February 28, 1871. Both signed their names.

ANSWER: I seen a strange lady there that was said to be the same. I was never introduced to her.

QUESTION: What do you know about his calling her his sister?

ANSWER: Well, I don't know anything about it, only from hearsay. I have heard him speak of her as Mary.

QUESTION: How often did you see her at Welch's house, and about when?

ANSWER: Twice, I dont remember any other times. It was this fall a year ago. She was said to have staid there over night. She was there to my knowledge at late bed time.

QUESTION: Did Mrs. Welch receive her as the sister of her husband, and treat her as such?

ANSWER: Yes sir, to the best of my knowledge.

QUESTION: How did Mrs. Welch treat her husband during all the time they were together, and how did she perform the duties of a wife towards him?

ANSWER: Well I always thought that she seemed to do her part, so far as I knew.

QUESTION: How near to her do you live?

ANSWER: Well, the next door, she lived in part of my house.

MARTHA BURNS

QUESTION: Are you acquainted with the plaintiff and defendant in this suit, and if so, how long have you know them?

ANSWER: Well, I have known Mrs. Welch for over two years. I have been acquainted with Mr. Welch for over a year. In fact I knew him before they were married, and before his wife met him.

QUESTION: State what you know of his bringing a woman to Mrs. Dunlevy's to board before he was married to Mrs. Welch?

ANSWER: Well, all I know about that is that I went into Mrs Dunlevy's; and Mrs. Dunlevy introduced her as Conner Welch's sister.

QUESTION: How long did she stay Mrs. Dunlevy's?

ANSWER: Well she was there several days. And I asked her who she was acquainted with in Wellsburg, because I had some acquaintances there, and what her husband done. He was a butcher, she said, in Wellsburg.

QUESTION: What attentions did Mr. Welch pay to that woman while she was there, to your knowledge?

ANSWER: I never saw any. I never met him and her there together. I spoke to Welch and said that his sister was here. And he said "Yes."

And I said to him at the same time, that I understood that her husband was a butcher in Wellsburg, and he said "Yes."

QUESTION: Did you see this same woman after the marriage, at his house? If so, at what time?

ANSWER: No Sir I never saw her there, but I saw her going there one afternoon. I saw her going up the steps, but I did not see her going in.

QUESTION: How did Mrs. Welch perform her duties as a wife while they lived together as husband and wife?

ANSWER: With regard to that I cant give any information as I never stood in their house after they were married. I never heard of anything between them but that which is correct. I always understood, and from what I seen, understood, that he was an industrious man trying to support his family, and I never heard of anything wrong in him till I heard of this.

CROSS EXAMINATION BY THE DEFENDANT

QUESTION: Do you know anything about Mrs Welch knocking me down on the Fourth of July?

ANSWER: No Sir. I never heard of it.

QUESTION: Did you ever hear anything of her putting my things out of the house in the mornings when I would go away to work, and leaving them out in the inclemency of the weather?

(Question excepted to by the plaintiff's counsel)

ANSWER: Not anything. In fact I know nothing of their family matters.

QUESTION: Do you believe from your knowledge of her and her daughter that their treatment of me has been such as a man should have had, who stepped in as a protector?

ANSWER: With regards to that Mr Welch, I cant answer. I know nothing of her treatment of you so as to give any satisfaction.

LOUIS LINGAMAN

QUESTION: Are you acquainted with Conner Welch and Elizabeth Welch, his wife?

ANSWER: I know him. He boarded with me once at the Pemberton House in this city. I don't know her.

QUESTION: How long did he board with you, and when?

ANSWER: Well he was boarding with me twice. The first time, I expect was about three years ago. His wife was with him then. The next time he was by himself, a year or six months since I can't exactly tell. It was before he was married this last time.

QUESTION: While he was boarding with you this last time, when he was a single man, state if he brought a woman to your house to stay a while, whom he called his sister, and how long she staid.

ANSWER: Well he brought a woman there. I can't say exactly whether more than one day for dinner and when he come to pay me he say Mr. Lingaman I pay you for the dinner for the lady and myself and he said she was a sister or cousin or some relation, I dont mind what.

QUESTION: Did he, at any other time, before or since that time, take that woman to your house and if so when?

ANSWER: No Sir, not to my recollection.

W. J. JOHNSTON

QUESTION: Are you acquainted with Conner Welch and Elizabeth his wife, the parties to this suit?

ANSWER: I am.

QUESTION: Were you acquainted with Conner Welch before he married this last time?

ANSWER: I was.

QUESTION: State if you was acquainted with a lady whom he brought to his house or boarding house and claimed to be his sister.

ANSWER: I was acquainted with the lady. I don't know that he took her to his boardinghouse. I saw her at my printing office where she called to see him, he being at work with me.

QUESTION: Was that before or after his last marriage?

ANSWER: Before and since, I have met the lady.

QUESTION: Did he claim her as his sister, or did she claim him for her brother, at those meetings?

ANSWER: Well I think that Mr. Welch introduced her as his sister, Mary. I wouldn't be positive.

QUESTION: How often did they meet in your printing office, or did you see them together there, or elsewhere?

ANSWER: Well I couldn't say positively. Two or three times at the printing office only, and each of those times she called on him.

QUESTION: State if they embraced as brother and sister when they met.

ANSWER: I couldn't say anything about that. I have no recollection as to how they met.

QUESTION: Did they retire at any one time into any private room, or did they stay in the room where you were while she was there?

ANSWER: They were in the room where I was. There was no *private* room there.

QUESTION: Did you ever see them together since his last marriage?
ANSWER: I think she called on him once since his last marriage, in the office.
QUESTION: How long were those interviews between them?
ANSWER: That I couldn't say positively.
QUESTION: Do you know whether she was his sister or not?
ANSWER: I dont know. I never saw her previous to her coming to the office.
QUESTION: What information, if any, have you as to whether she was his sister or not?
ANSWER: Well, I have none, only to the best of my knowledge she was introduced to me by him as his sister.
QUESTION: Do you know of her being at Mrs. Dunlevy's boarding house with him?
ANSWER: Not positively, I couldn't say.
QUESTION: What do you know about it?
ANSWER: Well I don't really know anything about it.
QUESTION: About how old a lady was this?
ANSWER: I would suppose about twenty eight years old.
QUESTION: Did Welch tell you that she was a married woman: and if so, where did he say her husband lived?
ANSWER: He told me she was a married woman, and I believe he said her husband lived in Wellsburg.
QUESTION: Did he tell you what her husbands name was?
ANSWER: It appears to me he did but I cant say positively what he said it was—R—— Roberts—or some such name.
QUESTION: Did he not say that her name was Mary Riddle?
ANSWER: Well I couldn't say that he did, for in speaking of her to me he always called her Mary.
QUESTION: Was you ever informed from any source that this lady was not his sister, and if so, did you afterwards ask him anything about it?
ANSWER: I was never informed until very recently and that was by his present wife, and I didn't ask him any thing about it.

ELIZABETH BROWN

QUESTION: Are you acquainted with Conner Welch and Elizabeth Welch, the parties to this suit, and if so, how long have you known them?
ANSWER: I am a little over a year acquainted with Mrs Welch and just about a year with Mr Welch.

QUESTION: Were you acquainted with Mr. Welch while he was boarding at Mrs. Dunlevy's before his last marriage?

ANSWER: Yes sir.

QUESTION: State if he brought any strange lady to Mrs Dunlevy's before his last marriage, and introduced her as his sister.

ANSWER: Yes sir, he did.

QUESTION: How long did she stay there, and how many times was she there?

ANSWER: She was there once. She staid a little over a week.

QUESTION: Did you know her name at that time, or have you found it out since?

ANSWER: I knowed her name before I knowed him.

QUESTION: State what it was.

ANSWER: Mrs. Riddle.

QUESTION: Were you acquainted with her before that time, and how long?

ANSWER: I was acquainted with her about eight years before.

QUESTION: Where was your acquaintance with her? At Wellsburg or here?

ANSWER: At Wellsburg.

QUESTION: Whose daughter was she?

ANSWER: Indeed I couldnt tell you. I don't mind the name any more. I have forgotten it, it has been so long.

QUESTION: About how long had she been married to Mr. Riddle when she was down here at Dunlevy's boarding house?

ANSWER: Oh, she's been married for the last nine or ten years if not longer. I used to live close neighbor to her.

QUESTION: Had she children or not, by Mr. Riddle?

ANSWER: No Sir, none at all as I know of.

QUESTION: Does her father live in Wellsburg, or did he when you were there?

ANSWER: I don't know if he lived there when I was there, but he lives below Wellsburg, the place that I heard of last.

QUESTION: What kind of attentions did Mr Welch pay Mrs Riddle when she was at Mrs Dunlevy's boarding house?

ANSWER: Well all I know, they was very sociable together.

QUESTION: Did they walk out together alone, any, or often?

ANSWER: Yes sir. I seen him twice walking out with her. I saw him taking her to his own house after he was married the last time.

QUESTION: How many times did you see him taking her to his own house?

ANSWER: Once, and then I seen him going once down street with her from his house.
QUESTION: While they were still at Dunlevy's, before his last marriage, did they walk out in daylight or at night?
ANSWER: In the evening they went out.
QUESTION: Do you know whether she was his sister or not?
ANSWER: No, I couldn't tell. I dont think she is.
QUESTION: Did you have any conversation with her when she was at Mrs Dunlevy's, in his presence or hearing?
ANSWER: No Sir, I just stood at my door and looked at them.
QUESTION: Do you know why Mrs Riddle left Dunlevy's at the time when she did leave?
ANSWER: I dont know, only what I heard.

CROSS EXAMINATION BY DEFENDANT

QUESTION: Do you *know* I introduced her to Mrs Dunlevy as my sister?
ANSWER: No, Mrs Dunlevy was telling me he introduced her as his sister, and Mrs Dunlevy, though she was a stranger to her, thought she was a very nice woman. She thought she was his sister till I told her who she was.
QUESTION: Do you know she was there over a week, and how do you know?
ANSWER: Why I seen it.
QUESTION: Where were you when you saw her and me go to my house?
ANSWER: I was going up towards Zane Street when I seen it.
QUESTION: When you stood in the door watching us, what did you see us do?
ANSWER: They was cutting up and laughing.
QUESTION: Did you see any thing improper in our conduct towards each other.
ANSWER: No I didn't.
QUESTION: Did you ever know of any improper intimacy between us?
ANSWER: No sir. All is, I saw him go into a house that didn't bear a very good name.
QUESTION: When you were watching me, whose house did I enter?
ANSWER: Why, he was standing at Mrs. Taylor's and Ella Newland was standing also at the door, and he spoke to her a little bit, and then he went in.
QUESTION: Did you see me when I came out?
ANSWER: No sir I didn't watch till you came out. I was standing at the door when he went in and I went in and shut my door.

QUESTION: When was this?
ANSWER: It was last summer here sometime
QUESTION: When did you next see me?
ANSWER: I saw him pass up and down in a day or two.

RE-EXAMINED BY PLAINTIFF'S ATTORNEY

QUESTION: What was the matter with Mrs Taylor's house? What was its reputation?
ANSWER: People said they saw men going in there on account of that girl she kept there.

VIRGINIA HANNA

QUESTION: What relation is the plaintiff, Mrs Welch, to you, and how old are you?
ANSWER: She is my mother, and I am sixteen years old.
QUESTION: State if Mr. Welch, your step father, brought a woman to your house claiming her to be his sister, and if so when was that, and how often?
ANSWER: He did: and I think she came about four or five times. It has been about nearly a year ago.
QUESTION: How did he claim her to be his sister?
ANSWER: Well, he just told us she was his sister.
QUESTION: State what familiarities you saw between him and her when they were alone at your house.
ANSWER: Well, as I went into the room to call them to supper she was lying on the bed, and he was standing by the bed, bending over her & talking in a low tone. And when they saw me she got up and they both walked across the floor and he had his arm around her, at the same time. I saw him kiss her once. She was sitting on the floor and he was sitting on the chair beside her, and he threw his arm around her neck and kissed her.
QUESTION: State if she staid at your house all night any one of the times she was there.
ANSWER: She staid one night.
QUESTION: State if he brought her there when she came, or if she came by herself.
ANSWER: The first time she came alone, and he brought her once or twice afterwards.
QUESTION: When she came the first time, what did she say, if anything, about being his sister?

ANSWER: Well she didn't say any thing. But mother says to her, "I suppose you are Connor's sister" and she answered "Yes," and she got up and shook hands.
QUESTION: Did you find out her name by herself or him at that time?
ANSWER: No sir. He just told us it was his sister Mary.

JOHN W. BORING

QUESTION: Are you acquainted with the parties to this suit?
ANSWER: Well, I know Mrs. Welch when I see her. I don't know Mr Welch the defendant.
QUESTION: Are you acquainted with Mary Riddle, and is she a relative of yours?
ANSWER: Yes sir, I am acquainted with her. She is a niece of mine; I believe she is my sister's child.
QUESTION: Is she a sister of Connor Welch's, or any relation whatever of his?
ANSWER: No I don't think she is.
QUESTION: What was the name of the father of Mary Riddle?
ANSWER: Jacob Robinson[37]
QUESTION: Was your sister ever married except to Jacob Robinson, or had she any children named Welch?
ANSWER: She was married before she married Robinson, and had one child only, and it died when a baby, before she seen Robinson. She was never married since. Her husband Robinson is living yet. She never had any children named Welch.

WILLIAM G. BROWN

QUESTION: State whether you are acquainted with the defendant, Connor Welch, and what your occupation has been for the last two or three years.
ANSWER: Well, in first place, I have been a little of everything, brakesman, baggage master, and Conductor at times, on the Hempfield R.R. I am acquainted with Connor Welch. I got acquainted with him at Henry Gill's binding establishment. Have since known him when he was on Water Street making boxes and binding books.
QUESTION: What business were you in habit of transacting for him last fall and before?
ANSWER: Well I would get orders from the tobaccoists in Washington

---

37. I cannot locate Jacob Robinson in the census records.

and take them down to him. These orders were for boxes. Then I would get sacks to put the cigar boxes in and would take the boxes to Washington and collect the money for him.

QUESTION: Do you remember last fall, perhaps in November, of Connor Welch going up as far as West Alexander with a woman? Who did he tell you that woman was, and where did they get off from the Hempfield train?

ANSWER: Well I was conductor at that time. He asked me whether he had better get a ticket or not. I told him, "Yes." I asked him where he was going. He said to West Alexander. He got on. I did not see her getting on. He got on himself. We talked along. Had some business about boxes. I gave him an introduction to Mr Waltz, a tobaccoist at West Alexander. The last I seen of him when the train left he was going up the hill with him at West Alexander. Waltz and him were talking together when they left the train. He got on the train and came back the next morning. I helped the ladies on but did not take notice to the lady. After the train left the station Welch & I got to talking. He got to talking about the transaction of the last night. He said he went up to Waltz's and got some sigars, and he said Waltz didn't deal in that kind of boxes. Then he said he went up to see the Squire's in the evening. He didn't say what time it was; and the Lawson folks at West Alexander, where he stopped, suspected something was wrong. He said one [of] the boys followed them up to the Squire's office. They went in, and he said he had a long chat with the squire. I asked him where his woman was; and he said she was on the train; and after we got away down the road a piece, when it was time to lift the tickets from the passengers, he was sitting beside her, and he gave me an introduction to her as his wife. I helped them off the train and that is the last I seen her till I seen them both down at the shop. She was working there.

QUESTION: Was that the woman you saw here just now?

ANSWER: No. I never saw this woman before.[38]

QUESTION: Did you ever see the other woman except at the times you have mentioned?

ANSWER: I saw her at the shop frequently, both before and after that time. She was working there like the rest of the girls.

---

38. Elizabeth Welch was in the room during the deposition, meaning that William Brown had never seen Conner's legal wife.

QUESTION: State as near as you can the time this took place on the train.
ANSWER: It was last fall. He told me to keep this as a secret and not to tell any body. I told him of course, I wouldn't be talking about it, and I didn't tell about it till I was brought here as a witness. I don't know how it come to be found out.

JOSEPH BENTER

QUESTION: Are you acquainted with the defendant, Conner Welch, and how long have you known him?
ANSWER: I am acquainted with him. Have known him about a year.
QUESTION: Do you remember Mr. Welch bringing a woman into his shop one Sunday night?
ANSWER: I do.
QUESTION: Do you know who she was?
ANSWER: I don't know her name. We have a latch or place to let barrels &c down from one story to another. I saw down through that.
QUESTION: Did you have any conversation with him about it?
ANSWER: Yes Sir. He let on as if he didn't have any body there but he afterwards acknowledged that he had.
QUESTION: What did you see them do?
ANSWER: I only saw that he had a woman down there.
QUESTION: When was this?
ANSWER: I think it was last fall.

[*In March 1871, the court ruled that Elizabeth and Connor Welch be forever divorced and that he pay her costs. I can find no record of either Elizabeth or Connor after their divorce.*]

William Hamilton v. Virginia Hamilton, 1872

[Hamilton, William v. Hamilton, Virginia *(1872), Records of the Circuit Court of Ohio County, WVRHC, env. 292 b-8. The case cost $32.47. William formally filed his petition in December 1872. The court issued summons to Virginia on November 11 and 16, although she was not served until November 30.*]

Unidentified Young Woman, ca. 1866;
West Virginia and Regional History Center.

Bill of Divorce

State of West Virginia, Ohio County Circuit Court
December Rules 1872
To the Hon. Thayer Melvin, Judge of said Court in Chancery sitting:
The plaintiff William Hamilton[39] says that he is now and for more than over year last past has been a resident of the said County of Ohio, that he and the defendant Virginia Hamilton were joined in marriage on or about the 29th day of August 1859 and for a number of years thence lived and cohabited together as man and wife. That plaintiff demeaned himself and provided for his family to the best of his abil-

---

39. There are too many William and Virginia Hamiltons to pinpoint these two specific people in the census records.

ity and as became a faithful husband, that defendant became and was unfaithful towards plaintiff, neglected her duty and sought the society and cohabitation of other men, & that plaintiff and defendant separated on or about the 4th day of July 1870 in consequence of the lewd and improper conduct of defendant, since which time plaintiff has not lived or cohabited with defendant. Plaintiff says that on the 8th day of November 1872 in the City of Wheeling and at divers times before and since that time and at divers places defendant committed adultery with and carnally knew one Ferdinand Debold,[40] and for months and years last past has been guilty of adultery with divers and sundry persons unknown to plaintiff. Plaintiff says there is no issue of said marriage living and prays that a summons may issue to the said defendant Virginia Hamilton and that on the final hearing of this he receive a divorce from the said bond of matrimony and such other and further relief as to the Court may seem meet.

William Hamilton by
Cochran & Hubbard his attys.

Marriage Certificate[41]

Mr William Hamilton of Triadelphia Ohio County and Miss Virginia Cochran of Peters Run Ohio County were married on the 29th day of August AD 1858 certificate given.

Depositions of Witnesses[42]

W. H. COCHRAN

QUESTION: Where do you reside?
ANSWER: I reside in the City of Wheeling.

---

40. Ferdinand Debold was born in Ohio in 1837 to French immigrant parents. In 1870, he lived in Wheeling's Sixth Ward with his wife, Mary, and their two young children. He worked at a rolling mill. They were still married and living together in 1880. United States Federal Census for 1870, 1880.

41. They were married by a justice of the peace in Washington County, Pennsylvania.

42. J. G. Pendleton, a notary public, recorded the first of these depositions on December 9, 1872, at the law offices of Cochran and Hubbard on Fourth Street. W. H. Cochran signed his name. William Frazier gave testimony on December 13, Isaac Kelly and William Hamilton on December 20, and Abraham Horne on December 23. All signed their names. Horne also demanded payment for giving his testimony.

QUESTION: Are you acquainted with William Hamilton & Virginia Hamilton the parties to this suit & if so, how long have you known them?

ANSWER: I know them & have known them for five years.

QUESTION: What opportunities have you had in that time to know how Mr Hamilton demeaned himself as a husband & provided for his family?

ANSWER: I have boarded with him frequently & have lived in the same house with him for a year or more at different times. He was always a good provider & his wife always admitted him to be such. He was always industrious & sober. He was a mechanic & always got good wages. When the wages of his profession were $2.25, he would get $2.50. He was always a very agreeable fellow about the House. He always treated her a great deal better than I thought he ought to any how, a great deal better than she treated him.

QUESTION: Please state how she treated him & how she behaved with other men.

ANSWER: She treated him at all times very hard & used vulgar & profane language to him. As to her behavior with other men, while he was living with her, I know nothing about it. When he left her he told her that if she would behave herself, lead a virtuous life & join the Church, he would come back to her, live with her & provide for her as before. She told him that if she lived so long without him, she would live without him always. After he left her she began to run after other men, or had other men running after her. A year or two before he left her, they were living in Martinsville, Belmont County, Ohio. I was boarding with them at the time. He & I were working at the Top Mill, building trestles to get coal to the furnaces. Hamilton & his wife had a difficulty about some of their domestic affairs & he went from home to the Cottage House to board, kept by a man name of Coss. After this I was one night walking up street & I met her going to his boarding house. She had a large carving knife up her sleeve & told me she was going to kill him with it. I told her not to make a fool of herself, & she said she would stick it in me if I didn't get out of the way. Her father took her home.

QUESTION: State how long they have been living in this State.

ANSWER: To my best knowledge they have been living here four or five years & may be longer, part of the time in Ohio County & part of the time in the City of Wheeling.

QUESTION: How long have they been living separately?

ANSWER: Since March 1870.

QUESTION: Are you acquainted with one Ferdinand, called "Fred Debold"?

ANSWER: I am, have known him for two years, about.

QUESTION: State what you know, if anything about Debold's associations with the defendant, Virginia Hamilton?

ANSWER: I know they used to run a great deal together. She lived here in Wheeling nearly a year after her husband left her; then she moved out to the neighborhood of Roney's Point to keep house for her brother. Debold used to come out there & he persuaded her to move back to Wheeling. This was in October or November 1871. This was the first time I saw them as closely connected as I did. I saw them in bed together & knew that they stayed all night together in the same room. I saw him give her money the next morning.

QUESTION: State when & where you last saw them in bed together.

ANSWER: On Friday night on the 8th of November 1872, I went to her residence on Fourth Street. I had told her that I would be there that night I went to the door & knocked. The windows & blinds were down. I knocked 3 or 4 times. This was about nine o'clock. I heard her jump, I thought, out of bed. At any rate it was sometime before she got to the door. I suppose she was putting on her clothes. She asked me who was there. I told her whom it was. She said she did not care for me, for me to come in. When I went in, the fire was covered & the lights were turned out & Debold was lying in bed undressed. He said he had heard from Hamilton & that he had threatened to take the law on him & said that now he was prepared for him & with that, he threw up his leg & patted his behind & said he didn't care a damn for any one. There was a bottle of Whiskey on the middle of the mantle & a pistol on each side of it & both were pretty full. As soon as I went out she locked the door & the light were put out, leaving Debold in there, in bed. At the time Debold said he "didn't care a damn for any one." He at the same time said, that he would come there now twice, where he done so once before. I went there the night before to notify her that her husband had written a note to Debold & that he was bringing a suit for divorce. Then she said that the note would bring Debold, that I must come there Friday night & would see them both there. Something over a year ago, she told me that she & Debold had gone to Bellaire Ohio & passed the night there as man & wife. She said that she was going to move into Wheeling as it was too inconvenient for her to come in here to meet him. This was when she lived in the neighborhood of Roney's Point. She spoke thus freely to me, because I had before seen them together in bed & supposed I was familiar with the subject. Their associations of late have been rather notorious & they have both admitted to me that he was keeping her & providing for her. I have known him frequently to go to her house in daylight & at night.

QUESTION: State what you know about any suspicious acts on her part, coming to the knowledge of Hamilton, before he left her.

ANSWER: He told me he thought she was not a decent woman & that he suspected her of consorting improperly with other men. He one time told her that if she would swear that she was virtuous, he would take the law on anyone that attacked her. This she would not do. He told me that he had told her this. He asked me if I would assist him in clearing her of these matters, & I told him that as long as he was trying to vindicate his wife's character I would stand by him. After this talk, he saw his wife & she told him he had better let these matters drop & that strengthened his suspicion. Sometime before Hamilton left her, he told me that he had contracted a veneral disorder from her. He said that he had gone to Dr. McGinnis, her physician & asked what was the matter with his wife & offered to pay the Doctor's bill if he would tell, but the Doctor would not. When I told her of this fact about a month ago, that the Doctor was likely to be a witness for her husband, she said she thanked God that Doctor McGinnis was dead.

QUESTION: State what you know; if anything, about her consorting with other men, besides Debold.

ANSWER: I have known her to go with a man from North Wheeling. I have seen him with her at her own house & at other houses, sometimes as late as 11 or 12 o'clock at night. From what I have seen & heard her say I know that she is not a virtuous woman. I know that she kept a house of ill fame, that she had bad women about her, that she was paid for it. I regarded her character as so bad that I have forbidden her to come to my house & told her that she wasn't fit for any respectable woman to associate with. I occupied a peculiar position towards some of her friends & was trying to put a stop to her evil ways & prevent her from becoming notorious. I was working more for her friends than for her to save them from the disgrace of her conduct. This was why I was so intimate with the case & so familiar with the facts.

WILLIAM T. FRAZIER

QUESTION: State your age, residence & occupation.
ANSWER: I am 31 years of age, reside in the city of Wheeling, and am employed by the Wheeler and Wilson Sewing Machine Company.
QUESTION: Are you acquainted with Virginia Hamilton, the defendant in this case?
ANSWER: I am
QUESTION: How long have you known her?
ANSWER: For about three years.
QUESTION: Are you acquainted with her reputation for virtue and chastity?
ANSWER: I am.
QUESTION: Is it good or bad?
ANSWER: It is bad.
QUESTION: Do you know of persons other than her husband having had carnal intercourse with the said Virginia Hamilton within the last three years?
ANSWER: I do.

ISAAC B. KELLY

I know the parties to this suit, William & Virginia Hamilton. Have known William Hamilton for three or four years. I know him to be an industrious hard working man and was inclined to work harder than his health allowed. He was a liberal provider for his family, and provided more than I thought his circumstances justified. At the time I know him he lived in Triadelphia. For some four or five months during the time I knew him he worked for me, and I know that at that time he was a member in good standing of the Methodist Church in Triadelphia.

WILLIAM HAMILTON

I am the plaintiff in this case. The defendant and I were married at the house of Joseph Lawson in West Alexander, Washington County, Pennsylvania, on the 29th day of August 1858 by Esquire Alexander. Joseph Lawson was a witness to the marriage but is dead. Esquire Alexander is also dead, I am informed. My wife has or had the certificate of marriage. We have no children living. I have no property except my tools and a few personal articles. When we separated my wife got all the household furniture. For a long time before I left my wife I was suspicious of her virtue, but did not leave her until I had convincing proof of her unfaithfulness.

ABRAHAM B. HORNE

QUESTION: State your age residence and occupation.
ANSWER: I am nearly 23 years of age. I reside in Triadelphia Ohio County. I am working at a saw mill.
QUESTION: Are you acquainted with Virginia Hamilton the defendant in this case?
ANSWER: I knew her formerly but have seen her only 2 or 3 times to recognize her in the last ten years and only spoke to her once or twice in that time. One of the times was at the old Hempfield Depot in this city and Ferdinand Debold was there at the same time.
QUESTION: Do you know the reputation of Virginia Hamilton for chastity and virtue?
ANSWER: I have heard persons speak of her as a bad character.
QUESTION: Since the marriage of the defendant to the plaintiff do you know anything of her having cohabited with any person other than her husband?
ANSWER: I know nothing.

[*After William's attorneys filed his depositions in April 1873, there was no activity on his suit. I can find no further record of either Virginia or William Hamilton.*]

CHAPTER 7

Abandonment

SHE HAD NEVER LIVED HAPPIER IN HER LIFE

Mary Kiefer v. Xavier Kiefer, 1868

[Keefer, Mary—by her next friend Winter, Philip v. Keefer, Xavier *(1868), Records of the Circuit Court of Ohio County, WVRHC, env. 275 b-6. This case cost $40.35. Mary filed her petition in March 1868. The court issued a summons on June 15, 1868, but found that Xavier no longer lived in West Virginia. Mary published notice of the divorce petition in the* Wheeling Register *for four weeks starting July 1, 1868, at the cost of $7.50. She published notice of the depositions in the same paper beginning August 3.*]

Bill of Divorce

State of West Virginia, Ohio County Circuit Court

To the Hon. E. H. Caldwell, Judge of the said Court in Chancery now Sitting,

Your Oratrix Mary Kiefer,[1] who sues by her next friend Philip Winter,[2] humbly complaining shows to the Court, that about the 23rd day of March 1856, she was legally married to her husband Xavier Kiefer,[3] in the city of Wheeling, West Virginia by Stephen Huber, a priest of St.

---

1. Mary was born in Germany in 1827. In 1860, four years after her marriage to Xavier, they lived with another German immigrant (Charles Rolph), as well as his wife and four children. Both Charles and Xavier were listed as laborers. United States Federal Census for 1860. Their names are also spelled Keeffer.

2. Philip Winter was also a German immigrant living in Wheeling, although his relationship to Mary Kiefer is unclear. United States Federal Census for 1870.

3. Xavier's background is tricky. The 1860 census lists him as having been born in Germany in 1824, but the marriage certificate, though difficult to read, lists his birthplace as France. It is possible that he was from the Alsace-Lorraine region of France, which was a contested area on the border of Germany and France where many residents still speak German. United States Federal Census for 1860.

James Cathedral[4] in said city, who was by the laws of the State of West Virginia (or then Virginia) duly authorized to solemnize marriages. That your Oratrix's maiden name was Mary Somer, and that for many years she has lived in the City of Wheeling, in the State of West Virginia, and that she has conducted herself with propriety and has always treated her said husband with kindness and that they lived and cohabited together as husband & wife until about February A.D. 1865, when her said husband abandoned her, since which time she has been unable, by diligent inquiry, to ascertain his whereabouts, and that your Oratrix has now been deserted by her said husband Xavier Kiefer for more than three years last past.

Your Oratrix further represents that of said marriage there was born one child Teresa Kieffer in the ninth year of her age, a child of her said husband who has been with your oratrix, and been supportd by the labor of her hands. That for more than three years last past, she, your oratrix, without any assistance of her said husband maintained herself and her child. That the said Xavier Kieffer is seized of the following described property, to wit: Lot No. 1 in Square No. 15 in the town of South Wheeling, in the County of Ohio and State of WV, which said lot is worth about three hundred & seventy five dollars. And also the South half of Lot No 12 in Square 27 in the town of South Wheeling, County and State aforesaid, worth about one hundred & fifty dollars, all of which is unencumbered by judgments, liens, or other charges, and household property of the value of 30 dollars, consisting of bed, table, and other necessary things.

All of which doings of the said Xavier Keefer are contrary to equity and conscience and inasmuch as your oratrix is wholly remediless by the rules of the Common Law and is only relievable in this Court as a Court of Equity, she prays the writ of Summons against the said Xavier Kieffer and that he be made Defendant hereto.

Your Oratrix prays that the said Xavier Kieffer may now be enjoined from selling or in any way incumbering the aforesaid lots of ground, or the aforesaid furniture or intermeddling with the same or in any way interfering with the said Teresa Kieffer — until the farther order of this Court and that your Honor would allow your Oratrix present support

---

4. Most likely, this refers to St. James Evangelical Lutheran Church, established by German immigrants around the time of the Kiefers' marriage. "St. James Evangelical Lutheran Church."

and money to carry on this suit, and that on the final hearing of this her cause your Oratrix prays that she may be finally divorced from her said husband and that sufficient Alimony be allowed her, and the custody of her said child, and such other and further relief as her case may require, or as the Court may deem proper, and your Oratrix will every pray.

Taylor & Barr,[5] Sols for Complt.

Marriage Certificate

To the Clerk of the County Court of Ohio County in the State of Virginia:

I hereby certify that the following is a correct statement of a marriage solemnized by me in the county aforesaid.

Date of Marriage: March 23
Place of Marriage: Wheeling
Full Names of parties married: Xavier Kiefer & Mary Somer
Age of husband: 30
Age of wife: 29
Condition of husband and wife: single
Place of husband's birth: [illegible], France
Place of wife's birth: [illegible]
Place of husband's residence: Benwood
Place of wife's residence: Wheeling
Names of husband's parents: Michael Kiefer & Catherine Schuable
Names of Wifes parents: Henry Somer and Ann Maria Wie
Occupation of husband: Laborer

Given under my hand as a priest of St. James Cathedral (legally authorized to solemnize marriages) this 23rd day of March A.D. 1856
Stephen Huber

---

5. Samuel Oliver Taylor was born in April 1838 in Washington County, Pennsylvania. He was admitted to the bar in Washington, Pennsylvania, in 1863. Robert G. Barr was born in June 1840 in Washington County, Pennsylvania, and attended Washington and Jefferson College. At the close of the war, he came to Wheeling to practice law. Atkinson and Gibbens, *Prominent Men of West Virginia*, 942; United States Federal Census for 1870, 1880; U.S. Find a Grave Index; West Virginia Marriages Index; U.S. City Directories; Ulman, *Lawyers' Record and Official Register*, 995.

Depositions of Witnesses[6]

MARY KEEFFER

QUESTION: State your age, place of residence, and if you are acquainted with the parties to this suit.

ANSWER: I am forty four years old. I live in South Wheeling. I am acquainted with the parties to this suit and am the complainant myself.

QUESTION: Look at this paper marked A, here shown to you, and state whether or not the Xavier Keeffer therein named is your husband and whether or not you are the Mary Somer therein named.

ANSWER: Xavier Keeffer is my husband and the Mary Somer named is myself.

QUESTION: State if your husband Xavier Keeffer is now living with you, and if not when did he leave you and where is he at the present time?

ANSWER: He is not living with me now. He went away three years and six months ago. I dont know where he is. I have not heard from him since he went away.

QUESTION: State what your relations with the defendant were previous to the time he went away.

ANSWER: Our relation to each other was friendly. We never had any quarrels.

QUESTION: State if you lived together and cohabited as man and wife from the dates of your marriage until the time your husband deserted you.

ANSWER: Yes we did.

QUESTION: If you had any children by your husband Xavier Keeffer, state how many their age and sex.

ANSWER: We had three children, two are now dead. The other is named Teresa Keeffer. She is eight years old. She lives with me and has lived with me all her life.

QUESTION: State in what manner you have supported yourself and child since your husbands desertion.

ANSWER: By washing and scrubbing and other such work. I have not received nothing from my husband since he deserted me.

QUESTION: State what property if any belongs to you and your husband.

---

6. J. S. Jones, a notary public, recorded these depositions on September 3, 1868, at the law offices of Taylor and Ban. All deponents signed their names.

ANSWER: We own the south half of lot no. 12 in square 27 in the town of South Wheeling and also Lot No 1 in square #15 in the town of South Wheeling and about thirty dollars worth of personal property.

QUESTION: Look at this paper now shown you marked No 1. J. S. Jones and state who the Mary Keeffer therein named is and also look at paper marked NO 2 J. S. Jones and state who the mary Keeffer therein named is.

ANSWER: I am the Mary Keeffer named in both papers marked No's 1 & 2.

QUESTION: State what buildings or other improvements if any are on the said south half of lot No 12 in square 27 in South Wheeling or on said Lot No 1 in square No 15 in the town of South Wheeling.

ANSWER: There are no buildings on either but there is a fence around lot No 1 in Square 15.

HENRY GAGER

QUESTION: State your age occupation and place of residence and if you are acquainted with the parties to this suit.

ANSWER: I am thirty eight years old. I am a stone mason. I live in Martinsville Ohio,[7] and I am acquainted with the parties to this suit.

QUESTION: State if you know the residence of Xavier Keeffer at this time.

ANSWER: I do not.

QUESTION: State if you know when he left Wheeling and deserted his wife Mary Keeffer.

ANSWER: He left here I think in March 1865. Yes, it was in March about the 25th.

QUESTION: If you had any conversation with Xavier Keeffer relative to leaving his family you can state and what that conversation was and when it took place.

ANSWER: In February 1863 I was watchman in the Top Mill and he was a boiler there.[8] He told me to come down to his house and see him. I went there, and as soon as I got there he told his wife to get the whiskey bottle, and he wanted me to drink, and he got so much that he got a quarreling with his wife. She told him not to get mad. He didn't whip

---

7. Martinsville is between Cincinnati and Columbus.
8. The Top Mill was part of the Wheeling Iron and Nail Company. "Wheeling Iron and Nail Co."

her but talked harshly to his wife and child. I told him if he went on that way that I never wanted to see him again. He said he did not care a damn he was going to switzerland. Afterwards about the 25th of March 1865 I met him at Barnesville Ohio.[9] He was in the big warehouse where the recruits were kept. When I saw him I said halloo Keeffer what you doing here. He didnt answer me but stepped aside. I stepped up to him and asked him what he was doing there. He said he had enlisted in the 28th Ohio Regement & I think he said in company F or K. I think it was K. He said as soon as I get this bounty, it will be five or six hundred dollars, I will run off from the company and go to Switzerland. I asked him what are you going to do about your family are you going to take them along or are you going to leave them. He answered I dont care a damn they can do as they please. From his actions there I infered that he had given a fictitious name when he enlisted. I have never heard from him since.

JOHN W. SCHULTZ

QUESTION: State your age occupation place of residence, and if you are acquainted to the parties to this suit.

ANSWER: I am thirty two years old. I am a justice of Richie Township and reside in Richietown. I am acquainted with the parties to this suit.

QUESTION: State how long you have known them.

ANSWER: I have known both parties five years.

QUESTION: State if you know where the complainant Mary Keeffer now resides.

ANSWER: She lives in South Wheeling.

QUESTION: State if you [know] where Xavier Keeffer is and where he has been for the last three years.

ANSWER: I dont know where he is. He has been away from South Wheeling for the last three years since March 1865.

QUESTION: Look at the papers marked nos 1 & 2. J. S. Jones and state whether or not the Mary keeffer therein named is the complainant in this suit.

ANSWER: To the best of my knowledge she is.

QUESTION: State if you know what other property if any they own at the present time.

---

9. Barnesville is about thirty miles west of Wheeling.

Top Mill, Wheeling Iron and Nail Company, 1834;
Ohio County Public Library Special Collections.

ANSWER: None that I know of

[*On October 8, 1868, the court ordered that Mary and Xavier Keefer be forever divorced. It awarded her the disputed property as alimony and custody of their daughter. In 1870, Mary and Teresa lived together in South Wheeling. Mary was listed as the head of her household.*[10] *By 1880, Mary had moved to Philadelphia, along with her daughter, Teresa, and her new son-in-law, a tailor named Jacob Rehm.*[11] *We may never know if Xavier was successful at skipping the country after obtaining his recruitment money from the military. He disappears from the records after his divorce.*]

---

10. United States Federal Census for 1870.
11. United States Federal Census for 1880.

Elizabeth Goudy v. James Goudy, 1868

[Goudy, Elizabeth O. by her next friend Milleger, James [her father] v. Goudy, James M. *(1868), Records of the Circuit Court of Ohio County, WVRHC, env. 274 e-9. This case cost $32.76. Elizabeth filed her petition in July 1868. The court summoned James Goudy in the same month, finding that he no longer lived in West Virginia. She then published notice in the* Wheeling Register *for four weeks starting on August 1, 1868.*]

Bill of Divorce

To Hon E. N. Caldwell Judge of the Circuit Court of Ohio County,

Your Oratrix, Elizabeth Goudy[12] by her Father & next friend John Milleger,[13] a resident of said County and State humbly complaining here shows to the Court, that for many years last past she has been a resident of said County and State and was prior to the foundation of said State a resident of the State of Virginia. That her maiden name before her marriage was Elizabeth Milleger and that on the seventeenth day of December A.D. 1860 at West Alexander in the County of Washington in the State of Pennsylvania, she was legally married to one James M. Goudy[14] by one John C. Hervey, a Justice of the Peace then resident in West Alexander in said State of PA but now a resident of the City of Wheeling in the State of West Virginia. That after their marriage as aforesaid to wit, from the 17th day of December A.D. 1860 up to the time of the institution of this suit they have not lived together as husband and wife, nor has the said James M. Goudy during that period of time contributed in any manner whatever to her maintenance and sup-

---

12. Only seventeen at the time of her marriage, Elizabeth was born in Germany in 1843. In 1860, she lived in Wheeling's Fifth Ward with her family and worked as a seamstress. United States Federal Census for 1860.

13. John Milleger was Elizabeth's father. Confusingly, this case lists him as both John and James, and the 1860 census lists him as Jacob. According to that document, Jacob "Meliker" had been born in Germany in 1810. He lived in Wheeling with his wife, Catherine, and his two daughters, Elizabeth and Fredericka, both of whom worked as seamstresses. He was listed as a laborer with only forty dollars to his name. United States Federal Census for 1860.

14. James Goudy was born in Wheeling in 1839. His father, Isaac, served as the "next friend" for his sister, Mary, in her 1858 divorce case, also found in this book. James lived with Isaac in 1860 at the time of his marriage. Isaac was a successful carpenter worth about $4,500. United States Federal Census for 1860.

port, but immediately after said marriage the said James M. Goudy without any cause or provocation on the part of your Oratrix abandoned and deserted her and so abandoned and deserted for all that period of time to wit from the 17th day of December A.D. 1860 to the time of the institution of this suit.

Your Oratrix further shews that under the laws of the State of Pennsylvania no record evidence of marriage was required and therefore she will have to rely on oral proof for the same.[15]

All of which is contrary to equity and inasmuch as your Oratrix is remediless by the strict rules of the Common law, and is only relievable in this Honorable Court, she prays that the said James M. Goudy her husband be made party defendant hereto and that he anser the same according to law.

She prays that on the hearing of this case, that the court would decree that she be divorced from the bonds of matrimony between her and her said husband for the causes of abandonment and desertion aforesaid and that such other and further relief as this Honorable Court may deem proper for her case be granted to her and she will ever pray &c.

G. L. Cranmer Solr. for Complainant

Depositions of Witnesses[16]

CATHARINE MILLEGER

QUESTION: State if Elizabeth Goudy the wife of James M. Goudy is your daughter and where does she reside?
ANSWER: She is my daughter. She resides in Ohio County, West Virginia.
QUESTION: State whether or not since December 17th 1860 the defendant in this suit has lived with the said wife Elizabeth Goudy. And if not why not?
ANSWER: He has not lived with her at all but I dont know why. I think because she is too poor for him.
QUESTION: State whether or not since the time of the marriage of the plaintiff & defendant (Dec 17 1860) the defendant James M. Goudy

---

15. John Hervey, a justice of the peace, testified that he married them at his house on the stated date.

16. All deponents gave their depositions on September 12, 1868. They signed their names.

has in any way [illegible] contributed to the support and maintenance of his said wife.

ANSWER: He never gave her a bit except when in the army the sum of sixty dollars in 1862 which was obtained through Mr. Thomas Hornbrook.[17] He was compelled by the Governor to send the money or he would have been removed from his Office of Lieutenant in one of the West Virginia Regiments.[18] This money was not sent voluntarily by him but in account of representation made to the Governor of the State at the time that his wife had been abandoned and deserted by him and left in a suffering condition.

QUESTION: State if you know where the defendant now is and where he has been for the last three years.

ANSWER: I do not know. His wife does not know where he has been three years nor has she heard, although she has made frequent inquiries by letter and other wise to ascertain his whereabouts but has failed. He left her in December 1864[19] and his wife has not heard from him since, and he has not been here since.

QUESTION: State if you know how and by whom the said Elizabeth his wife has been supported and maintained since December 1864.

ANSWER: She has been supported by me and sometimes when she was able, she worked for her sister Kate, who paid her for her labour, but owing to sickness she was unable to work only at intervals.

QUESTION: Did he ever give any reason why he would not live with her?
ANSWER: Yes Sir, he did. He said his parents were opposed to it.
QUESTION: Did he state why his parents were opposed to his living with her?
ANSWER: Yes, because she was poor and a german girl.

FREDRICKA MILLEGER

QUESTION: State what is your relation to the plaintiff in the case.
ANSWER: I am her sister.

---

17. The only Thomas Hornbrook I can find in Wheeling was listed as a surveyor and real estate agent. U.S. City Directories.

18. James M. Goudy was commissioned as an officer, eventually becoming a second lieutenant, in Company I of West Virginia's First Infantry Regiment. He was listed as a carpenter by trade. He mustered out on November 26, 1864. During 1864, his income was listed as $642 by the Internal Revenue Service. U.S. Civil War Soldier Records and Profiles; U.S. IRS Tax Assessment Lists.

19. This would have been within a month of him leaving the army.

QUESTION: State whether or not the defendant James Goudy has lived with his said wife since their said marriage December 17, 1860.
ANSWER: He has not.
QUESTION: State whether or not the defendant since their said marriage has contributed in any manner to her maintenance and support.
ANSWER: He has not.
QUESTION: State if you know where the defendant now is and has been for the last three years.
ANSWER: I do not.
QUESTION: State what if any efforts have been made to discover his whereabouts during the last three years.
ANSWER: There has. His wife has sent letters to different places and also made private inquiries and I have my self but have failed to learn anything about him.
QUESTION: How has she been supported and maintained since Dec. 17 1860?
ANSWER: By her mother.
QUESTION: What if any reason did he ever give why he did not live with her?
ANSWER: That his parents objected to his living with her.
QUESTION: Did he ever say why his parents objected to his living with her?
ANSWER: He did. because she was poor and because she was german.

TERESA HANKE

QUESTION: State if you are acquainted with the parties to this suit or either of them.
ANSWER: I am acquainted with Elizabeth Goudy but not with James M. Goudy.
QUESTION: State if you know who has supported and maintained Elizabeth Goudy since December 1860.
ANSWER: Her mother all the time.
QUESTION: State whether or not the said Elizabeth together with her parents lived in the same house with you and how long.
ANSWER: Yes Sir, they did for five years after the marriage of Elizabeth and James Goudy except about three months.

MARTIN SMITH

QUESTION: State if you are acquainted with the parties to this suit or either of them.

ANSWER: I am the brother-in-law of the plaintiff.[20] I am acquainted with her. I am not acquainted with James M. Goudy.

QUESTION: State whether or not the defendant James M. Goudy has lived with his wife Elizabeth Goudy since their marriage December 17, 1860.

ANSWER: He has never lived with her.

QUESTION: State whether or not James M. Goudy has since the marriage contributed towards the support or maintenance of his wife.

ANSWER: He never has only once while in the Army. The Governor made him send her sixty dollars which is all he ever gave her.

QUESTION: State if you know where the defendant is and where he has been for the last three years.

ANSWER: I do not know.

QUESTION: State what if any efforts have been made to discern his whereabouts during the last three years.

ANSWER: She wrote letters and inquired about him but failed to find where he was.

QUESTION: How has she been supported and maintained since December 1860?

ANSWER: By her parents and then she worked at my house part of the time.

JOHN C. HERVEY

QUESTION: State if you are acquainted with the parties to this suit.

ANSWER: I am. I recollect distinctly when they were married at my house.

QUESTION: Please state under what circumstances you met them and when and where.

ANSWER: They came to my house near West Alexander, Washington County, Pennsylvania on the evening of the 17th day of December 1860 to be married.

QUESTION: State whether or not any license was required by the law of Pennsylvania to celebrate the rites of matrimony.

ANSWER: None required.

QUESTION: State whether you made any private entry of the time you

---

20. Martin Smith married Elizabeth's sister Catherine on December 26, 1859, in Wheeling. Catherine's last name was listed as "Muhlier" and her father's name was listed as "Jacob Mushaker." Clearly, the Wheeling legal system struggled with this family's name. West Virginia Marriages Index.

celebrated the marriage of these parties and if so please furnish a copy of the same and file herewith.

ANSWER: I did and the copy herewith filed is a true and marked A.[21]

QUESTION: Was you not at the time of celebrating the rites of marriage between these parties duly commissioned and qualified as an acting Justice of the Peace ... for Washington County, Pennsylvania.

ANSWER: I was.

[*The court eventually ruled that Elizabeth and James Goudy be forever divorced.*[22] *I am unable to track either Elizabeth or James after their divorce.*]

James Kerr v. Louisa Kerr, 1869

[Kerr, James v. Kerr, Louisa *(1869)*, *Records of the Circuit Court of Ohio County, WVRHC, env. 281 b-2. The case cost $42.91. James filed his petition on August 18, 1869. The court summoned Louisa on August 15, and the sheriff stated that she no longer lived in West Virginia. James published notice in the* Wheeling Intelligencer *for four weeks starting on September 3, 1869; October 5, 1869; and April 8, 1870.*]

Bill of Divorce

To the honorable Thayer Melvin Judge of the Circuit Court of the County of Ohio:

Humbly complaining sheweth unto your honor your orator James Kerr,[23] of the city of Wheeling, a mechanic, that he has resided in the city of Wheeling for four years last past: that he was married to Louisa Louis,[24] now Louisa Kerr, on the 31st day of December 1862 by the Rev. William Hannah in the County of Washington and state of Penn-

---

21. This entry was only one line long and noted the date and parties married. I have not included it in this collection.

22. The court's decree is undated.

23. James Kerr was born in Pennsylvania in 1840. United States Federal Census for 1880.

24. Louisa Lewis (as her name is written elsewhere) was born in Pennsylvania in 1841. In 1860, she lived in her father's house in Morris Township, Pennsylvania, with her parents and her two siblings. Her father was a successful carpenter. United States Federal Census for 1860.

sylvania. That since that time he has been to her a faithful, affectionate, and dutiful husband. Yet so it is, his said wife Louisa Kerr has been negligent of her duty as a faithful and dutiful wife; in this, that your orator during the month of February 1865 came from Washington County Penn, to the city of Wheeling to pursue his occupation of house carpenter: that at the time he so came to Wheeling, he requested his said wife to accompany him which she refused to do: that your orator has repeatedly since the month of February 1865 requested his said wife to reside with him which she has as repeatedly refused to do. Whence your Orator charges the truth to be that the said Louisa Kerr did, about the month of February 1865, wilfully abandon and desert your orator by refusing to live with your orator although often requested so to do, and that the said Louisa Kerr has wilfully abandoned and deserted your orator for more than three years last past. All of which actings, doings, and pretences of the said Louisa Kerr are contrary to equity good conscience and tends to the manifest wrong and injury of your orator in the premises. In tender consideration whereof, and for as much as your orator is remediless in the premises of the strict rules of the common law, and cannot have adequate relief except in a court of equity where matters of this kind are properly cognizable and relievable. To the end therefore that justice may be done, your orator prays that the said Louisa Kerr may be made a defendant to this bill and required to render a full, true, and perfect answer to the same upon her corporal oath; that proper process be directed to the said Louisa Kerr; and that your orator may [be] divorced from her, and the marriage be dissolved, and for such other and further relief as his case may require, and to equity seems meet. And your orator will ever pray &c.

James Kerr
by Taylor & Barr, his solicitors

Depositions of Witnesses[25]

WILLIAM HANNA

QUESTION: What is your name, age, occupation & place of residence, & state whether you are acquainted with the parties to this suit.
ANSWER: William Hanna. Forty-nine. Minister of the Gospel. Linden, Washington County, Pennsylvania. I know the parties to this suit.

---

25. William Hanna, John Jones, and Samuel Rutan all gave testimony in November 1869 in Washington County, Pennsylvania. They signed their names.

QUESTION: State whether you ever solemnized the rites of matrimony between the parties to this suit, and if so state when and where it was; and whether such solemnization was in accordance with the laws of the State in which the same was solemnized.
ANSWER: I did—to the best of my recollection, aided of my journal, it was on the 31st day of December 1862 and at the house of the Brides father, Jacob Lewis, in Morris T[ownshi]p Washington County, Penn—it was solemnized in accordance with the laws of said State.
QUESTION: Do the laws of the State of Penn require persons solemnizing marriages to make a public record thereof?
ANSWER: To the best of my knowledge there is no such law in use.

JOHN JONES

QUESTION: What is your name, age, occupation, and place of residence, and state whether you are acquainted with the parties to this suit.
ANSWER: John Jones—Forty-four—Miller—Morris Tp. Washington County Pa. I know both the parties to this suit. Have known Defendant ever since she was a little child. I first became acquainted with the Complainant about the time the parties were married.
QUESTION: State whether the parties ever lived together as husband & wife, and if so, how long did they so live together?
ANSWER: I believe they lived together as husband & wife, for about a year after marriage. The Complainant then left and after being absent some time returned & they again lived together for a length of time—how long, I am unable to say.
QUESTION: State whether they ever separated & if so, when did they separate?
ANSWER: I know the parties separated—the complainant leaving his wife and going out of the neighborhood, the Defendant remaining in the house for sometime.
QUESTION: State whether they ever cohabited together as husband and wife, since the time of such separation.
ANSWER: They never did to my knowledge.
QUESTION: What declarations, if any, did you ever hear the Deft. Louisa Kerr make, in relation to her refusal to live with the Complainant James Kerr? State when and where it was, and all you know about it.
ANSWER: I once at my mill heard her say she could not live with him, that she had tried living with him twice and she couldn't do it, as he was jealous of her; this statement was made about a month after complainant had left the defendant the second time. I have fre-

quently at other times since heard her speak of the matter and she always spoke about the same way.

SAMUEL RUTAN

QUESTION: What is your name age, occupation and place of residence and state whether you are acquainted with the parties to this suit, and if so, how long have you known them?

ANSWER: Samuel Rutan—Sixty six—Broom-maker—Morris Tp. Washington County Penn—I know both the parties—I have known complainant about seven years & the Defendant all her life.

QUESTION: State whether the parties ever lived together as husband & wife, and if so, how long did they so live together?

ANSWER: They did so live together. I cant say how long.

QUESTION: State whether they ever separated, and if so, when did they separate?

ANSWER: The parties separated but at what time I cant state with certainty.

QUESTION: State whether they ever cohabited together as husband and wife, since the time of such separation.

ANSWER: I never knew of their being together after they separated.

QUESTION: What declarations if any did you ever hear the Deft. Louisa Kerr make, in relation to her refusal to live with the Complainant James Kerr, and state when it was, where it was, and all you know about it?

ANSWER: About the time she was going to Green Co. I wanted her to go and live with the Complainant when she told me she wouldn't, that she would never live with him, the reason that he was allways jealous of her to the best of my recollection this was said to me, about two years ago.

JOHN W. PATTERSON[26]

QUESTION: State your age residence occupation and if you are acquainted with the parties to this suit.

ANSWER: I am forty five years old. I live in Washington County Pennsylvania. Am a farmer and an acquaintance with the parties to this suit.

QUESTION: State if they have at any time cohabited as husband and wife and if they now cohabit as such.

---

26. J. S. Jones, a notary public, took the depositions of John Patterson and Andrew Kerr at the law offices of Taylor and Barr in Wheeling on April 30, 1870. Both signed their names.

ANSWER: They lived together as man and wife a while; they do not live together now.

QUESTION: When and how did they come to separate?

ANSWER: It is between four and five years since they separated. She went off and left him all that time and went to live with her mother and sister.

QUESTION: Has she at any time since lived with her husband?

ANSWER: I think not I have never known of it. If they had I would have known it. I saw letters he had written to her in which he offered to live with her if she would come back and live with him.

QUESTION: State if you know in what manner James Kerr treated his wife Louisa when she lived with him.

ANSWER: As far as I know he treated her well. I never heard any complaint.

ANDREW KERR

QUESTION: State your age residence occupation and if you are acquainted with the parties to this suit.

ANSWER: I am twenty nine years old. I live in Washington County Pennsylvania. Am a farmer and am acquainted with both the parties to this suit.

QUESTION: State if the parties have at any time cohabited as man and wife.

ANSWER: They have.

QUESTION: Are they now living together as husband and wife?

ANSWER: No sir.

QUESTION: When did they separate, and how did they come to separate?

ANSWER: It has been about five years since. She left him about five years ago.

QUESTION: With whom did she go to live and with whom has she lived ever since?

ANSWER: With her mother and sister

QUESTION: State if James Kerr and his said wife Louisa have lived together at any time since the separation you have spoken of.

ANSWER: They have not to the best of my knowledge.

QUESTION: State if you know in what manner the complainant James Kerr treated his said wife Louisa during the time they lived together.

ANSWER: He treated her well. I saw them together a great deal and he treated her as well as any person could treat his wife.

QUESTION: Do state if you know where the defendant Louisa Kerr now lives.

ANSWER: I dont know where she lives

QUESTION: State if you know in what manner the defendant Louisa Kerr conducted herself towards her said husband during the time they lived together.

ANSWER: Part of the time she treated him properly. As for the rest of the time I could not say that she did.

[*In June 1870, the court ruled in James Kerr's favor, divorcing him forever from his wife, Louisa. At that point, James lived in a saloon run by the Husman family. By 1880, James Kerr had remarried. He lived with his wife, Jennie, on South Benoit Way in Wheeling. They had two children, a six-year-old boy and a baby girl. He still worked as a carpenter.*[27] *James Kerr died in 1899, splitting his estate among his three children.*[28]]

Annie Green v. Augustus Green, 1870

[Green, Annie v. Green, Augustus *(1870)*, *Records of the Circuit Court of Ohio County, WVRHC, env. 282 b-5. Annie formally filed her petition in August 1870. The court summoned Augustus on July 28, 1870, and determined that he no longer lived in West Virginia. She published notice in the* Wheeling Intelligencer *for four weeks starting November 4, 1870.*]

Bill of Divorce

State of West Virginia, Ohio County Circuit Court.

To the Hon. T. Melvin, Judge of the said court in chancery now sitting:

Your oratrix Annie Green[29] of the said county, humbly complaining shows to the court, that on or about the 29th day of April 1862, she was

---

27. United States Federal Census for 1870, 1880.

28. While his daughter Ella (the baby girl mentioned above) received only ten dollars, James gave two-thirds of his real estate to his son, William, and one-third to his other daughter, Annette. He also bequeathed to them his library. West Virginia Wills and Probate Records.

29. According to the census, Ann Green was born in 1847 in Wheeling. In 1860, she lived with her father, Henry, and her mother, Barbara, as well as her sister in Wheeling's Second Ward. United States Federal Census for 1860.

lawfully married to Augustus Green,[30] then a resident of this county; that of said marriage, there was born a female child, Frances Green, who was six years old Sept. 23d 1869, & is still living.

That your oratrix & the said Augustus Green lived together as husband & wife, until about the 25 of March 1867, when he, the said Augustus Green, her said husband, wilfully abandoned & deserted her, his wife, & has so ever since wilfully abandoned & deserted her, your oratrix, for more than three years last past, & has not for that time contributed anything to the support of herself, or her said child, but has been all of that time absent from this state, & that it is reported, & is said in a newspaper printed in Ohio, that he has married another wife.

She avers, that before, & ever since her said marriage, she was a resident of the City of Wheeling, & is a citizen thereof, & has during all of that time supported herself & her said child, & that she has always conducted herself prudently & with affection towards her said husband, & that he left her without any cause whatever. She farther states that she had no property, nor had her husband any property, nor have either of them any property now, tho' she cannot say as to her said husband, who now lives in Allegheny city[31] in Pennsylvania, as she is informed.

She prays he may be made party defendant to this her bill of complaint, and that upon the hearing of her said cause the court would grant her a divorce from the bonds of the said marriage & [illegible] the same & give her the care & guardianship of the said child & such other relief as her case may require, or as to the court may seem proper, & she will ever pray &c.

Annie Green by Peck & Cochran her solicitors

Marriage License[32]

Time of Marriage: April 29, 1862
Place of Marriage: Wheeling Va

---

30. Augustus Green was born in Kentucky in 1830.
31. Allegheny was a city that existed at the time but has since been absorbed by the much larger city of Pittsburgh.
32. This marriage license was clearly made at the time of the divorce suit. The form was for "West Virginia" and the word "West" had been crossed out. Similarly, at another point, the "State of West" had been crossed out and replaced with the "Commonwealth of" to read "Commonwealth of Virginia." A legal document with the information for West Virginia would not have existed in April 1862, when the marriage took place, since West Virginia did not become a state until June 1863. If someone grabbed a marriage license form in 1870, though, it would not have reflected the reality of a marriage solemnized in Virginia in 1862. It is impossible to determine if the original was lost or never made.

Full Names of parties married: Augustus W. Green & Mary Ann Sly (both colored)[33]
Age of Husband: 32 years
Age of Wife: 19 years[34]
Condition of Husband and Wife: Single
Place of Husband's Birth: Bracken Co Ky[35]
Place of Wife's Birth: Wheeling Va
Place of Wife's Residence: Wheeling Va
Place of Husband's Residence: United States (Army)
Names of Husband's parents: John Green & Fanny Simmons
Names of Wife's parents: —— Sly & Barbara Sly[36]
Occupation of Husband: Servant U.S.A.
Given under my hand, this 29 day of April 1862
Jim McCulloch, clerk[37]

Depositions of Witnesses[38]

JOHN LUKER

QUESTION: State your age, residence, and occupation.
ANSWER: My age is 33. I reside in Wheeling and am a Barber by trade.
QUESTION: Do you know the plaintiff Anna Green, who is now present, and the defendant, Augustus Green, and if so, how long have you known them?

---

33. Black divorce did happen in the postwar period, but as other historians have shown, many Black elites frowned on the practice, believing that it would reinforce racist stereotypes about Black relationships and sexuality. Silkenat, *Moments of Despair*, 119–25. See also Penningroth, "African American Divorce."

34. This contradicts Annie's age in the 1860 census, where it is listed as thirteen. If the census is accurate, she would have been fifteen at the time of her marriage. United States Federal Census for 1860.

35. Bracken County, Kentucky, is on Kentucky's northern border, against the Ohio River.

36. This is the way the document reads. My research indicates that Annie's father was named Henry. He was a barber in Wheeling. United States Federal Census for 1860; U.S. City Directories.

37. The certificate was also signed by A. Paull, minister of the gospel, who married the couple.

38. John Luker, Eliza Snider, and Anna Green testified on December 5, 1870, at the law offices of Peck and Cochran before John Walton, a notary public. John and Anna signed with their names, Eliza with her mark.

ANSWER: I do, and have—Anna Green 20 years, and Augustus Green about 15 years.
QUESTION: Did you know them while they lived together as husband and wife?
ANSWER: Yes, Sir.
QUESTION: During that time how did she demean herself—as a prudent woman and a faithful, affectionate wife?
ANSWER: As far as I knew she was a prudent and affectionate wife.
QUESTION: During their married life was you frequently at their house and in their society?
ANSWER: Not very often at their house, but very frequently in their society.
QUESTION: Where does she now live and where has she lived during the last three or four years?
ANSWER: In the City of Wheeling.
QUESTION: Where is the defendant, Augustus Green, if you know?
ANSWER: I have understood he lived in Allegheny City, Pa.
QUESTION: State, if you know, when he left his wife.
ANSWER: He left her about four years ago.
QUESTION: Do you know anything of his having married another woman since he abandoned the plaintiff?
ANSWER: Nothing more than I was told by a man some four months ago, that he had visited his house in Alleghany City and seen a woman there that Green said was his wife.
QUESTION: Was the plaintiff that woman?
ANSWER: It was not.
QUESTION: Has he ever provided her or her child with any of the necessaries of life, or any support whatever since he abandoned her some four years ago.
ANSWER: Not to my knowledge or belief.
QUESTION: If he had, do you think you would have known it?
ANSWER: I would.
QUESTION: How has she been supported?
ANSWER: She has been washing for a living and working as a chambermaid on a steam-boat plying between Wheeling and Matamoras[39] a part of the time.
QUESTION: Has either of them any property or had they at their marriage?

---

39. Matamoras, Ohio, is a town fifty miles downriver from Wheeling.

ANSWER: Not that I know anything of.

QUESTION: Was there a child born of that marriage, and if so, state its name and about its age.

ANSWER: There was. Its name is Fanny or Frances and its age is about 7 years. It has been and is now living with its mother since he abandoned her.

QUESTION: Is she or not a fit person to have the care and custody of that child?

ANSWER: Yes, Sir—she is.

QUESTION: Does she bear, and has she borne, a good reputation among her neighbors and acquaintances?

ANSWER: Yes, Sir.

QUESTION: Has he since he abandoned his wife lived outside the State of West Virginia?

ANSWER: He has.

ELIZA SNIDER

QUESTION: State your age and residence.

ANSWER: I am 43 years of age, and my residence is Martins Ferry, Ohio.[40]

QUESTION: How long have you known the parties to this suit?

ANSWER: I have known the plaintiff all her life, and the defendant 8 or 9 years.

QUESTION: During the time they were married, were you a frequent visitor at their house?

ANSWER: I was.

QUESTION: How did she conduct herself—as a prudent and affectionate wife?

ANSWER: Very well, so far as I know or ever heard of.

QUESTION: How long has it been since they ceased to live together as man and wife?

ANSWER: Four years in April next.

QUESTION: During that time has he contributed anything to the support of herself or child?

ANSWER: Not anything to my knowledge.

QUESTION: How old is the child?

ANSWER: 7 years old last September.

---

40. Martins Ferry is across the river from Wheeling.

QUESTION: Is she a proper person to have the care and custody of her child?
ANSWER: She is.
QUESTION: Is he a fit person to have the care and custody of their child?
ANSWER: No, Sir.
QUESTION: Does she bear a good reputation among her neighbors and acquaintances?
ANSWER: Yes, she has always born a good character from her infancy to the present day.
QUESTION: So far as you know or belief has she had anything to do with him as a wife since he left her?
ANSWER: No, Sir.

ANNA GREEN

QUESTION: What is your age?
ANSWER: I am 25 years old.
QUESTION: When, where and by whom were you married to the defendant, Augustus Green?
ANSWER: I was married to the defendant on the 29th day of April, 1862, on Fourth Street, Wheeling by Alfred Paull, Pastor of the Fourth Presbyterian Church of this City.
QUESTION: When did you last live and cohabit together as man and wife?
ANSWER: It will be four years next April.
QUESTION: Has he contributed anything to the support of yourself and child since he left you?
ANSWER: He has not.
QUESTION: Has he been living in this part of the country since he left you?
ANSWER: No, Sir—not that I know of.
QUESTION: When did he leave here?
ANSWER: He left here about four years ago next April.
QUESTION: How have you and your child been supported since he left you?
ANSWER: Just by my own labor.
QUESTION: When was your child born?
ANSWER: September 3d, 1863.
QUESTION: What was your maiden name?

ANSWER: Anna Sly.

QUESTION: Look at the certificate now shown you, marked on the back "John Walton, Notary Public, Dec. 5, 1870," and state if you are the person therein named, Mary Ann Sly.

ANSWER: It is.

QUESTION: Why did you give your name as Anna Green when you applied to your Attorney to procure you a divorce?

ANSWER: Because I was always called Anna and did not think about giving my full name.

QUESTION: What was your husband's occupation?

ANSWER: His occupation was that of peddling Patent Medicines.

QUESTION: Do you know of any fault on your part that caused him to abandon you?

ANSWER: No, Sir, I do not.

QUESTION: Are there any persons now living who were at your wedding?

ANSWER: None but preacher Paull and my mother.

QUESTION: Where is Mr. Paull?

ANSWER: I am informed that he is in Philadelphia, Pennsylvania.

QUESTION: Where is your mother?

ANSWER: She is working on the steamboat "Hope."

[*In December 1870, the court ruled that Augustus had abandoned Annie, making her eligible for a divorce* a vinculo matrimonii. *She was given custody and alimony, too. Augustus was told to pay her costs. I can find no record of Annie or Augustus after their divorce. By 1880, their daughter, Frances, was living with Annie's younger sister, Lucinda, and her husband on Eoff Street in Wheeling.*[41]]

Belvidere Taylor v. Frank Taylor, 1871

[Taylor, Belvidere v. Taylor, Frank *(1871), Records of the Circuit Court of Ohio County, WVRHC, env. 288 b-2. This case cost $24.45. Belvidere filed her petition in September 1871. The court summoned Frank on September 30 and served him two days later.*]

---

41. Annie did not live with the family. She may have lived elsewhere, or she may have died prematurely, leaving Frances in the care of relatives. United States Federal Census for 1880.

Bill of Divorce

State of West Virginia, Ohio County Circuit Court

To the Hon. T. Melvin, Judge of the said court, in Chancery now sitting:

Your oratrix Belvidere Taylor,[42] humbly complaining here shows to the court, that on the first day of December 1867, in the city of Wheeling she was lawfully married to Frank Taylor,[43] both of the said city, which license issued to marry her & Ben F. Taylor, being the same as is known & designed as Frank Taylor, & that she & her husband have lived in this city ever since & now reside here. That they lived together as husband & wife but a short one month, when her said husband without any cause wilfully abandoned & deserted your oratrix from that day to this, & that during all of that time from the first day of January 1868, to the present time he has done nothing towards the support of herself or her children, being two infants, of tender years: & that her said husband has abandoned & deserted your oratrix for more than three years last past, before the commencement of this suit, & still does abandon her, & has for the whole of that time declared that he would not in any way support her & her children.

That before the said last mentioned marriage, she had been married to the said Frank Taylor, & then by him had two children, Charles Taylor, seven years old the 6th February 1871, & Harry Taylor six years old the 7th of July 1871, which she has always supported, entirely without his aid. That shortly before she was married as first above mentioned, her said husband obtained in this court a divorce against her; & then believing that he had done her a grievous wrong, proposed again to marry her, & she confiding in his promise of repentance again married him as first above stated.[44]

She states, that she has supported & educated, so far as their ages would permit their said children & is desirous to retain as heretofore the care & custody of the same & she avers that her said husband is en-

---

42. Belvidere Barkus was born in Ohio in 1843. Her father was a miner who had moved to Wheeling by 1850. United States Federal Census for 1850.

43. Frank Taylor was born in Troy, New York, in 1840. He enlisted in Company B of the West Virginia First Infantry Regiment on May 30, 1861. He mustered out at the end of August. U.S. Civil War Soldier Records and Profiles.

44. I can find no record of their first marriage. West Virginia Marriages Index. Similarly, there is no divorce record in the existing Ohio County records. It is plausible that the courts threw out that case when they remarried, but it is impossible to know.

gaged in no business, & is not a proper person, even if he would, to have their care & custody, & that he has no property of any description.

Your oratrix prays the writ of summons against the said Frank Taylor, & that upon hearing of her case, the court should order & decree a divorce from the bond of matrimony for the abandonment & desertion of your oratrix, & that she should have the custody & guardianship of her said children; & such other & farther relief as your oratrix's case may require, or as to the court may seem proper, & your oratrix will ever pray &c.

Peck & Cochran
Solrs. for complt.

Answer

I consent that this case may be heard at the present term of this court, but do not consent to, or agree to any fact stated in the bill, but on the contrary deny the same to be true.

Oct. 17 1871
B. F. Taylor

Marriage License

West Virginia, County of Ohio, to Wit:

To any Person Licensed to Celebrate Marriages:

You are hereby authorized to join together in the Holy State of Matrimony, according to the rites and ceremonies of your Church, or religious denomination, and the laws of the State of West Virginia, Benjamin F. Taylor and Bellvadier Barkus.

Given under my hand, as Recorder of said County, this 30th day of Nov. 1867.

B. B. Woods, Recorder[45]

Time of Marriage: Dec 1st 1867
Place of Marriage: Wheeling W. Va.
Full names of Parties Married: Benjamin F. Taylor & Bellvadier Barkus[46]

---

45. Rev. John Moffat also signed, confirming that he had married the couple.
46. It is interesting to note that Belvidere appears to have used her unmarried name in between her marriages.

Age of Husband: Twenty Seven Years
Age of Wife: Twenty Three years
Condition of Husband: Single[47]
Condition of Wife: Single
Place of Husband's Birth: Troy, N.Y.
Place of Wife's Birth: Ohio
Place of Husband's Residence: Wheeling W. Va
Place of Wife's Residence: Wheeling W. Va
Names of Husband's Parents: William & Caroline Taylor
Names of Wife's Parents: Thomas & Sarah Barkus
Occupation of Husband: Steam Boat

Depositions of Witnesses[48]

L. S. WOODS

QUESTION: Where do you reside, what is your age & are you acquainted with the parties to this suit?
ANSWER: I live in Wheeling, aged 28 years. I am acquainted with the parties.
QUESTION: State what you know about the defendant abandoning and deserting the plaintiff.
ANSWER: I know that he has done nothing for her for over three years. I know that he has several times said that he has deserted her without any cause at all & that he will do nothing for her. He does not live with her.
QUESTION: Where have they both lived for the past three years?
ANSWER: They have both lived in Wheeling.
QUESTION: State if you are acquainted with her two little boys?
ANSWER: I am.
QUESTION: Is the plaintiff a proper person to have the care & guardianship of those children?
ANSWER: Yes Sir, she is. She has always had them & always taken good care of them.

---

47. The marriage license form gives only two options here: widowed or single. There would be no way to indicate that a person was divorced.
48. L. S. Woods and Daniel Peck testified before William Caldwell, a notary public, on October 10, 1871, at Peck and Cochran. Both signed their names.

DANIEL PECK

In 1867 I procured a divorce for Frank Taylor the defendant here against the plaintiff. A short time after that divorce was obtained, he courted and married her again. I had been well acquainted with Frank Taylor for a good while before the commencement of that suit because of business for his father against the Belmont Iron Mill & I have seen him often since. He has been staying & living with his father & mother in Centre Wheeling & not engaged in any business that I know of. By that first marriage they had two children, boys that are now & all the while have been with her & her friends. He has said to me that he has done nothing for her or her family since a short time after they were married & for more than three years past & that he never would do anything for her. I do not believe that he has any property of any description whatever. His mother keeps a grocery in Centre Wheeling & it is very likely that he attends part of the time to that. I do not think that he ought to have either of the children on any account. The children appear to be well cared & provided for by her.

SUSAN STAMM[49]

QUESTION: Are you acquainted with the parties to this suit & if so how long have you known them?
ANSWER: I am. I have known Mrs. Taylor seven or eight years & him the same length of time.
QUESTION: State if you recollect the time that Mrs. Taylor & her husband were married the second time, & if so, how long has he lived with her since?
ANSWER: Yes Sir, but I could not tell how long he lived with her.
QUESTION: State if he has lived with or supported her or her family in any way for the last three years?
ANSWER: No sir, he has not done any thing for her to the best of my knowledge for the last three years. Nor to my knowledge he has not lived with her during that time.
QUESTION: How far from Mrs. Taylor have you lived for the last three years?
ANSWER: Not half a square & am there sometimes two or three times a day.

---

49. Susan Stamm and Ellen Newland testified before William Caldwell on November 11, 1871, at Peck and Cochran. Only Ellen signed her name.

QUESTION: How has she provided for her children during all this time?
ANSWER: She has taken good care of them.
QUESTION: Have you seen her husband at her house once for the last three years?
QUESTION: No Sir.

ELLEN NEWLAND

QUESTION: Are you acquainted with the parties to this suit & if so how long have you known them?
ANSWER: I am. I knew Mrs Taylor nearly four years. I have not known him more than a year.
QUESTION: Where have you lived the last three or four years?
ANSWER: I have lived with Mrs Taylor for over two years & before that I lived within half a square of her.
QUESTION: State how often you were at her house before that & how well you were acquainted with her before you came to live with her.
ANSWER: I was very well acquainted with her & I was at her house once or twice a week.
QUESTION: What do you know of her husband Frank Taylor deserting her & leaving her & providing for her family for the last three years?
ANSWER: I have known that he has not lived with her for four years next March. I know that he has not provided for her during that time & have heard him say that he would not provide for her or the children.
QUESTION: Where & when was it that he said he would not provide for the children?
ANSWER: It was at her house. She had sent for him to see if he would provide for them & he said he would not. She asked him to do something for the oldest boy & he said he would do nothing for the child or her either.
QUESTION: What care has Mrs. Taylor given to her children? Has she taken good care of them?
ANSWER: She has always taken the best care of them.

Attorney's Note

These parties were married before, & the husband obtained a divorce against the wife. After some time he again courted her & again 1 Dec. 1867 he married her again, & after living with her a short time he abandoned her & refused to support her or her children, ever since, tho' he lives in town. Of course he does not intend to even to live with, or support her, & having no property he cannot be compelled to do so, & no doubt is willing for a divorce. Nevertheless, he denies the charges against him. Mr. Cranmer is his attorney.

Agreeing that the case may be heard at this term is not agreeing to any part in the case.

The *admissions* of the parties made with a view to the divorce of course could not be evidence. The *reason* why it would be advisable is, that it would allow parties to divorce themselves. But there are many instances, what is said by the parties may be evidence under the circumstances of the case. For instance the interview between the husband & wife, testified by Ellen Newland, where the wife sent for the husband, & desired him to provide for the oldest child.

I think that the strongest evidence of the intentions of the husband not to do anything for the family.

Ellen lived with Mrs. Taylor for the last two years, but has known her about four years, & has been often at her house, before she went to live with her, almost daily. She says he has not lived with [her] since four years next March, & that he has done nothing for the family, all that time so far as she could see.

Mrs. Susan Stamm also testifies that she lived within a short distance of Mrs. Taylor's, & has known them about eight years.

She could not say how long he lived with her after the second marriage. She says that he has not done anything for her or the family for the last three years to her knowledge, nor has he lived with her for that time. She lived about one half square from Mrs. Taylor. She, Mrs. T., has provided for her children.

L. S. Woods testifies that he knows that the defendant has done nothing for the plaintiff & her family for over three years. This is an independent sentence, & then he says that he had deserted her without cause, & that he would do nothing for her. This may or may not be admissible.

I think the testimony is admissible that he deserted her, a very short time after the marriage, & has refused to do any thing for the family even on request. That is surely evidence.

I could not trouble the court again on this matter at this term, but the Plaintiff, a very smart woman & a business woman, is desirous of moving with her children to the West, & starting anew in the world.

[*In October 1871, the court divorced Belvidere and Frank Taylor for a second time, giving her custody and ordering him to pay costs. As her attorney notes, all of the witnesses testified that Frank Taylor had abandoned his wife for more than three years—specifically, that he had not lived with her during that time. However, according to the census, in 1870, just a year before this case, the pair lived together with their two children in Wheeling's Fourth Ward. Ellen Newland, one of the deponents, would have presumably known this, since she is listed as living with them.[50] Most likely, the pair had separated by the time Belvidere filed the divorce suit, but she had to exaggerate the length of time to meet the law's requirements. By 1880, Frank had remarried, and he and his wife, Sarah, lived with his mother on Chapline Street.[51] In 1887, Belvidere remarried. By 1900, she and her husband, Henry Hinders, lived in Martins Ferry, Ohio, with her two sons, Charles and Harry.[52]*]

Louis Lindemuth v. Augusta Lindemuth, 1871

[Lindemuth, Louis v. Lindemuth, Augusta *(1871), Records of the Circuit Court of Ohio County, WVRHC, env. 289 b-8. Louis filed his petition in May 1871. The court summoned Augusta on April 29 and served it to her two days later.*]

Bill of Divorce

In the Circuit Court of Ohio County, West Virginia
May Rules A.D. 1871 The Bill of Complaint of Louis Lindemuth[53] plaintiff against Augusta Lindemuth[54] defendant filed in the Circuit Court of Ohio County,

---

50. United States Federal Census for 1870.

51. Frank worked at the rolling mill by 1880. I can find a veterans' schedule that suggests Frank was still alive in 1890, but I have no more information about him. United States Federal Census for 1880; 1890s Veterans Schedules.

52. Henry was a German immigrant and thirteen years her junior. He worked as a heater in an iron mill. United States Federal Census for 1900.

53. Louis Lindemuth was born in Prussia and immigrated to the United States sometime before 1859. Around the time of this divorce suit, Louis Lindemuth was manufacturing caps and furs in Wheeling. U.S. City Directories; United States Federal Census for 1880.

54. Augusta Lindemuth was born Augusta Muegge in Brunswick, Germany, in September 1838. U.S. Find a Grave Index; United States Federal Census for 1880.

The plaintiff complains and says that on the fourth day of March A.D. 1859, at the City of Cincinnati in the State of Ohio he consummated a marriage and was joined in the holy bonds of matrimony with the said defendant which marriage was solemnized by one August Kroil, a minister of the Lutheran Church, a copy of which certificate of marriage is herewith filed as Exhibit "A" and is prayed to be taken as part of this Bill.[55]

That subsequent to the said marriage as aforesaid, they removed to this City and County and for some years lived happily together as man and wife until the 7th day of April A.D. 1867, when the defendant without just cause or provocation wilfully abandoned and deserted the bed and board of the plaintiff and without giving him any notice of such intention on her part and has remained absent ever since, although the plaintiff has repeatedly solicited the said defendant to return and resume her place in the household, she has persistently and wrongfully refused to do so, and still absents herself and refuses to return.

That the treatment of the plaintiff towards the defendant has been uniformly kind and considerate and that he always amply provided for all her wants and necessities. That for two years between the period of their marriage and the date of abandonment of the plaintiff by said defendant, the plaintiff was a soldier in the service of the United States[56] and during the whole of that period of time he sent home to said defendant all his earnings and wages as such, which were received and appropriated by said defendant to her own uses and purposes, and upon the return of the plaintiff to his home, she refused to account as to how, or in what manner they were spent, which earnings and wages, together with the property left with the defendant when the plaintiff enlisted in the service of the United States, was more than sufficient and largely in excess of what was necessary for the support of the defendant during the two years absence of said plaintiff as aforesaid.

That there is issue of the said marriage two children, both boys, of the names and ages following to wit: Lewis aged seven years, and Rudolph aged nine years, which said children are now both in the care and custody of said defendant and have been ever since the abandonment by said defendant of said plaintiff as aforesaid.

All of which is contrary to equity and inasmuch as the plaintiff is

---

55. This marriage certificate is no longer included in the records. They married on March 4, 1859. Ohio, U.S., County Marriage Records.

56. I can find no record of his service.

remediless by the strict rules of the common law and is only relievable in this Honorable Court, he prays that the said Augusta Lindemuth be made party defendant hereto, and that she answer to the same according to law.

He prays upon the hearing of this case that the Court would decree, that he be divorced from the bonds of matrimony between him and his said wife for the wilful desertion and abandonment by her of him for three years. He also asks such other and general relief as the Court may see fit to grant.

Louis Lindemuth by G. L. Cranmer his atto.

Depositions of Witnesses[57]

WILLIAM MAGGE

QUESTION: Are you acquainted with the parties to this suit, and if so how long have you known them?
ANSWER: I am and have known them for five years.
QUESTION: Where does Augusta Lindemuth, the deft, now live, and where has she been living for the three years last past?
ANSWER: She lives with her Father on the Corner of Third and Eoff streets in Centre Wheeling and has lived there for the three years last past.[58]
QUESTION: State if you know the date when she went to live with her Father, and why?
ANSWER: About four years ago last May. She would not stay with her husband.
QUESTION: State whether or not within the time you have mentioned, she has lived with her husband at any period?
ANSWER: Not that I know of.
QUESTION: How did she leave her husband's home in the daytime or in the nighttime?
ANSWER: In the daytime.
QUESTION: Did she or not take any of the house hold property with her when she left?

---

57. William Magge, Louis Grabe, Conrad Wasserman, August Hellenbriche, and Caroline Mader testified at Gibson Cranmer's law office on the northeast corner of Fourth and Monroe Streets on June 16, 1871. All signed their names.

58. Augusta's father, August Muegge, worked as a huckster. A huckster is a peddler or salesperson. U.S. City Directories.

ANSWER: She took some.

QUESTION: Who if any one assisted her in removing it?

ANSWER: Lindemuth lived in a part of the same house with her parents but as a separate family, and when they moved away from there, she moved with her parents. I assisted her in removing them with them [sic] with the others.

QUESTION: Where was her husband, the Complainant, at the time she so removed the goods?

ANSWER: He was out in the City at the time.

QUESTION: State whether or not she has refused to live with him as his wife since then.

ANSWER: I cannot tell sir.

QUESTION: Has she ever told you [she] would not live with him?

ANSWER: No.

QUESTION: State, if you know, how many children they had by this marriage.

ANSWER: They had two, one of them the oldest one is named Rudolph and the younger is Louis.

QUESTION: State if you know when and where they were married.

ANSWER: I dont know.

LOUIS H. GRABE

QUESTION: State if you are acquainted with the parties to this suit, and how long have you known them?

ANSWER: I am and have known them the last four or five years.

QUESTION: State whether during that period they have lived together as man and wife, or what portion of the time they lived together as man and wife.

ANSWER: They have not lived together as man and wife during that time. To the best of my knowledge they have not lived together for about three years.

QUESTION: State if you know where she has been living for the last three years.

ANSWER: With her father on the corner of Third and Eoff Streets, Centre Wheeling.

QUESTION: State whether you visited the house during the time they lived together as man and wife, and state how he treated his wife so far as you know.

ANSWER: I have been to the house where they lived, but dont know whether I was ever up stairs or not, and so far as I know he treated his wife well.

CONRAD WASSERMAN

QUESTION: State if you are acquainted with the parties to this suit and how long you have known them.
ANSWER: I have been acquainted with Mr Lindemuth the last three years. I only know Mrs Lindemuth when I see her and have no personal acquaintance with her.
QUESTION: State if during that period of time she has been living with her husband.
ANSWER: To the best of my knowledge she has not lived with him as long as I have known him.
QUESTION: State whose fault it is that she has not lived with him during the last three years.
ANSWER: I dont know.

AUGUST HELLENBRICHE

QUESTION: State if you are acquainted with the parties to this suit.
ANSWER: Yes.
QUESTION: State whether or not you ever applied to the defendant during her abandonment by her of her husband to return and live with him, and how you happened to do so.
ANSWER: I went up there to request her to come back and live with her husband. She said she would'nt do it.
QUESTION: How long has it been since she left her husband.
ANSWER: Three years as near as I can recollect.

CAROLINE MADER

QUESTION: State if you are acquainted with the parties to this suit, and if so, how long you have known them?
ANSWER: I am and have known them for twelve years.
QUESTION: State whether or not the defendant has refused to live with the plaintiff or not during the last three years.
ANSWER: It has been four years in last April since she refused to live with him.

[*In June 1871, the court ruled that Louis and Augusta Lindemuth be forever divorced and ordered her to pay the costs of the suit. I can find no re-*

cord of Louis after his divorce. In 1879, Augusta married Jacob Ehni, a cattle dealer and widower with eight children, and the couple moved to Ohio. In 1895, she died in Pease, Ohio, at the age of fifty-six. Her obituary stated that she had married twice and remarried "after the death of her first husband."[59]]

---

59. Pease is about seven miles north of Wheeling. Augusta left everything to her two sons, who had also moved to Ohio. Rudolph Lindemuth worked as a salesman and eventually sold insurance. Louis enrolled at West Virginia University in Morgantown in the late 1880s and became a Presbyterian minister. Ohio Wills and Probate Records; U.S. School Catalogs; Presbyterian Ministerial Directory; West Virginia Marriages Index; United States Federal Census for 1880.

CHAPTER 8

Cruelty

HOW FAR IN THE STREETS COULD HE BE HEARD?

Maggie Griffith v. Charles Griffith, 1869

[Griffith, Maggie C. v. Griffith, Charles E. *(1869), Records of the Circuit Court of Ohio County, WVRHC, env. 273 b-8. On September 1, 1869, someone paid $37.25 in costs to the court. Maggie Griffith filed her petition in July 1869.*]

Bill of Divorce

To the Hon. Thayer Melvin, judge of the said court in Chancery now sitting,

Your oratrix, Maggie C. Griffith,[1] humbly complaining, here shows to the court, that on the 27th day of October 1868 in the said county in the City of Wheeling she was legally married to Charles E. Griffith,[2] both of whom are citizens & residents of the said city of Wheeling, a transcript from the record of her said marriage is herewith filed, marked A & made a part of her bill of complaint. She farther shows that her maiden name was Maggie C. Stewart.

That at the time of their said intermarriage she & her brother James A. Stewart[3] owned the furniture now in the house & that he said brother rented the house in which your oratrix now lives, on Quincy Street, be-

---

1. Maggie Griffith (née Stewart) was born in Wheeling in 1837 to John Park Stewart and the former Sarah Ann Hughes. West Virginia Deaths Index; West Virginia Marriages Index.

2. Charles E. Griffith was born in Wheeling in 1834. His father, Luke, was a wealthy farmer and one of the few slaveholders in the area. In 1830, four years before Charles was born, Luke owned three slaves. Luke died when Charles was only four and left a detailed will, which allowed his wife, Rebecca, to retain half his estate if she never remarried. United States Federal Census for 1830; West Virginia Wills and Probate Records; United States Federal Census for 1870.

3. James Stewart, Maggie's younger brother, was born in 1843 in Wheeling. By the time of the divorce, he worked as a drug clerk. His testimony is in the depositions section.

tween 5th & 6th street in the City of Wheeling, & she & her husband lived together with her said brother, until lately, her brother could not longer reside with the said Charles E. Griffith & left her & her husband, & they are now living together therein.

That at the time of the said intermarriage her said husband was worth $16,000, $10,000 of which he put in the tobacco business in Wheeling, which business he is still carrying on in the said city, on main street, between Moulde & Quincy Street.[4]

Your oratrix does not know with what success her said husband has managed his said business since they were married, but from his terrible disposition, she fears it has not been very successful. That he has a larger amount of debts due him in the state of Ohio, & elsewhere.

That about two months after their intermarriage, her said husband, became dreadfully intemperate, & for the last nine weeks, has been in an awful state of intoxication & has abused your oratrix in the most cruel manner all of that time; that within a few days past, her said husband has so abused your oratrix by his beastly behavior, & most abusive language that she is now afraid to live with him, & has good reason to fear for her life.

That about two weeks ago she had born a female child, which is yet a most feble & very small child, & she is hardly able to sit up, or bear any ill treatment, yet during your oratrix' confinement & subsequent sickness, her husband has visited her room & has constantly abused her in the most shameful manner, & is in the habit of using the most vulgar & obscene & abusive language within his power & cursing her & swearing at her in the most blasphemous manner, & threatening to take from her, their little helpless infant.

Your oratrix further states, that she ever since their intermarriage has treated her said husband in the most considerate manner, & always, even in his drunkenness, that she always used him in a most affectionate manner, of which he has never complained.

That she has tried so far to reform her said husband, but finds that it is impossible now to do any thing with him in respite to his habits of drinking.

That the conduct of her said husband, is that of a madman, towards her & the family, & that she is afraid longer to have him about her, or the child, & asks the interference of this court for her relief.

---

4. James Stewart, in his deposition, describes Charles as a "wholesaler" in tobacco goods. Basically, he would travel to buy cigars and other tobacco products for sale in Wheeling.

Your oratrix further states that she has no property or money of her own, except as before mentioned, & has nothing with which to subsist herself or family.

Your oratrix prays, that your honor would now grant an injunction,[5] restraining her said husband from entering her said house or intermeding [sic] with the said child until the farther order of this court, but upon becoming sober, he may apply to this court for leave to see his wife & child.

Your oratrix further prays that her said husband, Charles E. Griffith, shall pay to some one to be named by your honor, a sufficient sum monthly for the support of herself & family, & that he, by some means be injoined from wasting, concealing or of disposing of his said stock of goods, & debts due him, until a sufficient alimony be secured for the support of herself & her family.

Your oratrix prays, that the said Charles E. Griffith be made party defendant hereto, & the . . . summons may issue against him, & that he may answer according to law, but no discovery is prayed of him.

Your oratrix prays, that on the final hearing of this, her bill, the court would divorce her from the said defendant, & that they be perpetually separated, & that the Plaintiff be awarded the said child, until she becomes of full age, & that your honor will order & decree that the said defendant shall put into the hands of the receiver general of this court, as sufficient sum for alimony, for the support of your oratrix & her family, as this court shall judge sufficient for that purpose, to be under the control of this court, & such other & farther relief, as the court may deem proper, or that her case may require, & she will every pray &c.

Maggie E. Griffith

Peck & Cochran Solr. for Complt.

Marriage License[6]

West Virginia, County of Ohio, to Wit:

To any Person Licensed to Celebrate Marriages:

You are hereby authorized to join together in the Holy State of Matrimony, according to the rites and ceremonies of your Church, or reli-

---

5. According to *Black's Law Dictionary*, an injunction is a "court order prohibiting someone from doing some specified act or commanding someone to undo some wrong or injury." Wagner, *Official Reports of the Supreme Court*, 428.

6. West Virginia Compiled Marriage Records.

gious denomination, and the laws of the State of West Virginia, Charles E. Griffith and Maggie C. H. Stewart.

Given under my hand, as Recorder of said County, this 24th of Oct. 1868

R. B. Woods, Recorder

> Time of Marriage: Oct 27 1868
> Place of Marriage: Wheeling W Va
> Full names: Charles E. Griffith & Maggie C. H. Stewart
> Age of Husband: Thirty four years
> Age of Wife: Twenty eight years
> Condition of Husband: single
> Condition of Wife: single
> Place of Husband's Birth: Wheeling Va
> Place of Wife's Birth: Wheeling Va
> Place of Husband's Residence: Wheeling Va
> Place of Wife's Residence: Wheeling Va
> Names of Husband's parents: Luke & Rebecca Griffith
> Names of wife's parents: John & Sarah Stewart
> Occupation of Husband: Merchant

Given under my hand, this 24 day of Oct 1869[7]

R. B. Woods, Recorder

I Certify, that on the Twenty seventh day of October 1868, at St Matthews Church Wheeling W Va, I united in Marriage the above named and described parties, under authority of the annexed License.

C. George Currie

Injunction[8]

State of WV, Ohio County, Circuit Court, July 29th 1869, In Chancery

On motion of the plaintiff by her counsel this case comes on to be heard upon the bill and affidavit thereto the affidavits of S Giffin, James A Stewart, and Henry Dobbins and the notice herewith returnd.

It is ordered by me at chambers in the clerks office of the said Court on the 29th day of July 1869 that the defendant Charles E Griffith be restrained from interfering with the liberty and movements of the plaintiff his wife and that he pay into the Receiver General of this Court the

---

7. This appears to be a mistake. The copy was made on July 29, 1869.
8. The court served this order on Charles Griffith on July 30, 1869.

sum of $100 to and for the use of the plaintiff and to enable her to prosecute her said suit and that he pay monthly on the first day of each month the farther sum of $75 for the support of the plaintiff and her family.

And it is further ordered that the plaintiff have the posession and custody of the said infant child of the parties and the defendant is enjoyined from intermeddling therewith until further order of the judges of the said Court.

It is further directed that the Clerk of the Circuit Court of Ohio County place this order in the chancery order book of said Court.

J. Melvin Judge of the First Judicial Court

Affidavits[9]

Samuel H. Giffen,[10] being sworn says that he is well acquainted with Charles E. Griffith, & lives next door to him, & that about nine weeks past, he commenced drinking, & that he has been drunk nearly all of the time ever since; that he is most abusive to his family & to his wife, that he stayed with him at his house all of last friday night, she kept awake nearly all of the night. He spoke very roughly to his wife, who was in a very feble condition, having been confined a short time before, & when this affiant[11] tried to restrain him by telling him he should [not] kill his wife, he said let her die, God damn her, in her hearing. This affiant, as well as other friends, have done all in their power to reform him, but is of [the] opinion that he cannot be reformed. When in a passion, he throws his cane, any thing else within his reach, about at every one. He believes his wife ought to be separated from him.

That the said C. E. Griffith is not fit to do any business. His business is the wholesale tobacco business, & he is not now [illegible due to a fold in the page] he continued drinking, his business as a retail business he believes would pay expenses.

That his conduct towards his wife is such as in his opinion ought to forfeit all confidence of his wife in him & she ought in justice be separated from him. He believes that he has had invested in his business, at different times, about ten thousand dollars.

The excitement his wife has now to endure is entirely too much for

---

9. The affidavits were taken on July 28, 1869. All affiants signed their names.
10. "Giffen" is sometimes spelled "Giffin."
11. A person who swears to an affidavit.

her. He is in the habit of abusing his wife on the streets of Wheeling, & behaving badly all of the time. This affiant talked with him, when he was with him last Friday night, & believes that he has not lost his sense, when so drunk, but does what he has done towards his wife & family from a malicious disposition.

James A. Stewart being sworn says that he is the brother of the said Maggie Griffith, & lived with her until the 5th of July 1869 & having heard [and] read the deposition of Samuel H. Giffen, concurs fully in what he has said, & believes all he said to be true, & is acquainted with the facts stated by him, mainly & is sure that his sister ought to be seperated from her said husband & that it is not safe for her to live with him.

Henry Dobbins being sworn says that he has been boarding with Mrs Griffith until last Monday morning: says that the testimony of S. H. Giffen is a very mild statement of the case; that he has heard C. E. Griffith call his wife a whore, & every thing base. Mrs. Griffith was confined on Sunday & Saturday night before, he raised his cane to her, & when she remonstrated with him, he in the most offensive manner bid her kiss his a —

She conducted herself towards him in a very kind manner, & always tried mild means to pacify him. His conduct towards his wife for the time, since he has been drinking, has been the most outrageous ever witnessed.

Depositions of Witnesses[12]

JAMES A. STEWART

QUESTION: State your age, residence, & occupation & what relation do you sustain to the parties to this suit?
ANSWER: Age 26 years. Reside in Wheeling, Ohio County, West Virginia. Occupation—a Drug Clerk. I am a brother of the plaintiff Maggie C. Griffith.
QUESTION: State what you know of the general habits of the defendant within the last nine or ten weeks.
ANSWER: His general habits have been drunkeness. I have not seen him

---

12. James A. Stewart, Samuel Giffen, Mary Mix, Jennie Duncan, A. M. Adams, L. T. Busbey, William McPhail, Dr. James Cummins, W. M. Curtis, A. M. Johnson, Henry Dobbins, and John Russell all testified beginning August 2, 1869. All signed their names. The depositions alone cost $43.15.

during that time unless he was drunk. I think I have seen him ten or twelve times during that time.

QUESTION: What is [his] general conduct when intoxicated?

ANSWER: He is the most abusive and violent man in his conduct that I ever saw or heard of during the time that I have seen him. During that time he has been using the most profane & obscene language about different persons, any person he thinks of at the time & threatening to violently abuse myself & his wife in the presence of his wife. When he would come in the house I would order him out & would have put him out if it had not been for affecting his wife as she would say that if we had a fight it would kill her. The reason of my ordering him out was of his being intoxicated & for fear he would offer some personal injury to his wife. I did not fear for myself.

QUESTION: Why did you fear he would injure his wife?

ANSWER: From threats that he made to her in my presence. I heard him say that he would kick hell out of her frequently and he would often tell her to go to hell God damn you & also said he would kick her out of the house. I have seen him place his closed fist in her face and threaten to kick her out of the house.

QUESTION: In what tone or manner as to violence or otherwise were these threats made?

ANSWER: In the most violent & abusive manner.

QUESTION: What was her conduct towards him during such and all other times as a faithful obedient and affectionate wife?

ANSWER: She always treated him in the most kind and affectionate manner even when he was cursing & abusing her.

QUESTION: Where, with whom, & under what circumstances since their marriage until recently have you been residing?

ANSWER: I resided on Quincy Street in this City with my sister the plaintiff & her husband until the 6th of July 1869. The house was rented by myself. They were boarding with me, & I left at the request of my sister, the plaintiff, to stay away for a short time, she saying she thought that if I was away from the house she might sober him up.

QUESTION: What property had your sister at her marriage?

ANSWER: She owned one half of the personal effects in the house & nothing else but her clothes.

QUESTION: What was that one half worth?

ANSWER: At the time she was married I offered to sell the defendant the whole of the effects at five hundred dollars, which is about what I think they are worth.

QUESTION: What is the defendant's business? & in what condition has he been to give attention to that business during the last nine or ten weeks?

ANSWER: He is a wholesale & retail dealer in tobacco & cigars. His principal business has been at wholesaling by traveling which he does himself although intending to go out traveling. He has neglected to do so & been at home drunk & unfit for business.

QUESTION: How does his neglect to travel and inattention effect his business?

ANSWER: His not traveling prevents him from selling stock which he has on hand & which he cant sell otherwise & gives his customers a chance to purchase from other persons by him not coming around regular & gives an opportunity to those owing him to fail before collecting, as I have heard him remark that if he had attended to his business and not neglected it he would have collected sums of money which he otherwise lost.

QUESTION: State his present condition and how that condition effects his general business.

ANSWER: His present condition renders him unfit to attend to business as he is under the influence of liquor and as he is unfit to attend to his business, and his business suffers on that account. He has no person to attend to his business except a boy.

QUESTION: From your knowledge of him and her, his general habits, & what you have seen, what prospect is there if any of reformation on his part and of them getting along harmoniously together?

ANSWER: Decidedly none in my opinion, as within nine months he has been induced & tried in the kindest manner as many as six times to sober up & remain so which he has failed to do as many times, although he promised reformation each time.

QUESTION: Since you left there at the request of your sister, what change if any has there been in his general conduct & conduct towards her?

ANSWER: He was never so abusive either by language or otherwise so much as he was after I left. During my absence he would destroy the goods & chattel belonging to myself & his wife. He would take a drink of water & throw the goblet against the wall, would pick up a piece of meat & throw it out of the door, would kick the furniture about the house. He would catch a hold of the table cloth and throw every thing on the floor, which in my opinion he would not have done had I been there.

QUESTION: State whether in your opinion your living in the family was any just cause or provocation for the treatment you witnessed & which she sufferd at his hands.
ANSWER: None what ever.

SAMUEL H. GIFFEN

QUESTION: State your age, residence, & occupation, and how long have you known the parties to this suit.
ANSWER: Aged 28 years. Reside on Quincy Street next door to the parties to this suit. Occupation—hat & cap business. I have known Mrs Griffith about two years. I have known him about six years.
QUESTION: State in detail his conduct so far as it has come to your knowledge in the presence of his wife during the last nine or ten weeks.
ANSWER: The last spree has been a repetition of the others. He commenced on the spree the same as usual & continued and was part of the time at the house & part of the time at the store, & every time he came home there was a row cursing his wife & her brother & every person about the house, generally broke something terrible & called his wife hard names. I have heard him call her frequently a damned slut & whore, & said that *thing* up stairs, meaning his wife, was the cause of the whole trouble, & when I would remonstrate with him & tell him that he must not talk that way, that his wife was not in a condition for to hear such language, that it might kill her, he would say let her die, damn her, she ought to die. Then he was all the time harping on her brother. He used to say that he had the greatest contempt for the whole Stewart family, that his connection with the Stewart family had ruined one of the best business men in the City (meaning himself). When I would remonstrate with him in regard to his actions, he always would say that he was going to rule his own house God Damn me. He said he acused his wife with being connected with a clique to beat him down. He said those parties connected with his wife was A. N. Johnson, J. C. Acheson, M. C. Good, Muro Stone, and her petty & contemptable brother Jimmie Stewart & all the balance of the damn Good Templars.[13] I have of-

---

13. The International Organisation of Good Templars was a temperance-focused fraternal organization. The organization took its name from the Knights Templar, stating that the Good Templars were fighting a crusade against alcohol. Schwalm, *Emancipation's Diaspora*, 171; Cabiniss and Easterly, "Fraternal Groups," 70.

ten told Charlie about the disgrace that he was bringing on his family & himself by acting in such a manner. He said that he did [not] care a damn what any of them said, that they could kiss his ass god damn them. The last week or two, my wife & family being absent in the country, I returned home about two oclock at night. Sometimes he would be in the house, and sometimes he would be down street. I would retire and hardly get in bed until the door bell would ring, & the nurse would say that Mrs Griffith wanted me, that Charles had returned & was crazy drunk & was raising hell. I would dress as quick as possible & rush in there. Sometimes I would find Mr Griffith with his clothes on & sometimes with them off, walking back & forth across the floor swinging his cane & cursing every person about the house especially his wife, using the most fearful oaths & slang phrases I ever heard used by a man in my life. Sometimes I could quiet him by talking to him & other times I had to put him down with man force & threats of what I would do if he did not keep quiet.

QUESTION: In whose presence & in what time & with what degree of violence were these things done?

ANSWER: The tone was pretty much as the tone of all drunken men—very loud, could be heard in the street. I dont think I ever heard his wife speak to him or remonstrate with him, but he give her a cursing.

QUESTION: How long has he been on this last spree?

ANSWER: I cant give the exact date. I think about ten weeks.

QUESTION: About how often during the last nine or ten weeks have you been called upon to pacify him?

ANSWER: I have been either called or gone into his house to quiet him on an average of five nights out of a week since his wife's confinement.

QUESTION: What do you know of his conduct towards her or in her presence immediately before her confinement?

ANSWER: She was confined on Sabbath evening. I was down to dinner and had just come home, & Mr Griffith came to the door & told me that his wife was very sick & wished Mr Dobbius to go up for Mrs Mix. Mr Dobbius being absent, & I having an idea of what was the matter with Mrs Griffith, I volunteered to go myself for Mrs Mix. After her arrival the Doctor was sent for & in about a half hour the child was born. Mr Griffith had been more quiet on that day and the following two or three days & I think less liquor in him than any other time during the whole spree. On the Friday night before the child was born he was as boisterous as usual.

QUESTION: State what occurred on Friday night the 22nd of July.

ANSWER: When I closed the store there was quite a severe storm threatening, & I hurried home before it rained. Mr Griffith was already home & drunker & crazier than usual. After the first gust of the storm had passed over & it had commenced raining, I was called to the door by a violent jerk of the bell. The nurse stated that Mr Griffith had no clothes on & wanted me to come in & quiet him. I went in as quick as possible & found his clothes all off, except his shirt & drawers, had his cane in his hand swinging it violently around his head, prominading back & forth through the house & swearing terribly at every thing that come in contact with him. I tried to get him to go & lay down. After laying down on the sofa I requested him to have a cover over him for the reason that his person was partially exposed, and he told me to kiss his ass, that he would cover every thing in the house before morning. This was in the presence of the nurse, Miss Duncan. Then he got up & wanted some fresh air and wanted to go & open the front door, & I remonstrated with him as the storm was raging terribly & the lightning was very vivid, but he would go. After going to the door I followed him out, & while standing there there was a very vivid flash of lightning and says I, Charles did you see that? Come in, it is not safe to stand here. He remarked & said, How do you like that for long? Says I, You will get struck with lightning if you do not go in out of this door. Let her strike God damn her. Then I took him by the arm & pulled him in & threw the door, took him back & got him to lay down in the sofa. I told him if he did not behave himself he would be struck by lightning & killed & go to the bad place certain, & he said certainly I am going to hell. Old Jesus Christ and me are going to run hell & the first fellow they will ask for will be where is Griffith bring him down here I have got a good position for him, and in course of a half hour afterward he went asleep. I went off and left him that is the last I had to do with him

QUESTION: At such times about how far in the neighborhood & in the streets could he be heard?

ANSWER: From his house he always talked louder than any place. I have heard him cursing & swearing when I was fully fifty yards below his house.

QUESTION: During this & all other times how has she demeaned herself as a virtuous & prudent woman & affectionate & dutiful wife?

ANSWER: I never saw anything unbecoming in Mrs Griffith. She has always conducted herself as any ordinary married woman should. She has always treated Mr Griffith with respect & tried to make home as comfortable & plesant as she could. Her reputation for chastity so far as I know is above reproach.

QUESTION: In what business is he engaged & if you know about what is he worth?

ANSWER: He is engaged in the wholesale tobacco & cigar business. From what I know I think he has now in his business about seven or eight thousand dollars. What he is worth outside of that I dont know.

QUESTION: In what condition is he now & has he for months been in to attend to business?

ANSWER: Well, his condition is a terrible one, & as far as I am a judge of doing, I think the man has not been in a fit condition to attend to business.

QUESTION: How has his business suffered or prospered during that time?

ANSWER: His business has suffered terribly. His business is done by traveling, & his retailing that he does in the store at home I do not think will pay expenses.

QUESTION: As a business man what in your opinion must be the result if things are permitted to go on as they have?

ANSWER: I think if his business is conducted in the same manner that it has been for the last two weeks, that in a short time Mr Griffith will not have anything left.

QUESTION: What expedient has been left untried to reform him, if any?

ANSWER: None. I think that everything has been done. He has been coaxed, threatened, and nothing will do any good.

QUESTION: What foundation, if any, is there for his complaints against his wife & her family, which he is in the habit of making?

ANSWER: None whatsoever as far as I am capable of knowing. I believe them all to be imaginary on the part of Mr Griffith, & I have told him so frequently, and I think that he only used them as a pretext to his drinking.

QUESTION: Are you a man of a family, and if so, what, in your opinion, would be a necessary & proper amount for the monthly support of the plaintiff & her child?

ANSWER: I am, and I dont think that Mrs Griffith having no other resources could sustain herself & child on much less than one hundred dollars per month.

QUESTION: In what mental & physical condition has the plaintiff been in during the last nine or ten weeks?

International Organization of Good Templars Certificate of Membership, 1868; Library of Congress.

ANSWER: Physically I believe Mrs Griffith would have recovered much sooner had she not been annoyed by her husband. Mentally I think that he would set the devil crazy, let alone a delicate woman & one in her condition.

QUESTION: What effect did his condition have on her the night of the storm?

ANSWER: The same effect it had the previous night when she had to send to her Doctor.

MARY W. MIX

QUESTION: What is your age, and where do you reside?

ANSWER: Aged 47 years & reside in Wheeling.

QUESTION: Have you been much about the house of Charles E. Griffith during the last six months?

ANSWER: I have.

QUESTION: State what has been his habits condition & treatment of his wife & those about his house.

ANSWER: In march last I was there. First he was very violent. He accused his wife of infidelity by reason of want of chastity, also threatened violence. He would disown her as his wife. He would go up to her & threaten to strike her in the face. Every time he has indulged in those fits of intoxication he would abuse her in that same way, from that time to this. These things were done in my presence and often in the presence of others.

QUESTION: In what language were these imputations against her chastity made?

ANSWER: The language was very bad. A few days ago he said you are a damn thing and there is nothing decent in you, and other language I would not repeat. I told him that he must not use such language before me. This was about a week ago. I have seen him walk up to her and threaten to knock her down & also to throw things at her. The night she was confined he was in a state of atmost imbecility from the effects of drink, rather in the second state from the effect. This was on Sunday night July 11th 1869 that the child was born. On Tuesday night he was raving, & I was sent for at such times. He was very violent in the room and about her, alarming her to such an extent that she become delirious. This was repeated for one or two weeks, every night successively, two weeks at least. His conduct to me was perfectly shocking, such oaths & violence. Every one in the house became frightened.

QUESTION: In what mental & physical condition was she at that time & how did this conduct effect her generally?
ANSWER: She had so little rest that she has debilitated physically & quite beside herself mentally—both day & night. I think it was entirely traceable to his conduct.
QUESTION: What reply would she make to his accusations?
ANSWER: You know better. I will not hear it. He would be checked but a few moments & then repeat it.
QUESTION: What during all this time has been her demeanor towards him?
ANSWER: She bore with a great deal of patience until at last one day he had been throwing the cane at her while she was lying in bed, & she told him if he did not let her alone, she would use the cane over his head, and I suppose she was at a loss for an expedient & she thought she would try that as she was not in a condition to carry the threat into execution.
QUESTION: What is her character for chastity, and with what grounds, if you know, did he charge her of unchastity?
ANSWER: I never saw or knew anything against her character. Her character by those who knew her is regarded above reproach. I could see no grounds; I simply thought him a monamania in the subject. During the last ten weeks he has rarely had a lucid interval. I regarded him as constantly under the influence of drink or a softening of the brain, and I regard him as a dangerous man, and he was dangerous. On one occasion we were obliged to drive him down stairs, as we could not stand to have him in the next room, and about three oclock we got all quiet, and at five oclock he screamed terribly and came up stairs. The reason was that a servant came into the room, and he was so delirious that he imagined he saw a man coming in at the window. This was shortly after his wifes confinement. And for two or three days he kept this up, imagining that a man was after him.
QUESTION: How has his condition affected the people in neighbourhood, and how notorious has it been?
ANSWER: They have all felt that it was outrajious, and men have heard him scream & got up thinking there was danger at the house. One night I was returning from church and other ladies were in company, and he was so drunk that his clerk was leading him home. When at the Corner of 5th & Quincy Streets, he hallowed out that he was going home to that damn bitch and she may kiss —— (the language I will not repeat but it was very low & vulgar). These were all common

phrases of his. He would come home & ask the servants how that bitch was up stairs.

QUESTION: Are you a mother?

ANSWER: I am of five children.

QUESTION: From your knowledge of his conduct & his wife during that conduct, what effect did it have upon the birth of the child?

ANSWER: Through excitement & want of sleep, it produced a premature birth. The night previous to the birth he was very violent so that she could not lay down at all. He was so violent that servants would not stay in the house, and she had to stay with him alone.

QUESTION: Do you regard it safe for her and her child to be left with him?

ANSWER: I do not.

QUESTION: What apprehensions had she for her safety & life, & with what grounds in your opinion?

ANSWER: His violent threats and his seeming to have no affection for her and her child. She stated to me that she feared for her life. Whenever he come in sight, she would catch up the child through fear of him and that at a time when she was not able to sit up. At times it was dangerous for any person to be with him and his threats of violence were promiscuous.

QUESTION: Do you know of any expedient that has not been resorted to for the purpose of reforming him?

ANSWER: I do not. First his wife left him and was absent two weeks, leaving a letter to inform him that it was impossible to live with him & hoping that would cause him to reform. Her brother also gave him up possession of his house & furniture to see if he would do better, which made bad matters worse. She has indulged him every way, having meals provided for him at all hours of the day & night.

QUESTION: Do you regard it possible for her and her child to live with him as he at present is and for a long time has been?

ANSWER: I do not.

QUESTION: What monthly allowance is reasonably necessary for the maintenance & support of her self & child?

ANSWER: I think that a hundred dollars will not be any too much.

JENNIE DUNCAN

QUESTION: How long have you been living with the defendant Charles E. Griffith & in what capacity?

ANSWER: I have been the nurse for three weeks to day.

QUESTION: Please state what has been his condition & conduct during that time.

ANSWER: On Monday after the birth of the child he was quiet, that is he had been drinking but was not very noisy—and on Tuesday evening he carried on so that she was delirious. Ever since I went there he has used the most profane language and names that could be used to a woman. He would go up to her & shake his fist in her face & tell her that he would knock her over & hit her in the face, & he would say she was a damn thing & other words I cant repeat. That was the first two weeks, and on last Monday evening he threw a goblet at her, but it hit the door & broke. If it had not struck the side of the door, I think it would have hit her in the face or the baby, which was lying in the bed by her side.

QUESTION: Were the words which you decline to repeat such words as charged her with unchastity?

ANSWER: They were.

QUESTION: Does this spell one of the words: W-H-O-R-E?

ANSWER: It does.

QUESTION: During such & all other times how has she demeaned herself towards him as a prudent faithful and affectionate wife?

ANSWER: By treating him kindly until one night this week he abused her mother, who has been dead some twenty years, when she told him she could not & would not stand it.

QUESTION: How has his treatment affected her mentally & physically?

ANSWER: She is not recovering rapidly at all. She is always crying unless there are strangers in. She seems to be greatly troubled and at every little noise she always starts, & if you go in the room you always find her crying.

QUESTION: When was he there last, & what was his conduct?

ANSWER: It was last Tuesday evening, the 20th of July. He went in the house about 7 o'clock in the evening. He came in & asked if Jim Stewart was in, the damned puppy[14] and to kick her & the damn brat (meaning his wife & baby) out of the house. He went up to his wifes room and ordered her out & said that every thing there belonged to him, that he was going to run the house, and that she should not stay. She told him to come & look at his baby. He said it was not his and that he wished both her & the baby would die.

---

14. A nineteenth-century way of saying "son of a bitch."

QUESTION: What are his habits as to extravagance & his conduct towards the members of the family?
ANSWER: He was very extravagant. He would break something every time he would come in the house. At meals he would eat what he would want & then throw the balance under the table.
QUESTION: Were you a witness to what Mrs Mix state[d] about the morning he immagined he saw a man coming through the window?
ANSWER: I was.
QUESTION: State what you have heard him say publicly in the streets & in the hearing of passers by?
ANSWER: I have heard him say that was not his child & that it was not the first one she had had and that she was damned *thing* before he married her & was still one. He was setting on the front door step at the time, and he said it loud enough for to be heard a half square.
QUESTION: Do you regard it safe for yourself, his wife, & child to be with him?
ANSWER: I do not.
QUESTION: State if you remember any instance in which all persons were driven from the house by him. Give the particulars.
ANSWER: One Evening last week he ran after the colored girl with his cane, & I started to run out, & then thought of her & I run upstairs to her & him after me & he went to her & was going to hit her, & I handed her a cane & she kept him off with it. She was in bed at the time, the child with her.
QUESTION: What is & has been the condition & that of her child since you was there?
ANSWER: She has been in a very critical condition until this week & she is very nervous & not able to sit up more than ten minutes at a time & the child is nervous, & you would think it would go into spasms every few minutes, & it is very weak & feeble.

A. M. ADAMS

QUESTION: Are you acquainted with the parties to this suit?
ANSWER: I am acquainted with Griffith but not with his wife.
QUESTION: What & where is your place of business?
ANSWER: No 37 Monroe Street and adjoining the business house of the defendant. I am a Merchant Tailor.[15]

---

15. Merchant tailors are tailors who own their materials, rather than using materials supplied by their customers.

QUESTION: What has been the defendant's general habits during the last three months?
ANSWER: Disipation.
QUESTION: To what extent?
ANSWER: So much so that I am afraid and have complained to Morgan Oth, his landlord, that I was afraid he would set the house on fire, and other parties were afraid & told me about his being there at night drunk as they saw him there.
QUESTION: State what attention his business has received & is receiving.
ANSWER: From him since my knowledge of him except two weeks it has been very bad attention & such as will lead a man to bankruptcy if he continues.
QUESTION: What effect has his conduct had upon the customers & those who might otherwise patronize him?
ANSWER: I should think it would have the tendency to drive them away if he was present. He has been the subject of universal remarks by parties on Monroe Street about his beastly drunkeness.
QUESTION: Since you have known him, what has been his capacity, & what now is his capacity to take care either of himself his family or his business?
ANSWER: I dont think he has had any capacity except the two weeks I mentioned.
QUESTION: What must be the inevitable result to himself & his business unless he soon reforms or is in some way restrained?
ANSWER: Insolvency.
QUESTION: Is it safe in your opinion for business of any kind to be left in the hands of such a man?
ANSWER: No Sir.
QUESTION: Is he a fit party for the care custody or companionship of a wife & child?
ANSWER: Not since I have known him or in his present condition.
QUESTION: From what you know & from popular repute what is he worth?
ANSWER: Twenty thousand dollars. I have never heard him estimate it less.
QUESTION: What is a fair monthly allowance for the maintenance of the plaintiff & her child?
ANSWER: Taking into consideration the way she was raised, his circumstances, & her conditions I think one hundred dollars is little enough.

QUESTION: Do you think his capacity and general demeanor any warranty that in six months hence his property will not all be squandered?

ANSWER: I should not think it would. I think he will die before that time, but if he lives that long, I do not think he will have much left.

QUESTION: What in your opinion would be a proper amount of alimony out of his Estate for the permanent support of herself & child?

ANSWER: If I was going to do it, I would give his wife & child the three fourths of it & appoint a Guardian to take care of the balance of it for him.

L. T. BUSBEY

QUESTION: State your age & business, place of business & whether or not you are acquainted with the defendant.

ANSWER: Age 28 years. Business—hardware merchant. Place of business—Corner of Market & Monroe Streets & next door to the defendants place of business. I am acquainted with the defendant & have been about two years.

QUESTION: State what has been his habits & condition since March last.

ANSWER: He was on a spree about two weeks in April & then took sick. After he got over his sick spell, he staid around the store getting things ready to take a trip to Ohio selling goods, & he staid in Ohio about a week or two days. He came back & had his goods all put up & was pleased with the success he had met with & told me that from this forward he would quit drinking and attend to his business. He was then sober about five or six days, since which time he has been on a spree. He told me last Tuesday that he had been on a spree for nine weeks, & it was time he was getting off.

QUESTION: What are his habits, temperament, & language when on such spree?

ANSWER: Very bad.

QUESTION: Give some details.

ANSWER: I have heard him curse Jim Stewart, and damn the Stewart family.

QUESTION: What attention has his business received during such sprees?

ANSWER: I dont think his business has been attended by himself at all, as I do not think he has been in a fit condition to attend to private business & was it not for Thomas Morris, a young man he has employed, his store would have been closed. It was closed two days &

Morris went to him & got the key & opened the store on the third day, thinking that it would be better for himself & family to have the store open.

QUESTION: State about what is the age of young Morris, & what is his experience in & capacity for business?

ANSWER: His age is 18 or 20 years—the tobacco business is a new business to him, as he has been staying with his father in the hardware business. He came to Griffith some time in April

QUESTION: From what you know & have seen, what have been the effects of the defendants habits upon himself, his customers, & his business?

ANSWER: I asked him one day what he was drinking for & he said it was all trouble about the Stewart family. It has give him a very bad character among the citizens as a businessman. When under the influence of liquor he would bring in his excuse that it was family trouble instead of liquor. I notice customers go in, & when Mr Morris was at dinner they would ask Griffith for cigars or tobacco. "I dont want to sell any God damn you sir" was his reply. Some people would come in, & he would say "what in the hell do you want Sir," and the people would turn around & go out. This would have a tendency to drive away any person who was a stranger to him. Since he has been on a spree his business is in a decrease as his business is more wholesale then retail, & he expects to make his profits by trading & expects the retail business to pay the expenses of the house.

QUESTION: State whether his retail business has been sufficient to defray expenses the last two or three months.

ANSWER: It would as he had a good stock of fine cigars & tobacco & was getting a good run of custom for the same, but when in these sprees, parties would go else where. If he had staid away from the store while in sprees, I think Morris could have carried the business along & made it pay, but as it is & has been it has been insufficient that is for the last ten weeks.

QUESTION: Unless his personal & business habits are reformed what in your opinion as a business man must be the inevitable result?

ANSWER: His business will go to a rack within a year. If he goes on the way he has for the last eight or ten weeks he would spend all he has in a year as his sprees are very expensive.

QUESTION: Unless his personal or business habits reform what in your opinion would be proper & necessary to be done for the protection & preservation of his property & business?

ANSWER: To have a Guardian or Reciever or some one appointed to take care of his business.

QUESTION: Are you acquainted with the plaintiffs character as a prudent virtuous & upright woman?

ANSWER: Yes Sir.

QUESTION: What is it?

ANSWER: Good.

QUESTION: What exhortation have you seen & heard about his store?

ANSWER: I could hear him through the partition swearing & using abuseive language so much so that a crowd would gather around the door, & I have asked them to go away so that an officer would not come. This was at his business, hence this would attract the attention of persons on both side of the street & could be heard at least a half square.

QUESTION: What are his abilities as a traveling & general business man when sober?

ANSWER: Good.

WILLIAM MCPHAIL

QUESTION: What is your occupation?

ANSWER: Deputy Sheriff of Ohio County

QUESTION: What paper do you now hold in your hand?

ANSWER: A copy of the order of the Court made by his Honor Judge Melvin on the 29th day of July 1869 and copied into the Chancery Order book of the Circuit Court of the County West Virginia in a cause in Chancery wherein Maggie C. Griffith is plaintiff & Charles E. Griffith is defendant.

QUESTION: By when on what day & about at what hour was a copy of that paper served on the defendant Charles E. Griffith?

ANSWER: By me as Deputy Sheriff on the 30th day of July 1869, not later than 2 ½ P.M. of that day, served on him personally.

JAMES CUMMINS[16]

QUESTION: What is your age & occupation?

ANSWER: Aged 42 years. I am a physician.

---

16. Dr. James Cummins was the brother of Dr. Robert Cummins, who served as a witness and doctor in both *Wehner v. Wehner* (1850) and *Leasure v. Leasure* (1871), which are featured in this book.

QUESTION: If at all, how long have you been treating the plaintiff Maggie C. Griffith?
ANSWER: My Brother left the 13th of July. I visited her that day. I have visited her about from 10 days to two weeks.
QUESTION: State what was her physical & mental condition.
ANSWER: Her physical condition was very good but considerable mental excitement most of the time I visited her. She was nervous & excited & attributed it all to the actions of her husband, and she several times mentioned to me that her husband was acting badly & that she feared him this mental excitement interfered greatly with her recovery.
QUESTION: What effect would such treatment & conduct of his, which has come to your knowledge, have upon a woman & child in their condition?
ANSWER: It might have a very serious effect & even a fatal effect, as it is very important to keep a lying in woman very still, and I think it endangers the life of both mother & child.
QUESTION: What results might reasonably be apprehended before the birth of the child to a woman in her condition and with her surroundings?
ANSWER: It would be calculated to bring about premature birth and might else endanger her life.
QUESTION: Do you regard it as safe or prudent for her & child to be subjected to the companionship of a man with his habits & temperament?
ANSWER: I do not consider it prudent.
QUESTION: What proportion of his Estate would be a reasonable allowance to her as alimony?
ANSWER: I would say one third any kind. If he continues his dissipation I think she should have the most of it.

W. M. CURTIS

QUESTION: Where do you reside & what is your business?
ANSWER: Wheeling—business bookkeeper at Hofts Jones Winston & Co.
QUESTION: Are you acquainted with the defendant Charles E. Griffith?
ANSWER: Yes Sir.
QUESTION: What knowledge have you of the cash capital with which he commenced business and of additions afterward made thereto?
ANSWER: About the last of December 1867, he received a Draft in New

York for a little less than 5000 dollars & commensed business in that & continued with that until about the 1st April 1868. He called in me some time in April 1868 to assist him in keeping his cash book & told me that he had another addition of about 5000 dollars, & his cash balance showed that he had an increase of about that amount. Since that time, I have never seen his books. I dont know that he has ever received another installment. I have heard it said that he has, but I dont know anything about it.

QUESTION: State whether in your opinion he has any capacity for business and whether any business is safe in his hands?

ANSWER: I dont think at the present time he has any business capacity at all. I dont think any business safe in his hands at the present time, although when he is sober & whisky is out of him he is a very competant salesman.

QUESTION: Are his habits & recent mismanagement any warranty that six months or a year hence he will have any property at all?

ANSWER: I don't think he would.

A. M. JOHNSON

QUESTION: Are you acquainted with the parties to this suit?

ANSWER: I am.

QUESTION: What have been the habits and condition for several months last past of the defendant?

ANSWER: Being frequently grossly intoxicated

QUESTION: What is his manner towards his family & others when in that condition?

ANSWER: From my own personal knowledge of being at his house one night, I consider him dangerous.

QUESTION: Give details of your reasons for so considering him?

ANSWER: I was called upon a few months back, some two or three months, by James A Stewart, the brother in law of the defendant, for the purpose of trying to get the defendant to stop using abusive & threatening language. I went to the house, found the defendant in what I should consider a moderate state of intoxication in the dining room. His wife at the same time was upstairs, confined to her bed sick, & he used lewd vulgar & abusive language & made threats so that his wife could hear them of such a nature that it tended to alarm her. The threats being of such a nature that his brother in law James Stewart procured Charles Exlay, one of the deputy sergeants, to come to the house for the purpose of arresting him. After the officer informed him for what purpose he came, he agreed to go with him & made excuse that he wanted to take a little more stimulant before he left & went to the cupboard & got two large knives, one a butcher knife & the other a carving knife, & made at the officer using threatening language at the time that he would not be taken, & the officer protected himself by drawing his mace in him & then arrested him & took him to the lock up.

QUESTION: State whether in your opinion he is a fit or safe person for the companionship of his family.

ANSWER: From my knowledge of him I do not think they are safe either in person & property.

QUESTION: When in these fits of intoxicated do you consider him a fit person to run at large?

ANSWER: I do not.

QUESTION: Do you consider any business or property safe under his management or control?

ANSWER: Not when under the influence of intoxicating drinks.

QUESTION: Has the defendant been recently before you as one of the justices of this County, & if so when for what & with what result?

ANSWER: He was before me July 21st 1869, arrested on a warrant for threatening to burn the house occupied by James A. Stewart & the plaintiff & family as boards. I required him after hearing the testimony to enter into a bond of 500 dollars for his good behavior for one year. He failed to give the bond and was committed to jail where he remained until August 2nd 1869, when he give a bond.

QUESTION: During the time you have known her how has she conducted herself as a patient prudent industrious & affectionate wife?

ANSWER: Well.

QUESTION: What is her character for chastity?

ANSWER: From my knowledge I consider it above suspicion.

QUESTION: How do you regard his use of the following words in regard to his wife: She is a whore? A damn thing? This is not the first child she has had & kindred expressions?

ANSWER: I consider them the worst insults he could give her, as I do not think there is a word of truth in them. I think it is very cruel and more particularly to a lady who has conducted herself with the propriety she has during a long acquaintance.

QUESTION: What proportion of her property would be a reasonable allowance to her for alimony?

ANSWER: Not less than two thirds.

QUESTION: Unless he reforms & his habits become changed, what in your opinion would be necessary and proper to preserve his property?
ANSWER: Place it in the hands of the Receiver of the Court or a Trustee. I do not think he is capable of manageing it. In fact I know he is not.

HENRY DOBBINS

QUESTION: Where have you been boarding during the last year?
ANSWER: At Mrs Griffith's until July 26th 1869.
QUESTION: What have been the conduct & habits of the defendant since January last?
ANSWER: He has been mighty bad while drunk, & every time he gets drunk he is worse. His first drunk commenced about the 29th of January. He came home drunk from the Country. He had been on the road selling goods. On that, the first drunk, he was very profane & made awful noise. The next drunk he commenced cursing his wife and charged her with unchastity. He said in my hearing of his wife "she is a God Damn whore," "she is a God Damn whore," she "would f—k a niger," repeating it. He said it in a loud manner, & I dont see how the girl could help hearing it. His wife was then away. He had to leave on account of his conduct. His last drunk commenced about ten weeks ago.
QUESTION: State some of the prominent features & treatment of his wife during the last ten weeks.
ANSWER: This last drunk he has been terrific. He droped the profane somewhat & went on the whore business. By that I mean calling her a damn whore. So far as I saw this was his general manner. I heard him say inside of two or three weeks, since the birth of the child "I have no more respect for that thing up stairs (meaning his wife) than I have for the lowest whore in Baltimore." I dont see how his wife could help hearing it as he said it loud enough, as he was no ways [careful] about how loud he spoke. On the night before the child was born, Saturday night, I wanted to go down street, & I just steped into the hall and wanted to see how soon supper would be ready, & his wife heard me upon the door, & she came out to tell me not to go in as he was breaking goblets up in the dining room, & after I had stood there & his wife began talking to me he came out flourishing his cane, & she tried to get him to go back and he said "kiss my ass. God damn you." She had a gun in her hand and said you must "not use such language as that to me or I will slap you,"

& he said "You will slap my ass. God damn you." That was the only time I thought he would strike her.

QUESTION: From your knowledge of the defendant is or is it not in your opinion whiskey alone which prompts him to such conduct?

ANSWER: I think it must be whisky, as he acts well enough when sober, although I think he knows what he is doing when he is drunk, although he pretends he does not. At one time while drunk he acted well enough when he thought there was an officer present, but when he found there was not he went on the rampage. This was at night. This helped to convince me that he knew what he was doing when drunk.

QUESTION: During all the time that you have known them how has she treated him?

ANSWER: First rate always.

QUESTION: What effect has his treatment had upon her?

ANSWER: It made her nervous, & she frequently had sick spells she told me it was killing her.

QUESTION: Do you regard him a fit person for the companionship of his wife & child?

ANSWER: No Sir.

QUESTION: Do you regard business or property safe in his hands?

ANSWER: No I do not.

QUESTION: Did you ever see anything in her conduct that was imprudent or unwifelike?

ANSWER: No Sir I never did.

JAMES A. STEWART, RECALLED

QUESTION: What have you heard if anything the defendant say about his money, & what he was worth & expected?

ANSWER: I have heard him say several times that he had ten thousand dollars invested in his business & six thousand in bank, & at the time he got the first installment from his Uncles Estate, he said he would get about twenty thousand dollars. I mean this to include the sixteen thousand before mentioned. He said he had expected to get seventy five thousand but would only get twenty.

QUESTION: About when to your knowledge did he receive the last installment of 5000 dollars from the estate of his Uncle Edward Griffith, late of Maryland?

ANSWER: I think it was about July 1868. I myself received the draft & handed it to him when he came home.

QUESTION: What money has he since received from the Estate of Edward Griffith dec[ease]d?
ANSWER: He showed me during April 1869 a receipt which the executor had sent him from Baltimore to sign for thirteen hundred & some odd dollars which he said he had received. He told me he had signed the receipt afterwards received the money on it and deposited the money in the 14 National Bank. I knew that he had money in that bank but dont know the amount as the bank officers told me so.
QUESTION: Who was your sisters family physician before & at the birth of her child?
ANSWER: Dr Robert H. Cummins[17]
QUESTION: Where is he now?
ANSWER: Absent from the city.

JOHN RUSSELL

QUESTION: What is your age & profession?
ANSWER: Aged 59. Profession—medicine.
QUESTION: Have you heard the testimony of Henry Dobbins in this case?
ANSWER: I have heard it read.
QUESTION: What in your opinion would be the effect of such conduct upon a woman in her condition?
ANSWER: It would have a depressing effect upon her nervous system & impare her general health I should think.
QUESTION: Were you called upon to visit her in a professional capacity since her confinement? If so when & in what condition was she?
ANSWER: I visited her one night in the fore part of last week when they said her physician could not be found. I found her sufering with [illegible] pains in the bow[e]ls & nervous excitement & perscribed for her abdominal trouble & left her.
QUESTION: How would such conduct before & since the birth of the child effect the general health of both?
ANSWER: It would be calculated to depress the mother in body & mind & impare her general health & also that of the child through the imparement of her own health as she was nursing it.

---

17. Robert Cummins served as a witness in both *Wehner v. Wehner* (1850) and *Leasure v. Leasure* (1871).

QUESTION: What in your opinion would be a fair & reasonable mon[th]ly allowance for the maintenance & support of the plaintiff & her child?

ANSWER: In counting that up I would count the rent of the house in the first place & count the wages of a girl to do the kitchen work & that of a regular nurse to take care of her & her child—provisions sufficient for the support of three persons & the child & all that is necessary for the clothing & bedding of her & the child and such necessary amount as would be proper for contingent expenses. Aside from these things I dont know what they would be & such medical attentions as might be necessary—during the time she is sick, & would require close medical attention, she would require at the rate of 150 dollars per month. If she could dispense with a nurse & medical attention a hundred & perhaps less would cover her expenses.

Report of Receiver

To the Hon. Thayer Melvin, Judge of said Court,

I, D. C. List, Receiver General of said Court have the honor herewith to report, that the defendant, Charles E. Griffith, has not paid nor caused to be paid to me any money under the order in this cause made on the 29th day of July 1869.

Wheeling, W. Va., August 24, 1869 2 o'clock P.M.

Order of Arrest

State of West Virginia, Ohio County, Circuit Court, August 24, 1869
In Chancery, At Chambers

On motion of the Plaintiff, by her counsel, this cause comes on further to be heard at chambers. And it appearing to the Court that a true copy of the former order of this court in this cause made at chambers on the 29th day of July 1869, was, by the Sheriff of this county duly and personally served on the defendant Charles E. Griffith on the 30th day of July 1869;

And it further appearing to the satisfaction of the Court that the said defendant has wholly neglected and refused to pay to the Receiver General of this court the sums heretofore ordered to be paid to wit, the sum of $175 and that he has so neglected and refused since the first day of August 1869:

And it further appearing that the said defendant on the 18th day of August 1869, was by the Sheriff of this county duly and personally served with a written notice, herewith ordered to be filed to the effect that a motion would this day be made to this court of chambers, at the Clerks' office of this court, at 2 o'clock to attach the said defendant for failing and refusing to obey the former order of this Court so made as aforesaid on said 29th day of July 1869:

The Court, at chambers, in consideration of the premises, find that the said Charles E. Griffith hath not yet paid to the Receiver General of this Court the sum of $175 nor any part thereof, as aforesaid ordered on said 29th day of July 1869 to be paid, and that he hath disobeyed said order and is guilty of contempt.

It is therefore ordered that an attachment against the said Charles E. Griffith, directed to the Sheriff of Ohio County requiring him to arrest the said Griffith and commit him to the jail of Ohio County, there to remain in custody until he shall comply with and obey said order of this Court, or until the Court shall otherwise order.

It is further ordered that the Clerk of the Circuit Court of Ohio County place this order in the chancery order book of this court.

T. Melvin, Judge, Circuit Court, Ohio County

Contempt of Court

The State of West Virginia

To the Sheriff of Ohio County Greeting:

We command you that you take Charles E. Griffith if he be found in your bailiwick and him safely keep until he shall satisfy us in the sum of one hundred and seventy five dollars by us heretofore to wit on the 29th day of July 1869 in a cause in chancery in our Circuit Court of Ohio County wherein Maggie C. Griffith is plaintiff and the said Charles E Griffith is defendant, ordered to be paid by the said defendant to the Receiver General of our said Court on the 1st day of August 1869 and which said order the said Charles E Griffith has disobeyed and for which said disobedience he has by our said Court been found and adjudged guilty of contempt as appears to us of record, and you the said Sheriff are hereby further required to convey and deliver the said Charles E Griffith to the jailor of your said County in whose said jail and custody he is directed safely to be kept until he shall comply with and obey said order or until the Court shall otherwise order. And how you have executed this writ make known immediately after its Execution to our said Court at Chambers in the Clerks Office of our said Court and have you then and there this writ, Witness Michael J. Brewing Clerk of our said Court at the Court House of our said County in the city of Wheeling this 25th day of August 1869 and in the 7th year of the State of West Virginia.

Michael J. Brewing Clerk

Receipt

Received of Charles E. Griffith one hundred seventy five dollars, on August 25th 1869

Executed by taking into custody the within named Defendant Charles E. Griffith who was released from custody by order of Hon. T. Meloin Judge of the Circuit Court of Ohio Co. under reason endorsed August 25, 1869

> [After this payment, there are no documents. Despite the arrest and injunction, the court never officially divorced Maggie and Charles Griffith, and the pair still lived together in 1870. Her brother still maintained his distance, and their baby had died.[18] Whether or not Charles continued his drunken, abusive behavior is impossible to determine, but he died a mere five years after this suit. Maggie Griffith never remarried and lived until 1903.[19] They were both buried at Stone Church Cemetery in Elm Grove, West Virginia.[20]]

Mary Norman v. John Norman, 1871

> [Norman, Mary v. Norman, John *(1871)*, *Records of the Circuit Court of Ohio County*, WVRHC, env. 289 b-5. Mary filed her petition on December 13, 1869. The court summoned John three days later, and he accepted the summons.]

---

18. Charles listed his personal estate as being worth $6,000 and his real estate as the same value. The only other person in their house was an eighteen-year-old white domestic servant from Maryland named Jemima Smith. United States Federal Census for 1870.

19. Charles appointed Maggie as the administrator of his will. At one point, she worked as a schoolteacher. West Virginia Wills and Probate Records; West Virginia Deaths Index; United States Federal Census for 1880.

20. U.S. Find a Grave Index.

Bill of Divorce

State of West Virginia, Ohio County Circuit Court

To the Hon. T. Melvin, Judge of the said court in Chancery now sitting:

Your oratrix Mary A. Norman,[21] of the said county, humbly complaining here shows to the court, that on or about the 12 day of July 1861, at West Alexander, Washington county in the state of Pennsylvania, she was married legally to John Norman,[22] also of the county, by one William Alexander, a justice of the peace of the said Washington county, & who had authority in the said state of Pennsylvania to solemnize the contract of marriage, & that she exhibits here a certificate of the said marriage so made by the said Alexander.[23]

That the said John Norman had been before married, & then had a family of children by his first wife, who are all but one over 21 years of age, & that one & he quite able to take care of himself. That he has three children of the said marriage with your said oratrix to wit, George A. Norman, seven years old the last day of March 1869, Ida Lee Norman four years old the 28 day of Nov. 1869, and Charles D. Norman two years old the 9 of next April.

That she has on her part been a true & faithful wife to her said husband, John Norman, yet the said John Norman, without cause has conducted himself toward her in the most cruel manner, in every way that he could devise: He has for a long time been in the habit of becoming intoxicated, & when drunk he has often beat & struck your oratrix & threatened her life, & that on the [blank] day of December 1869 & divers other days before that day he cruelly beat your oratrix without any cause, & threatened to take her life, & that she has good reason to fear, & does fear that her said husband will take her life.

And that her said husband has been extremely cruel to her in this: he has on or about the [blank] day of December 1869, falsely charged your oratrix with being a prostitute, & has in a most cruel & false manner repeated the said charge to the great distress & mortification of your oratrix, not only to her privately, but before others.[24]

---

21. Mary Stewart was born in 1840 in Maine. Her parents, Joseph and Dianna Stewart, moved with Mary to Virginia sometime before 1856. United States Federal Census for 1870; West Virginia Marriages Index.

22. John Norman was born in 1832 in Virginia. United States Federal Census for 1870.

23. No marriage certificate remains in the records.

24. Increasingly, as the nineteenth century wore on, judges accepted a husband's defa-

For the said cruel treatment of her said husband, & because she feared for her life, she has now, on the 13 day of December 1869 left her said husband, & has come into the city of Wheeling to reside, seperate & apart from her said husband, where she with her children expect to reside, where she will do all she has in her power to support them & herself.

Your oratrix further here shows, that the said John Norman owns a small farm on which he resides, in this county, about one mile from Roney's Point, which has hitherto supported him & his family, with your oratrix' labor & the labor of his children. The said small farm is worth about $2,500, & that John Norman asks $2,600 for it. That he has advanced none of his other children by a conveyance of land.

That your oratrix has a bed made by herself, at the house of her said husband, & bedding, which she is in want of to keep house with here: that he has one horse one cow, over 50 sheep & farming tools, & good common furniture in the house: that she has no clothing of any consequence, only the suit she wears daily.

That she is without means except the proceeds of the sale of one 80 acre tract of land in Iowa, given her by her father Joseph Stewart who lives at that point,[25] but she is ignorant, but supposes that it did not sell for much if any over government prices, nor does she know if the money has been paid therefore. Inasmuch as your oratrix is wholly remediless by the strict rules of the common law & only relievable in the court, she prays process against her said husband John Norman, & that he be made defendant to this her bill of complaint; & she now prays, that sufficient alimony be awarded her for her present support & that a sum sufficient to enable her to prosecute her said suit be ordered & be now paid by the said John Norman, & that he be directed & ordered to devise to her the said bed & bedding so claimed as her own above & that the said John Norman be injoined from selling or incumbering the said tract of land until the farther order of this court, & that upon the final hearing of this case the court would order & decree divorce of separation from the bed & board of her said husband, & that she have sufficient alimony for her reasonable support, & such other &

---

mation of a wife's moral character as evidence of mental cruelty. According to Schweninger, "The act of humiliating women in the presence of others carried special weight . . . in a society where it was important to uphold the sanctity of the ideal southern white woman." Schweninger, *Families in Crisis*, 52–56.

25. A footnote in the original text of the divorce bill reads: "not to be enjoyed until after the death of her said father, who is still alive."

farther relief as her case may require, or to the court may seem proper, & she will ever pray &c.

Mary A. Norman by Peck & Cochran, her Sltrs.[26]

Depositions of Winesses[27]

MORGAN VERMILLION

QUESTION: What is your age, & where do you live?

ANSWER: Aged 25 years. I live about a mile north of Roney's Point in this County.

QUESTION: How far do you live from the home of the defendant, John Norman?

ANSWER: Not more than a quarter of a mile.

QUESTION: How long have you known him & his wife, Mary A. Norman?

ANSWER: Two years

QUESTION: State what you know about the plaintiff coming to your house in the night about the 3rd of July last, what condition she was in, & how long she remained.

ANSWER: She came to my house between the hours of 9 & 12 o'clock & brought her youngest child, a babe, & remained until morning. I think it was about the 3rd of July last.

QUESTION: State whether she came alone.

ANSWER: I could not state that.

QUESTION: State where you were when you first knew she was at your house, what you did & all about it.

ANSWER: I was in bed when I first knew she was there. She called & I knew it was her. My wife got up & let her in & she went to bed & remained there until morning.

QUESTION: What if anything did she say was the cause of her coming there at that time of night?

(Question objected to)

---

26. A footnote in the original text asked for "the care and custody of the said children." Another note at the bottom of her petition reflects the court's order that John pay Mary fifteen dollars a month for her support, twenty-five dollars for attorney fees, and thirty-five dollars for the cost of the suit.

27. Morgan Vermillion and Robert Norman testified on December 28, 1869, at the law offices of Peck and Cochran. Both signed their names.

ANSWER: I dont believe that I could answer that question. She might have said a good deal but for me to say she said any thing I dont mind it, as anything of that kind soon slips my memory.
QUESTION: Have you any recollection of anything she said?
(Question objected to)
ANSWER: No positive recollection.
QUESTION: Have you any means of knowing at about what hour in the night it was she came there?
ANSWER: No means of knowing, only just by the head.
QUESTION: Well, what does your head think about it?
ANSWER: I think I am not wrong in saying between the hours of 9 & 2 oclock.

ROBERT S. NORMAN

QUESTION: What is your age?
ANSWER: 22 years old.
QUESTION: Are you a son of the defendant, John Norman?
ANSWER: Yes Sir.
QUESTION: About when was your father married to the plaintiff?
ANSWER: It was in July 1861, I think.
QUESTION: Did they come to your fathers & your home on the day they were married?
ANSWER: Yes Sir.
QUESTION: How many children have been born of that marriage?
ANSWER: Three.
QUESTION: Please do name them & give their ages as near as you can.
ANSWER: George A. Norman, the first one, is about 8 years old, I think. The next was Ida Lee, I think, 4 years old, & the next Charles D., over a year old. They are all living.
QUESTION: When did your step mother leave the house of John Norman?
ANSWER: Last Wednesday evening the 13th of December.
QUESTION: Were you at home the Sunday before that?
ANSWER: No Sir.
QUESTION: Were you at home on Wednesday before that, December 8th?
ANSWER: Yes.
QUESTION: State what condition your father was in that night & what took place.
ANSWER: He was in a state of intoxication. He came home drunk, &

he was talking loud & ordered her (his wife) to get up & get away. I got up & went to him & caught him & told him to behave himself, & then he commenced to lecture me, & then she got up & was going to go away, & I told her not to do it.

QUESTION: What time in the night did he come home drunk?

ANSWER: I cant tell exactly, but it was about 10 o'clock.

QUESTION: Did you hear what he was saying when he came through the gate before he came up to the house?

ANSWER: I heard him say he was going to rid the shanty of the trash.

QUESTION: What other threats if any did he make?

ANSWER: If she did not get up & get, he would kick her into the road & I think he said he would kick her girls out.

QUESTION: Was there a gun in the house?

ANSWER: Yes Sir, there was.

QUESTION: State what he did with that & all he did & said so far as you can.

ANSWER: He took the gun down & laid it on the floor & said it was his & said he would take it where he pleased, & I took the gun & hung it up again on the rack & I took the powder horn from him too. He had it in his hand.

QUESTION: State whether you saw him draw the poker on his wife.

ANSWER: I belive he did not draw the poker. He had the poker in his hand, but I dont think he drew it to strike her with it.

QUESTION: What if anything did you do to prevent him from doing violence to his wife on that occasion?

ANSWER: I told you all that I did do. I dont know whether I prevented him from doing anything or not.

QUESTION: State whether you pushed him down on that occasion & if so why you did it.

(Question objected to)

ANSWER: I did not push him down.

QUESTION: Where were you when you heard him coming in the house?

ANSWER: I was up stairs in bed.

QUESTION: What did you first do after you got out of bed & why did you get out?

ANSWER: I went down to see what he was making a fuss about.

QUESTION: What did you see when you got in the room?

ANSWER: He was in the house telling her what I told you.

QUESTION: Where was Mrs Norman?

ANSWER: In bed.
QUESTION: Who else were in the room?
ANSWER: None but the children I believe.
QUESTION: Why was Mrs Norman about to leave?
ANSWER: He had told her to leave & that was the reason.
QUESTION: Do you know about how long he carried on that night?
ANSWER: No, I dont exactly. It was not very long, not more than five minutes, I reckon.
QUESTION: What effect did his conduct on that occasion have on the children? What did they do if anything?
ANSWER: They did not do any thing until she went to start & then they commenced to cry.
QUESTION: What names, if any, did he call her on that night?
ANSWER: I dont recollect, but I think he called her a whore for one thing.
QUESTION: State whether or not he was in the habit of calling her such names.
ANSWER: Yes, when he was drunk I have heard him call her such names as that.
QUESTION: In whose presence at sundry times?
ANSWER: I cant remember whether in any persons presence or not.
QUESTION: I mean, in whose presence of the members of the family?
ANSWER: I could not say whether it was in the presence of any other member of the family. I could not be sure about it.
QUESTION: Has he or not to your knowledge called her such names in the presence of her children?
(Question objected to)
ANSWER: I could not be certain whether the children were present at any time or not they were there that night.
QUESTION: State whether George is old & intelligent enough to know that such names are improper when applied to a respectable & deacent mother?
ANSWER: I dont think he knows the definition, of those words.
QUESTION: Do you remember the time that she in the night went to Morgan Vermillion's house?
ANSWER: I remember the circumstance but dont remember the time.
QUESTION: What took place on that night to cause her to leave?
ANSWER: I think he came home intoxicated again & ordered her to leave, I think.

QUESTION: About what hour did she leave?
ANSWER: I think about 10 o'clock, I could not be sure about that, I think.
QUESTION: What do you know if any thing about him choking her that night?
ANSWER: I dont know anything about that. I did not see anything of that.
QUESTION: Did you hear her say anything about it in his presence? If so, state what she said he did.
(Question objected to)
ANSWER: I dont recollect of hearing her say anything about it to him.
QUESTION: What do you remember if anything about throwing him on the floor that night & breaking his whisky bottles?
ANSWER: I did not throw him on the floor. I caught a hold of him & he fell down on the floor. I broke his bottle.
QUESTION: Why did you do that, what was he doing?
ANSWER: He was drunk & talking pretty loud to her.
QUESTION: What was he saying to her?
ANSWER: I cant remember just exactly what.
QUESTION: State what you do remember.
ANSWER: I told you all there I believe what I do remember. I cant remember what he did say though.
QUESTION: Do you remember what names if any he called her mother who had recently died?
ANSWER: No, I do not remember him saying any thing about her mother.
QUESTION: Do you remember of him making threats to kill her?
(Question objected to)
ANSWER: No, I believe I did not hear it.
QUESTION: State what you remember if anything about it being a rainy night & about her going out & sitting in the coal house door before starting to Vermillions.
ANSWER: I did not know that she sit in the coal house door. I think it did rain that night. I dont know whether it was raining at the time or not. I dont remember about it.
QUESTION: What frame of mind was she in that night in consequence of his conduct & treatment?
(Question objected to)
ANSWER: I dont know. I could not tell you. I did not see her after she went out.

QUESTION: Do you recollect anything of him throwing a knife at her about the first day of December?
(Question objected to)
ANSWER: I mind he threw a case knife[28] at her, but I did not see him throw it. I heard the knife drop on the floor.
QUESTION: What did she say if anything?
ANSWER: I think she said she would make him pay for it.
QUESTION: What did he say in reply to that?
ANSWER: I dont mind what he did say.
QUESTION: Do you remember that he said he would split her brains out or something to that effect?
(Question objected to)
ANSWER: No, I did not hear that.
QUESTION: What do you remember, if anything, about him then calling her Ike Burkham's Miss & whore?
(Question objected to)
ANSWER: I think he did say something about Ike Burkham, but I dont mind what it was.
QUESTION: Was that knife throwing operation at breakfast, dinner or supper?
ANSWER: At supper.
QUESTION: Who were present?
ANSWER: I dont remember who all, whether any person besides the family or not the three children we spoke of, him & I, & I cant say positively whether my brother was there or not.
QUESTION: What, if anything, have you ever at any time heard him say about her daughter Ida Lee being a Burkham?
ANSWER: Yes, I have heard him tell her that she was a Burkham.
QUESTION: State generally what you knew about him charging her (his wife) with improper intimacy with Ike Burkham.
ANSWER: I have heard him tell her that, that was Ike Burkhams child & that it was not his.
QUESTION: What do you know if anything about the defendant running his wife and your sister, Mary Ellen, through the rye & wheat in the night about July 1862?
ANSWER: I mind the time, but I dont think he run them. I think they run themselves. He did not run after them.
QUESTION: Why did they run?

---

28. Before the 1880s, "case knife" would have referred to a table knife.

ANSWER: I dont know. I did not see them run.
QUESTION: What do you know about them being frightened?
ANSWER: I dont know whether they were frightened or not.
QUESTION: Was he drunk on that occasion or sober?
ANSWER: He was drunk.
QUESTION: Do you remember about catching your father on that occasion & holding him until his wife & you[r] sister got off the porch?
ANSWER: No, I dont remember of doing it.
QUESTION: Do you know what time they returned?
ANSWER: No, I dont remember what time.
QUESTION: How old was her child at that time?
ANSWER: I could not say. 16 months old, I suppose. I could not be positive. I dont recollect.
QUESTION: Was it not about 9 (months) old?
(Question objected to)
ANSWER: I could not say whether it was or not. To the best of my recollection it was about 16 months.
QUESTION: About how long after they were married was the first child born?
ANSWER: I think about the first of March after that.
QUESTION: At the time of this knife throwing operation, was your father drunk or sober?
ANSWER: He was sober, I believe.
QUESTION: When he was on these sprees what was his usual time & manner as to being loud, savage boisterous or otherwise?
(Question objected to)
ANSWER: He talked very loud & sassy & independent.
QUESTION: How did Mrs Norman usually treat you & her own children as a mother?
ANSWER: Tolerable well.
QUESTION: At about the time Mrs Norman left what did you advise her, if anything, as to its being impossible for her to stand your fathers treatment any longer?
(Question objected to)
ANSWER: I believe I told her they had better seperate if they could not live peaceable.
QUESTION: About how frequently during the last four years has your father, to your knowledge, come home intoxicated?
ANSWER: I could not tell exactly. Sometimes once a month & sometimes more.

QUESTION: Sometimes once a week?
ANSWER: Yes. I have knew him to be drinking once a week for two weeks.
QUESTION: How many horses has your father?
ANSWER: He has two.
QUESTION: What are they worth?
ANSWER: I dont really know what.
QUESTION: How many cows & what worth?
ANSWER: One. I dont know what it is worth. Is a pretty good cow & worth $40.00, I reckon.
QUESTION: How many sheep what kind & what worth?
ANSWER: I dont know exactly how many, about 30 head, I believe. I guess they are saxon breed. I dont know exactly what they are worth. They are worth a dollar a head any how.
QUESTION: How many acres of land has your father?
ANSWER: 15 acres, I think.
QUESTION: Has he any interest in any other land that you know of?
ANSWER: He has a piece bought, but he has no deed for it.
QUESTION: How many acres?
ANSWER: Twelve, I think.
QUESTION: Who did he buy it from & when?
ANSWER: From Perry Parson. He bought this last piece—it was in 1868.
QUESTION: For how much?
ANSWER: I think $50 per acre.
QUESTION: How much has he paid on it?
ANSWER: That is what I dont know.
QUESTION: Is it as valuable per acre as the other 15 acres he owns?
ANSWER: I dont know that.
QUESTION: Has he the ordinary supply of household good & farming utensils?
ANSWER: He has the household goods. He has no farming utensils. He sold them all off last year.
QUESTION: Do you remember Mrs Norman showing you a mark on her face about a year ago when her sister was visiting your house, & if so what she said about it what caused it in your fathers presence?
(Question objected to)
ANSWER: I believe I remember about that. I think she said he struck her with the handle of a knife. I dont mind anything more about it.
QUESTION: What kind of a mark was it & where?
ANSWER: It was right on her cheek bone, I think a sort of a red spot.

QUESTION: Where is your brother James?
ANSWER: He was at home this morning.
QUESTION: Where is your sister Mary Ellen?
ANSWER: She is in Marshall County, Illinois.
QUESTION: Have you ever seen this paper marked W.H.C. Notary Public? If so where?
ANSWER: Yes, I have seen that before. I dont know exactly where it was. It was at home among some papers.
QUESTION: State whether the accompanying envelope marked W.H.C. Notary Public was the envelope containing the papers.
ANSWER: To the best of my knowledge I think it was.

CROSS EXAMINATION

QUESTION: Was you present at the marriage between the plaintiff & defendant?
ANSWER: No Sir, I was not.
QUESTION: Did you know the plaintiff before her marriage with your father? If so, was she a maiden lady, or had she been married before?
ANSWER: I did not know her before, but she had been married before.
QUESTION: What was her first husband's name?
ANSWER: John Forker, as far as I can understand.[29]
QUESTION: Was he dead at the time of her marriage with your father?
ANSWER: He was not.
QUESTION: Where was he living then?
ANSWER: I dont know.
QUESTION: What is your fathers trade or business?
ANSWER: Stone mason.
QUESTION: When the complainant & defendant were married, did she own any property?
ANSWER: None as I know of.
QUESTION: Did she bring any property—to your fathers house with her?
ANSWER: None as I know of.
QUESTION: What was the general character of your fathers treatment of her when he was sober?
ANSWER: At times he treated her well enough.

---

29. Mary Ann Stewart married John Forquer Jr. on February 28, 1856, in Brooke County, Virginia (now West Virginia). She was barely seventeen. Brooke County is the county just north of Ohio County. I can find no record of how their marriage ended or what happened to John Forquer after the marriage. West Virginia Marriages Index.

QUESTION: What is the general character of her treatment of your father?
ANSWER: I guess she was about the same as him—sometimes good & sometimes not so good.
QUESTION: What had she done to him that caused him to throw a case knife at her as you have stated in your examination in chief?
ANSWER: He had just set a grate. She was sweeping up the floor, & he told her not to slap the dirt on where he had plastered on the grate, & she kept on sweeping & then he threw the knife he told her not to sweep.
QUESTION: Did she ever drink any intoxicating liquors?
ANSWER: I have seen her take a drink of whisky, but I never saw her drunk.

WILLIAM MAXWELL[30]

QUESTION: What is your age, & where do you live?
ANSWER: Aged 61 years. Live near Roney's Point, Ohio County, West Va.
QUESTION: Are you acquainted with the parties to this suit?
ANSWER: I have known them ever since they come on the run there, which was a great many years ago. I have known Mrs Norman ever since she was John Normans' wife.
QUESTION: What are the habits of the defendant, John Norman, as to intoxication & drunkenness, & what have they been for the last eight or nine years if you know?
ANSWER: It has been a good deal that way & where ever he could get it, he got it. When ever he come to town, I guess, he went home intoxicated. I have seen him drunk a great many times but not half the number of times I have heard of it. I think he makes a business of getting intoxicated. This has been the case for a number of years.
QUESTION: How does he behave himself when intoxicated?
ANSWER: He is pretty noisy. He has quite an abusive tongue when he gets that way, particularly to any person he has anything against.
QUESTION: So far as you have seen when you have been about their house, how has Mrs Norman demeaned herself as a faithful & industrious wife?
ANSWER: I saw nothing but what she done what she could & but what was right.
QUESTION: How near does your farm lay to John Norman?

---

30. William Maxwell, James Norman, Hamilton Frazier, and Robert Norman testified on December 29, 1869. All signed their names.

ANSWER: About a half mile where we live from where he lives but the farms are about a hundred rods from each other.[31]

QUESTION: Are you acquainted with the value of lands in your neighborhood?

ANSWER: I am a little.

QUESTION: Please state the value of John Normans lands?

ANSWER: I would not suppose that both tracts are worth more than 55 dollars per acre.

QUESTION: Are you a farmer?

ANSWER: Yes Sir.

QUESTION: What is John Normans occupation?

ANSWER: A stone mason by trade & when he dont get work at that, he works on the farm.

QUESTION: State whether he is a man who earns a good deal of money.

ANSWER: He earns right smart of money.

QUESTION: How many children has he living of his first marriage? And which of them is the youngest & how old is he?

ANSWER: He has four. James is the youngest about 20 years old.

QUESTION: If you know please state the value of his horses & sheep?

ANSWER: I dont know the value of them at all.

JAMES NORMAN

QUESTION: Are you a son of the defendant?

ANSWER: Yes Sir.

QUESTION: What difficulty, if any, took place between your father & the plaintiff shortly before she left?

ANSWER: I dont just remember now.

QUESTION: State if you remember what names, if any, he called her or what threats if any he made to & against her.

ANSWER: I dont mind whether I was in the house that morning at the time, & I dont remember what names were called. There might have been, but I dont remember whether there were or not.

QUESTION: State what you remember if anything about him then threatening to kick her in the run & calling her a whore.

ANSWER: I dont remember any threats, & I did not pay any attention what it was. I don't remember whether he called her a whore or not.

QUESTION: Have you any recollection on the subject?

ANSWER: No Sir.

---

31. A rod is five and a half yards.

QUESTION: Were you present at any time when a knife was thrown? If so, state at when, by whom, when, & where?
ANSWER: Yes sir, I was. My father threw it at his wife. I dont just remember, just the evening it was. It was about the first of this month. It was at home.
QUESTION: State whether it hit her?
ANSWER: Yes Sir, it hit on the back, about the shoulder I think.
QUESTION: State what she did if anything to provoke such an act.
ANSWER: She was sweeping up the ashes of the hearth & he had been setting a grate & he told her to stop & she did not & he threw the knife.
QUESTION: Do you know whether she continued to sweep purposely to provoke him?
ANSWER: No, I know not. I dont know whether she did or not.
QUESTION: If she had done it for that purpose could you not have so known by her manner & countenance?
ANSWER: I did not pay any attention to her countenance.
QUESTION: What did she say when he thus struck her?
ANSWER: I am not sure, but I think she said that would be the last night that he would throw at her.
QUESTION: What if anything did he say in reply to that?
ANSWER: I dont remember now what he said.
QUESTION: Do you remember that he said that he would split her brains out & called her Ike Burkham's Miss?
(Question objected to)
ANSWER: I dont remember.
QUESTION: Is Mrs Norman a stout, robust, or small & delicate woman?
ANSWER: She is a small woman & not very stout & hearty.
QUESTION: What if anything have you ever heard him say to her concerning herself, Ida Lee, & Ike Burkham?
ANSWER: I have heard him call her his child. He said that Ike Burkham was the father of Ida Lee.

HAMILTON FRAZIER

QUESTION: What is your age, where do you live, & what is your occupation?
ANSWER: Aged 54 years. I live in Ohio County near the parties to this suit and am a farmer.
QUESTION: How long have you known the defendant?
ANSWER: For 15 or 20 years.

QUESTION: During the last few years, what have been his habits as to drunkenness?
ANSWER: I am not out much from home, but I have seen him when I thought he had too much liquor.
QUESTION: How does he behave or misbehave when intoxicated?
ANSWER: He is rather abusive in his language. He is both vulgar and profane.
QUESTION: Are you acquainted with the value of real estate in your neighborhood?
ANSWER: Some little.
QUESTION: Are you acquainted with the lands of John Norman?
ANSWER: Yes Sir.
QUESTION: What in your judgment are they worth?
ANSWER: I would say that the 15 acre lot is worth from 60 to 65 dollars per acre with improvements & the other tract is worth 50 dollars per acre.
QUESTION: Is Mrs Norman a large & rugged or small & delicate looking woman?
ANSWER: I would say she was delicate.

CROSS EXAMINATION

QUESTION: What is the defendants general character for industry & peaceable & quiet conduct when sober?
ANSWER: I believe he has the reputation for being industrious & as a general thing peaceable & quiet when sober.

ROBERT NORMAN, RECALLED FOR FURTHER CROSS EXAMINATION

QUESTION: State particularly the conduct of the complainant towards the defendant at the time you say he threw a knife at her at the supper table.
ANSWER: He had just set the grate & she was sweeping up the dust & dirt & he told her not to until the plastering got dry & she kept on sweeping was all I noticed.
QUESTION: Did you ever know the defendant [to] strike or beat or offer to strike or beat the complainant when he was sober?
ANSWER: No, I dont think I did.
QUESTION: Was not he a good provider for his family?
ANSWER: He was, as far as I know. I lived in the family.
(The witness wishes to correct the answer to question 2nd by saying that he was sober when he threw the knife.)

QUESTION: What kind of a knife was it?
ANSWER: It was a table knife, a case knife.
QUESTION: Could it, used as it was at that time, have inflicted upon her any injury?
ANSWER: I dont know.
QUESTION: Did it inflict any injury upon her?
ANSWER: It caused no cut, but she complained of it afterwards hurting her.
QUESTION: Could it have hurt her any worse than a stick of the same weight?
ANSWER: I dont know that.
QUESTION: Do you know of any cause she ever give the defendant for being jealous of Ike Burkham, if so state it.
ANSWER: I believe I dont know of any.
QUESTION: Was Ike Burkham at any time since complainants alledged marriage with the defendant in the habit of visiting her?
ANSWER: Not as I know of.

EXAMINATION IN CHIEF, RESUMED

QUESTION: At the time she was sweeping after he had set the grate, was not the floor muddied & dirtied up & the ashes scatered about, & was she not hurrying the work to get an opportunity to put the small children to bed?
(Question objected to)
ANSWER: Yes, after the grate was set, it was muddy & dirty, certainly & I suppose that was the reason she was sweeping up to get through.
QUESTION: Did you see anything in her conduct on that occasion indicating an intention to provoke him?
ANSWER: No, I did not notice any.
QUESTION: How long after he had thus struck her with a knife did she complain of it hurting her?
ANSWER: I believe it was the next day I heard her complaining. I am not certain. I think it was.
QUESTION: Was not the mortar used in setting that grate a mixture of mud & clay?
ANSWER: Yes, the mortar was in setting the grate, but he covered the outside with cement.
QUESTION: Was it such a nice & fancy job that a little sprinkle of ashes would [cause] an irreprable injury?
ANSWER: It was not such a fancy job, I did not think, but it was good enough, I guess.

QUESTION: Did not the drinking by her which you spoke of yesterday in your cross examination consist in this, that on one occasion she was nervous & frightened & had a cramp in her stomach & drank some liquor mixed with black pepper as a remedy on the advice of her husband & on an other occasion you had made some right nice toddy & very kindly requested her to taste of it?
ANSWER: I dont know any thing about the mixing up of the pepper, but I mind of giving her some mixed with water & a little sugar & I think I saw her drink some that had no water in once & may be twice.
QUESTION: Under any of the circumstances in which you saw her take liquor was there any thing objectionable that you noted?
ANSWER: No, I believe not.
QUESTION: How long has it been since they have not bedded together as man & wife?
ANSWER: I think it is something over a year as far as I know.

CROSS EXAMINATION, RESUMED

QUESTION: What things did she take with her when she left during this month?
ANSWER: I dont know what all she took. I think she took a feather bed, about two sheets, & a blanket, & she took some canned fruit & I think some apple butter & some quince butter, & I think she took most of a set of dishes & about 3 quilts & some other little things, & I think she took her trunk, & I think it was full of clothes & things too.
QUESTION: Did she leave any dishes in the house?
ANSWER: Yes, she left a few.
QUESTION: Were not the goods she took with her purchased by the defendant & his property?
ANSWER: Some of them were & some were not.
QUESTION: What portion of them were not his property & where were they?
ANSWER: She claimed her dishes & her trunk.
QUESTION: Who bought the dishes that she claimed?
ANSWER: I think she bought them, but I dont know who paid for them.

EXAMINATION IN CHIEF, RESUMED

QUESTION: If she only took a part of a set & there were only a few left, she had a very small stock to take from had she not?
ANSWER: Yes, there was a good many of them broke, I believe. She left two cups, & I think maybe three saucers.

QUESTION: Did she not only take five cups & saucers?
ANSWER: I dont know how many she did take.
QUESTION: Was the trunk not a small one & her own when she married your father?
ANSWER: It was hers. It was not a large trunk, just an ordinary sized one.
QUESTION: Were the sheet, blanket & 2 quilts that she took sufficient to protect her & her two little children from the cold?
ANSWER: With the bed I suppose it would be sufficient.
QUESTION: Were the quilts not those made by her since she came to your house?
ANSWER: I think they were made by her.
QUESTION: Did she take any table or has she any now in the house, & are she & the children not now using a store box for a table?
(Question objected to)
ANSWER: She took no table with her. She was using a store box for a table the last time I was at her house, but she told me she was getting one made & was to get it the day I was there, one day last week.
QUESTION: Did she take with her any bed stead or chairs?
ANSWER: No Sir, she did not.
QUESTION: Did not the def[endan]t object to her taking even as much as she did, & did you not have to intercede for her to get what she had?
ANSWER: He objected to some things. I told her to take the box & what things she had in it.
QUESTION: Were the box & contents a portion of what he objected to her taking?
ANSWER: I believe he did object to the box.
QUESTION: Were the quilts & childrens clothing in that box?
ANSWER: The quilts were, I believe. I dont know about the childrens clothing I did not see any.
QUESTION: Do you know how she is now making a living for herself & children?
(Question objected to)
ANSWER: She told me she was sewing & washing.
QUESTION: Where is George, their eldest child?
ANSWER: He is staying at his fathers.

JAMES NORMAN, RECALLED FOR CROSS EXAMINATION

QUESTION: Was you present at the marriage of the complainant & defendant?
ANSWER: No Sir.

QUESTION: Did you know complainant before she was married to your father?
ANSWER: No Sir.
QUESTION: Do you know whether she had ever been married before?
ANSWER: No Sir, only by her own say so.
QUESTION: What did she say about it?
ANSWER: She said she was married once, before she was married to my father.
QUESTION: When did she say that?
ANSWER: Some time after she was married. I cant mind the year or when it was.
QUESTION: Who did she say she had been married to before?
ANSWER: I believe she said the mans name was Forquer.
QUESTION: Was he living or dead?
ANSWER: She said he was living.
QUESTION: Did she say where?
ANSWER: I dont remember whether she said where he was living at.
QUESTION: What did she say about him & about her marriage with him?
ANSWER: I dont know of any thing particular.
QUESTION: State as near as you can, the value of all your fathers property together?
ANSWER: I dont know, but I suppose there is between 1500 & 2000 dollars.
QUESTION: Does not your father provide sufficient clothing & provisions for his family?
ANSWER: I believe he does.
QUESTION: Is not his general character towards his family good when sober?
(Question objected to)
ANSWER: Yes Sir, as a general thing.
QUESTION: What has been the character of the complainant towards him as a general thing?
ANSWER: I guess she treated him well enough.
QUESTION: Do you know why he spoke to her about Ike Burkham in the manner you have stated in your answer to the 16th chief interrogation?
ANSWER: No, I have no idea what he spoke to her in that way for.
QUESTION: Do you know of any reason he had to be jealous of Ike Burkham?

ANSWER: No Sir, I do not.

QUESTION: Do you remember of she & Ike Burkham being up stairs together when your father made her go down?

ANSWER: No Sir.

(Plaintiffs counsel objects to all cross interrogations and answers thereto in the testimony of Robert & James Norman relating to former marriage of complainant)

EXAMINATION IN CHIEF, RESUMED

QUESTION: Who is Ike Burkham, & how related to your father?

ANSWER: My fathers mother & his mother are sisters, which would make them cousins.

QUESTION: Was this conversation which you had with Mrs Norman about a former marriage not a short time after her marriage with your father, & did not your father not know all about it?

ANSWER: I could not say how long afterwards. He knew that she had been married once.

QUESTION: Why did you so long hesitate to answer Cross Interrogatory No 11?

ANSWER: Well I have not been at home any of any account for the last six years. I have been staying away from home the most of the time.

[*Mary filed her divorce petition in December 1869. When the census taker arrived on her doorstep in 1870, she was still living with John Norman, in Liberty, Ohio County. George, Ida Lee, and Charles Norman, their children, all lived with them, and John was working as a farm laborer.*[32] *In March 1872, Mary and John Norman appeared in court with their attorneys and asked that the case be dismissed. John agreed to pay the costs of the suit, fifty dollars for Peck and Cochran. By 1880, Robert Norman, John Norman's son from his first marriage, had moved to Bennington, Illinois. There, he and his wife were raising their two sons, alongside his half brother, Charles, now twelve.*[33] *The whereabouts of Charles's two siblings and their parents remain a mystery.*]

---

32. United States Federal Census for 1870.
33. United States Federal Census for 1880.

James Leasure v. Elizabeth Leasure, 1871

[Leasure, James v. Leasure, Elizabeth *(1871)*, *Records of the Circuit Court of Ohio County, WVRHC, env. 290 b-5. This case cost $44.38. James filed his petition in September 1871. The court summoned Elizabeth on August 25 and served her notice four days later.*]

Bill of Divorce

The Bill of complaint of James A. Leasure[34] against Mary W. Leasure[35] filed in the Circuit Court of Ohio County.

The plaintiff complains & says, that heretofore, to wit, on the 16th day of January 1862, at Wheeling in Ohio County, the plaintiff & the defendant herein named, were married, which will fully appear by reference to a certified copy of their marriage certificate, herewith filed & marked exhibit (1), and prayed to be made a part hereof.[36] That since the said marriage, the said plaintiff & defendant have resided in Ohio County, West Virginia, & now reside therein.

That the said plaintiff & defendant last cohabited in said County. That since the said marriage, they have had three children, to wit; William C. aged nine years, Margaret aged five years and Charles, aged three years; That the defendant, totally disregarding her marriage vows & her duty towards this plaintiff, has for a long period, to wit; for the space of two years at Ohio County aforesaid, been guilty of cruel & inhuman treatment towards this plaintiff, & has caused him to have reasonable apprehension of bodily hurt. In this, that the said defendant, has almost constantly during that time, been in a state of intoxication, produced by excessive use of intoxicating beverages, & also by the excessive use of opium in various forms; that so addicted is she to the use of these stimulants that she daily uses large quantities of Brandy, or

---

34. James, a glasshouse worker, was born in Ohio in 1832. He was twenty-eight when he married Elizabeth. James served very briefly as a corporal during the Civil War. He was a member of the First Virginia Infantry from June to August 1861. U.S. Civil War Soldier Records and Profiles; U.S. Civil War Pension Index: General Index to Pension Files.

35. Elizabeth's maiden name was Collins. It does not appear that she ever went by Mary, so this is most likely a clerical error. She was born in Belmont County, Ohio, in 1837. She was twenty-four when she married James and already a widow with a young daughter. Her first husband's last name was Winters. West Virginia Marriages Index; United States Federal Census for 1870.

36. No marriage certificate remains with the divorce records.

Whiskey, and large quantities of Laudanum,[37] rendering her entirely unfit for her duties as a wife & mother, and causing this plaintiff, to apprehend that she will inflict bodily harm to himself & his children; that sometimes she becomes so violent from the effects of intoxication, that he is utterly unable to restrain her; that at times she will become entirely insane, attack & assault this plaintiff in a most violent manner; that this plaintiff by reason of her violence, has for a long space of time, become so apprehensive that she would inflict some bodily injury upon him, that he has been compelled to live apart from her, fearing that when asleep, she in her drunken frenzy might injure him, as she has frequently attempted to do. That so disregardful is she of her duty towards this plaintiff, her said husband, and her said children, that she frequently appears on the public streets in a state of intoxication, exposing her person to the public in such a manner as to mortify and wound the feelings of this plaintiff.

That so disregardful is she of her duty towards this plaintiff, her husband, that although this plaintiff has always been a kind & dutiful husband, & has always provided & furnished her with everything necessary for her comfort, and although well knowing this plaintiff to be a man of moderate means, yet by her extravagant & foolish expenditure of money, & her utter recklessness, she has contracted large debts, which this plaintiff has been compelled to pay, although in so doing, he has been subjected to great financial embarrassment.

And this plaintiff hoped that he could dissuade her from her evil practices & could induce her to reform, so that he might live with her without apprehension of bodily harm; but so persistent has she been, that she has refused & entirely disregarded his entreaties, and still persists in her conduct as aforesaid. This plaintiff therefore prays that this Court will grant unto him a divorce a mensa et thoro & for such other relief as the Court may see fit to grant.

Pendleton[38] & Davenport, Attorneys for Plaintiff

---

37. Dormandy, *Opium: Reality's Dark Dream*.

38. Joseph Henry Pendleton was born in Louisa County, Virginia, in January 1827. By the 1850s, he had moved to Virginia's northern panhandle and become a successful (and wealthy) lawyer. Thirty-three years old at the time Virginia seceded, Pendleton moved his family to eastern Virginia and enlisted in the Confederate army, serving in Company S of the Twenty-Third Virginia Infantry. He also served as a member of the Virginia General Assembly during the war. After the war, he returned to Wheeling and took up his legal practice again. United States Federal Census for 1860; U.S. Civil War Soldier Records and

Depositions of Witnesses[39]

ROBERT H. CUMMINS

QUESTION: Are you a practising physician in this city, & if so, have you treated the defendant?

ANSWER: Yes, I have during the last two years, & have been so since her marriage.

QUESTION: Has she been in the habit of using stimulants, & if so, to what extent?

ANSWER: She has for the last two years. I have never seen her taking alcohol but from her appearance, should judge she did. I have never seen her taking laudanum, but she has confessed to me that she made immoderate use of it—& had been attempting to quit it. I have also treated her for it at the request of her husband. My visits to her home have only been for a short time & at long intervals.

QUESTION: Suppose the defendant was to be in the daily habit of using from 1 to 6 ozs of opium, what would be the consequence?

ANSWER: It would unfit her for every duty of life.

MATTIE BENEDICT

QUESTION: Have you lived with the plaintiff & the defendant, if so, how long; & when did you live there?

ANSWER: I did live there sixteen weeks, & left about the first of Jan[uar]y 1871.

QUESTION: What were Mrs Leasures habits during that time?

ANSWER: She was drinking all the time, and drank about 2 quarts a day; this would be gotten for her in a quart Bucket. When she had not the money to get that, she would get it of Mr Bocking. She would *also* use large quantities of Laudanum. She would use six bottles of Laudanum a day, 2 oz. bottles. She never was sober, being constantly drunk night and day.

QUESTION: What was her disposition?

ANSWER: There was no peace in the house with her. She was at all times

---

Profiles; United States Federal Census for 1880; U.S. Find a Grave Index; *Journal of the House of Delegates of the State of Virginia for the Called Session of 1863*, 160.

39. Robert Cummins (who also appears in *Wehner v. Wehner*, 1850), Mattie Benedict, Mrs. William Haller, Ella O'Donnell, Mattie Benedict, and Edmund Bocking testified on October 2, 1871, at the law office of Pendleton and Davenport on Fourth Street. All signed their names, except Mattie Benedict, who signed only with her mark.

very violent. She was always cross and quarrelsome, was very cross to her children & would whip them unreasonably. She was also very cross to her husband, & gave him no peace whatever.

QUESTION: How did she manage her domestic affairs?

ANSWER: He would give her $11.00 a week for marketing regularly, he being at work at Bellaire during the time. The money she spent for Laudanum & Whiskey, instead of buying her marketing with it. For one whole week she bought nothing to eat, and we had to live off of what we could borrow from the neighbors. She had three children in the house at the time. She paid no attention whatever to her household, entirely neglected her children, never paying any attention to washing, or dressing them. She would swear at times that she would burn the house down, & was only prevented from so doing by a strict watch being kept upon her. She sold all the dishes out of her house except one cup, for whiskey. She has sold the clothes off her back for the same thing.

QUESTION: Is she fit to have charge of a family?

ANSWER: I do not consider her capable of so doing. She never keeps herself clean, & she could not at times have told her & her children from beggars.

MRS. WILLIAM HALLER

QUESTION: Have you lived with the plaintiff & the def[endan]t, & if so, when did you live there?

ANSWER: I never lived there, but was called in when their little boy got hurt. I was there after that, off & on for a year. I have lived four years as a near neighbor.

QUESTION: What were Mrs Leasure's habits?

ANSWER: For the last two, or three years, she has been constantly drunk, & has been in the habit of using laudanum. I cant say the amount of liquor she uses. She uses from three to six bottles of Laudanum a day. I have often seen her staggering along the streets.

QUESTION: What is her disposition?

ANSWER: I was sitting up there one evening with her sick boy, and she was very drunk & very violent. She was always quarrelsome & violent. I have at times heard her threaten to burn the house, & never knew a man, or woman so inebriate. She was very cross to her children & often beat them. I have frequently heard her threaten her husband with violence.

QUESTION: How did she manage her domestic affairs?

ANSWER: She didn't manage them at all. She left them to her children, or let everything go to ruin. She neglected her children, & the neighbors had to take care of them. She sometimes set her clothes on fire, and was entirely unfit to look after her household affairs, to have the care & management of children. She is very profane & obscene in her language, & uses it before her children, & will often keep her children from school to send them for Whiskey.

QUESTION: How did her husband treat her?

ANSWER: He was a good husband & furnished her with everything that was necessary, & she would take the goods he bought, & sell them for whiskey. He did everything in his power to reform her. She would sell the bed clothing, some fine sheets for fifty cents, & was perfectly reckless in her domestic affairs. She was perfectly filthy in her habits & person, & let her children remain in the same condition.

ELLA O'DONNELL

QUESTION: Did you ever live with the plaintiff & defendant?

ANSWER: Yes, I lived with them about two months. I left about the last of July 1871.

QUESTION: What were Mrs Leasure's habits?

ANSWER: She had very bad habits, was always drunk, used a great deal of laudanum & whiskey, about six bottles of Laudanum & about 3 or 4 quarts of Whiskey. Everyday when her husband came home from work, he would find her drunk on the floor. She was very profane & obscene in her language, & filthy in her person.

QUESTION: What was her dispositions?

ANSWER: She had a very bad disposition, would fight with the children, or any one with whom she could get a chance, would quarrel with Mr. Leasure at the table & elsewhere, & be very violent & abusive to him.

QUESTION: How did she manage her domestic affairs?

ANSWER: She did not manage them at all. She didnt care how anything was done & let everything take care of itself. He would give her market money, and she would spend it on whiskey. She would sell her own clothing, her childrens clothing & everything in the house to get liquor. When her little child Maggie about 7 years old of age, went away; all the clothes she had, was an old pair of shoes picked up in the yard, & an old calico dress, & an old hat & a dirty underskirt & her husband was ashamed to take her on the street with him.

QUESTION: What was Mr Leasure's conduct towards his said wife?

ANSWER: He was a very good husband, provided her with every thing necessary to her comfort.

MATTIE BENEDICT, RECALLED

QUESTION: State if you have seen Mrs Leasure guilty of any improper conduct, and please state what it was.
ANSWER: Sometime last summer, I was going to the grocery about nine Oclock at night, and as I passed their house, I saw a couple of men in her back yard, and they went into a frame stable that was in the back yard, & she went in with them. I dont know how long she staid in there, as I kept on my way to the grocery.

EDMUND BOCKING

QUESTION: What is your occupation, & are you acquainted with the parties to this suit?
ANSWER: I am a Druggist & am acquainted with both the parties.
QUESTION: Please state the amount of the bill of the plaintiff in your store from January 1st 1871, until [blank].
ANSWER: Something over $100.00
QUESTION: Please state what proportion of that bill was Laudanum.
ANSWER: Three fourths. There was about $20.00 of it for Hostiller's Billers.
QUESTION: Who purchased these articles, & for whom were they?
ANSWER: They were generally gotten by the children, & were represented to be for Mrs Leasure.
QUESTION: About how much Tincture of Opium did she get a day?
ANSWER: About a quarter of a pint.
QUESTION: Have you in the course of your business known of any one using so much Laudanum per day, or nearly so much?
ANSWER: I do not.

ALLEN C. SCROGGINS[40]

QUESTION: Do you know the parties to this suit; if so, how long have you known them, & state whether you have ever lived in their house?
ANSWER: Yes, I have known Mr Leasure for five years, & Mrs Leasure for one & half years. I have lived in their house from July 11th 1871 to August 14th 1871.

---

40. Allen Scroggins, Sallie Scroggins, Nettie Sleepack, Mrs. John Boring, and Anna Arbison testified on October 3, 1871. All signed their names.

QUESTION: Please state what were Mrs. Leasure's habits?
ANSWER: She drinks, & uses Laudanum. She is most of the time under the influence of liquor; she is very crabid, disagreeable & violent while under its influence.
QUESTION: How did she manage her domestic affairs?
ANSWER: Very poorly as to taking care of her house & children. I went there with my wife for the purpose of taking care of the house & the youngest child because she would not look after them & left on account of her violence & bad behavior. Mr Leasure's desire was what brought us there.
QUESTION: What kind of language does she use?
ANSWER: She uses profane language & is abusive to her husband, & is often obscene in her talk, and is not capable of taking care of a house & children.

SALLIE SCROGGINS

QUESTION: Do you know the parties to this suit; if so, how long have you known them, & state whether you have ever lived in their house?
ANSWER: I have known Mr Leasure for two years, & have seen Mrs Leasure frequently, but never was acquainted with her until I moved to her house last July, where I remained about one month.
QUESTION: Please state what were Mrs Leasure's habits.
ANSWER: She was always trying to borrow money of me to buy liquor. She has been in the habit of getting drunk. I have seen her lying on the floor in a state of intoxication. She was at those times very hateful in her behavior to me.
QUESTION: How did she manage her domestic affairs?
ANSWER: When myself & husband were there she didn't look after her house at all, everything was left lying around loose & dirty.
QUESTION: How did she take care of her little child?
ANSWER: She paid but little attention to him, would seldom wash & clean him, & several times swore at me & threatened me when I wished to wash him. She was very uncleanly & untidy herself, extremely dirty.
QUESTION: What kind of language did she use?
ANSWER: She frequently used profane & obscene language to me & her husband. She was very vulgar in her language.
QUESTION: Did you think her fit to manage a house, or have charge of children?
ANSWER: I do not. I think she was not fit to have charge of any house

or any child by reason of her drunkenness. I have heard her threaten to burn the house down.

NETTIE SLEEPACK

QUESTION: How long have you known the parties to this suit, & whether you have lived in their neighborhood?
ANSWER: I have known Mr & Mrs Leasure for about three years, & have lived near them ever since I knew them.
QUESTION: What have been Mrs Leasure's habits during that time?
ANSWER: She has been drinking ever since I knew her, uses immoderate quantities of Laudanum. She would sometimes when intoxicated act very violently, & at other times would not.
QUESTION: How did she manage her domestic affairs?
ANSWER: She would sometimes let the children run around very dirty, at other times she would have them clean.
QUESTION: What kind of language did she use?
ANSWER: I never heard her use good language often. I have heard her swear about her husband, but have never heard her swear at him, because I was not there. She was very vulgar in her talk. She has sworn to burn down both her house & mine. I know of her pawning her shawl & a black Alpaca dress for liquor.

ELIZA BORING

QUESTION: Do you know the parties to this suit, & how long have you known them?
ANSWER: Yes, I have known them for a number of years. She rented a house from me for over a year.
QUESTION: State her habits & mode of life.
ANSWER: When she moved into my house she was seldom drunk. She afterwards came to drink excessively & neglected her duties as a wife & mother, & [I] have seen her have three bottles of brandy taken from Mr Bocking's. She would drink beer as one drank water. I have seen her swallow a pint at the barrel, at the time, & then start home from my house with another pint in her hand.

ANNA ARBISON

QUESTION: If you have lived with the plaintiff & defendant, please state how long.
ANSWER: I went there in October & left in March 1871.
QUESTION: What were Mrs Leasure's habits during that time?

ANSWER: She drank to excess all the time. She also used Laudanum. I have known her frequently to be in a state of intoxication. When she was drunk, she was sometimes very violent, at other times she would not be so. As a wife she was very negligent. She used very profane & obscene language. Also, towards the latter part of the time I was there, she paid no attention to her household affairs.
QUESTION: What kind of a husband was Mr Leasure?
ANSWER: He was as good a husband as ever a woman had.

[*After these October 1871 depositions, there are no further documents in this case. According to the 1880 census, James Leasure and his son, William, were living as boarders in John Boring's house. James was still listed as "married."*[41] *Elizabeth Leasure died in 1884. After her death, James was promoted and became the manager of the local glass factory. He also remarried. When he died in 1896, he left a generous will. In it, he distributed his money among his children—and stepchildren, including Alice, Elizabeth's daughter from her first marriage. He also left his piano to his "beloved wife," Margaret E. Leasure.*[42] *Despite the conflict revealed in this case, James was buried with his first wife, Elizabeth, in Peninsula Cemetery. Their joint headstone reads: "Till the day break and the shadows flee away."*[43]]

---

41. John Boring's wife, Eliza, had testified in the original divorce suit. United States Federal Census for 1880.

42. U.S. City Directories; West Virginia Deaths Index; West Virginia Wills and Probate Records.

43. U.S. Find a Grave Index.

APPENDIX A

The Code of Virginia, 1849

Chapter CIX. Of Divorces.

1. All marriages between a white person and a negro, and all marriages which are prohibited by law on account of either of the parties having a former wife or husband then living, shall be absolutely void, without any decree of divorce, or other legal process. All marriages which are prohibited by law on account of consanguinity or affinity between the parties, all marriages solemnized when either of the parties was insane, or inescapable from physical causes of entering into the marriage state, shall, if solemnized within this state, be void from the time they shall be so declared by a decree of divorce or nullity, or from the time of the conviction of the parties under the third section of the one hundred and ninety-sixth chapter.
2. If any person resident in this state, and being within the degree of relationship within which marriages are prohibited by law, shall, in order to evade the law, and with an intention of returning to reside in this state, go into another state or country, and there intermarry, and shall afterwards return and reside here, cohabiting as man and wife, such marriage shall be governed by the same law, in all respects, as if it had been solemnized in this state.
3. In case of a marriage solemnized when either of the parties was under the age of consent, if they shall separate during such nonage, and not cohabit afterwards, the marriage shall be deemed void, without any decree of divorce or other legal process. The age of consent of the male shall be fourteen years, and of the female twelve years.
4. When a marriage is supposed to be void for any of the causes mentioned in the foregoing sections of this chapter, either party may institute a suit for annulling the same; and, upon due proof of the nullity of the marriage, it shall be decreed to be void by a decree of divorce or nullity. But a party who at the time of marriage, as men-

tioned in the third section, was capable of consenting, with a party not so capable, shall not have power to institute such suit, for the purpose of annulling such marriage.

5. When the validity of any marriage shall be denied or doubted by either of the parties, the other party may institute a suit for affirming the marriage; and, upon due proof of the validity thereof, it shall be decreed to be valid; and such decree shall be conclusive upon all persons concerned.

6. A divorce from the bond of matrimony may be decreed for adultery; for natural or incurable impotency of body existing at the time of entering into the marital contract; where either of the parties is sentenced to confinement in the penitentiary for life or for seven years or more; and no pardon granted to the party so sentenced, after a divorce for that cause, shall restore such party to his or her conjugal rights.

7. A divorce from bed and board may be decreed for cruelty, reasonable apprehension of bodily hurt, abandonment, or desertion.

8. The circuit courts, on the chancery side thereof, shall have jurisdiction of suits for annulling or affirming marriages, or for divorces. No such suit shall be maintainable unless the parties have cohabited as husband and wife in this state, nor unless the plaintiff is a resident of the state at the time of bringing the suit. The suit shall be brought in the county or corporation in which the parties last cohabited, or (at the option of the plaintiff) in the county or corporation in which the defendant resides, if a resident of this state; but if not, then in the county or corporation in which the plaintiff resides.

9. Such suit shall be instituted and conducted as other suits in equity, except that the bill shall not be taken for confessed, and, whether the defendant answer or not, the cause shall be heard independently of the admissions of either party, in the pleadings or otherwise. Costs may be awarded to either party, as equity or justice may require.

10. The court in term or the judge in vacation, may, at any time pending the suit, make any order that may be proper to compel the man to pay any sums necessary for the maintenance of the woman, and to enable her to carry on the suit, or to prevent him from imposing any restraint on her personal liberty, or to provide for the custody and maintenance of the minor children of the parties, during the pendency of the suit, or to preserve the estate of the man, so that it

be forthcoming to meet any decree which may be made in the suit, or to compel him to give security to abide such decree.

11. When the suit is for a divorce for adultery, the divorce shall not be granted if it appear that the parties voluntarily cohabited after the knowledge of the fact of adultery, or that it occurred more than five years before the institution of the suit, or that it was committed by the procurement or connivance of the plaintiff.

12. Upon decreeing the dissolution of a marriage, and also upon decreeing a divorce, whether from the bond of matrimony or from bed and board, the court may make such further decree as it shall deem expedient, concerning the estate and maintenance of the parties or either of them, and the care, custody and maintenance of their minor children, and may determine with which of the parents the children, or any of them, shall remain; and the court may, from time to time afterwards, on the petition of either of the parents, revise and alter such decree concerning the care, custody and maintenance of the children, and make a new decree concerning the same, as the circumstances of the parents and the benefits of the children may require.

13. In granting a divorce from bed and board, the court may decree that the parties be perpetually separated and protected in their persons and property. Such decree shall operate upon property thereafter acquired, and upon the personal rights and legal capacities of the parties, as a divorce from the bond of matrimony, except that neither party shall marry again during the life of the other.

14. In granting a divorce for adultery, the court may decree that the guilty party shall not marry again; in which case, the bond of matrimony shall be deemed not to be dissolved as to any future marriage of such party, or in any prosecution on account thereof.

15. When a decree for a separation forever, or for a limited period, shall have been pronounced in a suit for divorce from bed and board, it may be revoked at any time thereafter by the same court by which it was pronounced, under such regulations and restrictions as the court may impose, upon the joint application of the parties, and upon their producing satisfactory evidence of their reconciliation.

APPENDIX B

The Code of West Virginia, 1870

Chapter LXIV. Of Divorces.

1. All marriages between a white person and a negro; all marriages which are prohibited by law on account of either of the parties having a former wife or husband then living; all marriages which are prohibited by law on account of consanguinity or affinity between the parties; all marriages solemnized when either of the parties was insane, or incapable from physical causes of entering into the marriage state, or under the age of consent, shall, if solemnized within this state, be void from the time they are so declared by a decree of divorce or nullity.
2. The age of consent of the male shall be fourteen years, and of the female twelve years.
3. If any persons resident in this state shall, in order to evade the law, and with an intention of returning to reside in this state, go into another state or country, and there intermarry in violation of the provisions of the first section of this chapter, and shall afterwards return and reside here, cohabiting as man and wife, such marriage shall be governed by the same law, in all respects, as if it had been solemnized in this state.
4. When a marriage is supposed to be void, or any doubt exists as to its validity, for any of the causes mentioned in the first section of this chapter, either party may institute a suit for affirming or annulling the same, and upon hearing the proofs and allegations of the parties, the court shall render a decree affirming or annulling the marriage, according to the right of the case. In every such case, and in every other case where the validity of a marriage is called in question, it shall be presumed that the marriage is valid, unless the contrary be clearly proven.
5. A divorce from the bond of matrimony may be decreed for adultery,

or for natural or incurable impotency of body, existing at the time of entering into the matrimonial contract; where either of the parties is sentenced to confinement in the penitentiary, (and no pardon granted to the party so sentenced shall restore such party to his or her conjugal rights); where, prior to the marriage, either party, without the knowledge of the other, had been convicted of an infamous offense; where either party willfully abandons or deserts the other for three years, a divorce may be decreed to the party abandoned; where, at the time of marriage, the wife, without the knowledge of the husband, was enceinte by some person other than the husband, or prior to such marriage had been, without the knowledge of the husband; or where, prior to such marriage, the husband, without the knowledge of the wife, had been notoriously a licentious person, such divorce may be decreed to the wife: but no such divorce shall be decreed if it appear that the party applying for the same has cohabited with the other after knowledge of such conviction of an infamous offense, or has cohabited with the wife after knowledge of the fact that she was enceinte or had been a prostitute, or has cohabited with the husband after knowledge of the fact that he had been notoriously a licentious person as aforesaid.

6. A divorce from bed and board may be decreed for cruel or inhuman treatment, reasonable apprehension of bodily hurt, abandonment, or desertion. A charge of prostitution made by the husband against the wife, falsely, shall be deemed cruel treatment within the meaning of this section.

7. The circuit court, on the chancery side thereof, shall have jurisdiction of suits for annulling or affirming marriages, or for divorces. No such suit shall be maintainable unless the parties, or one of them, is a resident of the state at the time of bringing the suit. The suit shall be brought in the county in which the parties last cohabited, or, (at the option of the plaintiff,) in the county in which the defendant resides, if a resident of this state; but if not, then in the county in which the plaintiff resides. Such suit may be brought and prosecuted by the wife in her own name, without a next friend, and a decree may be rendered in the case upon the publication of the summons and statement as provided in chapter one hundred and twenty-four of this act.

8. Such suit shall be instituted and conducted as other suits in equity, except that the bill shall not be taken for confessed, and whether the

defendant answer or not, the cause shall be heard independently of the admissions of either party, in the pleadings or otherwise. Costs may be awarded to either party, as equity and justice may require.

9. The court in term, or the judge in vacation, may, at any time pending the suit, make any order that may be proper to compel the man to pay any sum necessary for the maintenance of the woman, and to enable her to carry on the suit, or to prevent him from imposing any restraint on her personal liberty, or to provide for the custody and maintenance of the minor children of the parties, during the pendency of the suit, or to preserve the estate of the man, so that it be forthcoming to meet any decree which may be made in the suit, or to compel him to give security to abide such decree.

10. When the suit is for a divorce for adultery, the divorce shall not be granted if it appear that the parties voluntarily cohabited after the knowledge of the fact of adultery, or that it occurred more than five years before the institution of the suit, or that it was committed by the procurement or connivance of the plaintiff.

11. Upon decreeing the dissolution of a marriage, and also upon decreeing a divorce, whether from the bond of matrimony or from bed and board, the court may make such further decree as it shall deem expedient, concerning the estate and maintenance of the parties, or either of them, and the care, custody, and maintenance of the minor children, and may determine with which of the parents the children, or any of them, may remain; and the court may, from time to time afterwards, on the petition of either of the parents, revise and alter such decree concerning the care, custody, and maintenance of the children, and make a new decree concerning the same, as the circumstances of the parents and the benefit of the children may require.

12. In granting a divorce from bed and board, the court may decree that the parties be perpetually separated and protected in their persons and property. Such decree shall operate upon property thereafter acquired, and upon the personal rights and legal capacities of the parties, as a decree for a divorce from the bond of matrimony, except that neither party shall marry again during the life of the other.

13. When a decree from a separation forever, or for a limited period, shall have been pronounced in a suit for a divorce from bed and board, it may be revoked at any time thereafter by the same court by which it was pronounced, under such regulations and restrictions

as the court may impose, upon the joint application of the parties, and upon their producing satisfactory evidence of their reconciliation; and when a divorce from bed and board has been decreed for abandonment or desertion, and three years shall have elapsed from the abandonment or desertion, without such reconciliation, the court may, upon the application of the injured party, and the production of satisfactory evidence, whether taken theretofore or in support of such application, decree a divorce from the bond of matrimony; provided the court shall be of the opinion that such a decree would have been proper when the decree from bed and board was pronounced had three years then elapsed and the whole evidence adduced upon said application been before the court, and that no reconciliation is probable.

Bibliography

Primary Sources

GOVERNMENT DOCUMENTS

Acts and Joint Resolutions Passed by the General Assembly of the State of Virginia during the Extra Session of 1902-3-4. Richmond: J. H. O'Bannon, 1902.
Ambler, Charles H., Frances H. Atwood, and William B. Mathews, eds. *Debates and Proceedings of the First Constitutional Convention of West Virginia (1861–1863)*. Huntington, W.Va.: Gentry Bros., 1939.
The Code of Virginia. Richmond: William F. Ritchie, 1849.
The Code of Virginia. Richmond: Ritchie, Dunnavant and Co., 1860.
The Code of West Virginia. Wheeling: J. Frew, 1871.
Journal of the Constitutional Convention, Assembled at Charleston, West Virginia, January 16, 1872. Charleston: H. S. Walker, 1872.
Journal of the House of Delegates of the State of Virginia for the Called Session of 1863. Richmond: William F. Ritchie, 1863.
Journal of the House of Delegates of Virginia, 1850–1851. Richmond: William F. Ritchie, 1851.
Pennsylvania v. Wheeling and the Belmont Bridge. 54 U.S. 518. 1852.
The Revised Statutes of Kentucky. Cincinnati: Robert Clarke and Co., 1860.

MANUSCRIPTS, NEWSPAPERS, AND ARCHIVES

Library of Virginia
Fauquier County Circuit Court Records
West Virginia and Regional History Center (WVRHC), West Virginia University Libraries, Morgantown, W.Va.
Francis H. Pierpont Civil War Telegrams
Records of the Circuit Court of Ohio County: Case Files 1850–73
Wheeling Intelligencer (1856, 1866–67, 1869–70)
Wheeling Daily Register (1902)
Wheeling Register (1868, 1897)

PUBLISHED PRIMARY DOCUMENTS

Atkinson, George W., ed. *Bench and Bar of West Virginia*. Charleston, W.Va.: Virginian Law Book Co., 1919.
Atkinson, George W., and Alvaro F. Gibbens. *Prominent Men of West Virginia: Biographical Sketches of Representative Men in Every Honorable Vocation, includ-*

ing Politics, the Law, Theology, Medicine, Education, Finance, Journalism, Trade, Commerce and Agriculture. Wheeling, W.Va.: W. L. Callin, 1890.

Biographical and Portrait Cyclopedia of Monongalia, Marion, and Taylor Counties, West Virginia. Philadelphia: Rush, West & Co., 1895.

Blackstone, William. *Commentaries on the Laws of England*. Edited by W. G. Hammond. San Francisco: Bancroft-Whitney Company, 1898.

Cranmer, G. L. *History of the Upper Ohio Valley*, vol. 1. Madison: Brant & Fuller, 1890.

Cranmer, G. L., ed. *History of Wheeling City and Ohio County, West Virginia*. Chicago: Biographical Publishing Company, 1902.

Davis, Rebecca Harding. *Bits of Gossip*. Boston: Houghton, Mifflin & Co., 1904.

Federal Cases Comprising Cases Argued and Determined in the Circuit and District Courts of the United States, Book 24. St. Paul, Minn.: West Publishing Co., 1896.

Garland, David Shepard, and Thomas Johnson Michie. *The American and English Encyclopaedia of Law*. Long Island, N.Y.: Edward Thompson Co., 1903.

History of West Virginia, Old and New, vol. 2. Chicago: American Historical Society, 1923.

Lewis, Virgil A. *History and Government of West Virginia*. Chicago: Werner School Book Co., 1896.

Luther, Martin. *Martin Luther's Table Talk: Abridged from Luther's Works, Volume 54*. Minneapolis: Fortress Press, 2017.

Negley, W. B. *Allegheny County: Its Formation, Its Cities, Wards, Boroughs, and Townships*. Pittsburgh: G. M. Hopkins & Co., 1876.

Reeve, Tapping. *The Law of Baron and Femme, of Parent and Child, Guardian and Ward, Master and Servant, and of the Powers of the Courts of Chancery; with an Essay on the Terms Heir, Heirs, Heirs of the Body*. Albany: William Gould, 1862.

Representative Men of the South. Philadelphia: Chas. Robson & Co., 1880.

Sanger, William W. *The History of Prostitution: Its Extent, Causes, and Effects throughout the World*. New York: Medical Publishing, 1921.

Stanton, Elizabeth Cady. "The Need of Liberal Divorce Laws." *North American Review* 139, no. 334 (September 1884): 234–45.

Stowe, Harriet Beecher. *Uncle Tom's Cabin*. New York: Dover, 2005.

Ulman, H. Charles. *Lawyers' Record and Official Register of the United States*. New York: A. S. Barnes & Co., 1872.

Wagner, Frank, ed. *Official Reports of the Supreme Court*. Washington, D.C.: United States Government Printing Office, 2009.

WEBSITES

Ancestry.com Databases
Civil War Pension Index
1860 United States Federal Census—Slave Schedules
General Index to Pension Files, 1861–1934
1980s Veterans Schedules

Ohio, U.S., County Marriage Records, 1774–1993
Ohio Wills and Probate Records, 1786–1998
Pennsylvania Death Certificates, 1906–68
Presbyterian Ministerial Directory, 1898
Saarland, Germany, Births, Marriages, and Deaths, 1776–1875
Schedules Enumerating Union Veterans and Widows of Union Veterans of the Civil War, 1890
United States Federal Census for 1830, 1840, 1850, 1860, 1870, 1880, 1900, and 1910
U.S. City Directories, 1822–1995
U.S. Civil War Draft Registrations Records, 1863–65
U.S. Civil War Soldiers, 1861–65
U.S. Civil War Soldier Records and Profiles, 1861–65
U.S. Encyclopedia of American Quaker Genealogy, Vol. 1–6, 1607–1943
U.S. Find a Grave Index, 1600s–current
U.S. Freedmen's Bureau Marriage Records, 1846–67
U.S. IRS Tax Assessment Lists, 1862–1918
U.S. School Catalogs, 1765–1935
Veterans Administration Pension Payment Cards, 1907–33
Virginia Death Records, 1912–2014
West Virginia Births Index, 1804–1938
West Virginia City Directory, 1898
West Virginia Compiled Marriage Records, 1863–1900
West Virginia Deaths Index, 1853–1973
West Virginia Marriages Index, 1785–1971
West Virginia Naturalization Records, 1814–1991
West Virginia Wills and Probate Records, 1724–1985
Williams' Wheeling Directory City Guide and Business Mirror for 1864

Secondary Sources

Ambler, Charles H. *Sectionalism in Virginia from 1776–1861*. Chicago: University of Chicago Press, 1910.
Ambler, Charles H., and Festus P. Summers. *West Virginia: The Mountain State*. Glenwood Cliffs, N.J.: Prentice-Hall, 1958.
Astor, Aaron. *Rebels on the Border: Civil War, Emancipation, and the Reconstruction of Kentucky and Missouri*. Baton Rouge: Louisiana State University Press, 2012.
Attie, Jeanie. *Patriotic Toil: Northern Women and the American Civil War*. Ithaca, N.Y.: Cornell University Press, 1998.
Bardaglio, Peter W. *Reconstructing the Household: Families, Sex, and the Law in the Nineteenth-Century South*. Chapel Hill: University of North Carolina Press, 1995.
Barton, Keith C. "'Good Cooks and Washers': Slave Hiring, Domestic Labor, and the Market in Bourbon County, Kentucky," *Journal of American History* 84, no. 2 (September 1997): 436–60.

Basch, Norma. *Framing American Divorce: From the Revolutionary Generation to the Victorians*. Berkeley: University of California Press, 1999.

——. *In the Eyes of the Law: Women, Marriage, and Property in Nineteenth-Century New York*. Ithaca, N.Y.: Cornell University Press, 1982.

——. "Relief in the Premises: Divorce as a Woman's Remedy in New York and Indiana, 1815–1870." *Law and History Review* 8, no. 1 (Spring 1990): 1–24.

"Battle Unit Details." National Park Service. https://www.nps.gov/civilwar/search-battle-units-detail.htm?battleUniteCode=UWV0001RAL. Accessed June 12, 2019.

Bercaw, Nancy. *Gendered Freedoms: Race, Rights, and the Politics of Household in the Delta, 1861–1875*. Gainesville: University Press of Florida, 2003.

Berry, Mary Frances. *The Pig Farmer's Daughter and Other Tales of American Justice: Episodes of Racism and Sexism in the Courts from 1865 to the Present*. New York: Knopf, 1999.

Blake, Nelson. *The Road to Reno: A History of Divorce in the United States*. New York: Macmillan, 1962.

Block, Sharon. "Lines of Color, Sex, and Service: Comparative Sexual Coercion in Early America." In *Sex, Love, Race: Crossing Boundaries in North American History*, edited by Martha Hodes, 141–63. New York: New York University Press, 1999.

Boswell, Angela. *Her Act and Deed: Women's Lives in a Rural Southern County, 1837–1873*. College Station: Texas A&M University Press, 2001.

Boydston, Jeanne. *Home and Work: Housework, Wages, and the Ideology of Labor in the Early Republic*. New York: Oxford University Press, 1990.

Broomall, James J. *Private Confederacies: The Emotional Worlds of Southern Men as Citizens and Soldiers*. Chapel Hill: University of North Carolina Press, 2019.

Buckley, Thomas E. *The Great Catastrophe of My Life: Divorce in the Old Dominion*. Chapel Hill: University of North Carolina Press, 2001.

Burke, Diane Mutti. *On Slavery's Border: Missouri's Small-Slaveholding Households, 1815–1865*. Athens: University of Georgia Press, 2010.

Bynum, Victoria. "Reshaping the Bonds of Womanhood: Divorce in Reconstruction North Carolina." In *Divided Houses: Gender and the Civil War*, edited by Catherine Clinton and Nina Silber, 320–33. New York: Oxford University Press, 1992.

Cabiniss, Allen, and Ernest Easterly III. "Fraternal Groups." In *The New Encyclopedia of Southern Culture. Vol. 4, Myth, Manners, and Memory*, edited by Charles Reagan Wilson, 70-74. Chapel Hill: University of North Carolina Press, 2006.

Carlson, A. Cheree. *The Crimes of Womanhood: Defining Femininity in a Court of Law*. Urbana: University of Illinois Press, 2009.

Carroll, Dillon J. *Invisible Wounds: Mental Illness and Civil War Soldiers*. Baton Rouge: Louisiana State University Press, 2021.

Catte, Elizabeth. *What You Are Getting Wrong about Appalachia*. Cleveland, OH: Belt Publishing, 2018.

Censer, Jane Turner. *The Reconstruction of White Southern Womanhood, 1865–1895*. Baton Rouge: Louisiana State University Press, 2003.

———. "'Smiling through Her Tears': Ante-Bellum Southern Women and Divorce." *American Journal of Legal History* 25 (January 1981): 24–47.
Chused, Richard H. "Married Women's Property Law: 1800–1850." *Georgetown Law Journal* 71 (June 1983): 1359–425.
———. *Private Acts in Public Places: A Social History of Divorce in the Formative Era of American Family Law*. Philadelphia: University of Pennsylvania Press, 1994.
Clinton, Catherine. *Plantation Mistress: Woman's World in the Old South*. New York: Pantheon, 1982.
Cohen, Patricia Cline. *The Murder of Helen Jewett*. New York: Vintage, 1999.
Cohn, Henry S. "Connecticut's Divorce Mechanism: 1636–1969." *American Journal of Legal History* 14, no. 1 (January 1970): 35–54.
Conley, Phil, and William Thomas Doherty. *West Virginia History*. Charleston, W.Va.: Education Foundation, 1974.
Coontz, Stephanie. *Marriage: A History*. New York: Viking, 2005.
Cott, Nancy. *The Bonds of Womanhood: "Woman's Sphere" in New England, 1780–1835*. New Haven, Conn.: Yale University Press, 1977.
———. "Divorce and the Changing Status of Women in Eighteenth-Century Massachusetts." *William and Mary Quarterly* 33 (1976): 586–614.
———. "Eighteenth-Century Family and Social Life Revealed in Massachusetts Divorce Records." *Journal of Social History* 10 (Fall 1976): 20–43.
———. "Passionlessness: An Interpretation of Victorian Sexual Ideology, 1790–1850." *Signs* 4, no. 2 (Winter 1978): 219–36.
———. *Public Vows: A History of Marriage and the Nation*. Cambridge, Mass.: Harvard University Press, 2000.
Cox, Karen L. *Dixie's Daughters: The United Daughters of the Confederacy and the Preservation of Confederate Culture*. Gainesville: University Press of Florida, 2019.
Currie-McDaniel, Ruth. "Northern Women in the South, 1860-1880." *Georgia Historical Quarterly* 76, no. 2 (1992): 284-312.
Curry, Richard Orr. *A House Divided: A Study of Statehood Politics and the Copperhead Movement in West Virginia*. Pittsburgh: University of Pittsburgh Press, 1964.
Daniels, Roger. *Coming to America: A History of Immigration and Ethnicity in American Life*. New York: HarperCollins, 1991.
Davy, Daniel. *Gold Rush Societies and Migrant Networks in the Tasman World*. Edinburgh: Edinburgh University Press, 2021.
Dayton, Cornelia Hughes. *Women before the Bar: Gender, Law, and Society in Connecticut, 1639–1789*. Chapel Hill: University of North Carolina Press, 1995.
Delfino, Susanna, Michele Gillespie, and Louis Kyriakoudes. "Editors' Introduction." In *Southern Society and Its Transformations, 1790–1860*, edited by Susanna Delfino, Michele Gillespie, and Louis Kyriakoudes, 9–22. Columbia: University of Missouri Press, 2011.
D'Emilio, John, and Estelle Freedman. *Intimate Matters: A History of Sexuality in America*. Chicago: University of Chicago Press, 1998.

Dormandy, Thomas. *Opium: Reality's Dark Dream*. New Haven, Conn.: Yale University Press, 2012.
Doyle, Nora. *Maternal Bodies: Redefining Motherhood in Early America*. Chapel Hill: University of North Carolina Press, 2018.
DuBois, Ellen. *Feminism and Suffrage: The Emergence of an Independent Women's Movement in America, 1848–1869*. Ithaca, N.Y.: Cornell University Press, 1999.
Dunaway, Wilma A. *The African-American Family in Slavery and Emancipation*. New York: Cambridge University Press, 2003.
——. *Women, Work, and Family in the Antebellum Mountain South*. Cambridge: Cambridge University Press, 2008.
Edwards, Laura. *Gendered Strife and Confusion: The Political Culture of Reconstruction*. Urbana: University of Illinois Press, 1997.
——. "Law, Domestic Violence, and the Limits of Patriarchal Authority in the Antebellum South." *Journal of Southern History* 65 (1999): 733–70.
——. "'The Marriage Covenant Is at the Foundation of All Our Rights': The Politics of Slavery Marriages in North Carolina after Emancipation." *Law and History Review* 14 (1996): 81–124.
——. *The People and Their Peace: Legal Culture and the Transformation of Inequality in the Post-revolutionary South*. Chapel Hill: University of North Carolina Press, 2009.
——. *Scarlett Doesn't Live Here Anymore: Southern Women in the Civil War Era*. Urbana: University of Illinois Press, 2000.
Farnham, Christie. *The Education of the Southern Belle: Higher Education and Student Socialization in the Antebellum South*. New York: New York University Press, 1994.
Faust, Drew Gilpin. *Mothers of Invention: Women of the Slaveholding South in the American Civil War*. Chapel Hill: University of North Carolina Press, 1996.
Fetherling, George. *Wheeling: An Illustrated History*. New York: Windsor, 1983.
Foner, Eric. *Reconstruction: America's Unfinished Revolution, 1863–1877*. New York: Harper and Row, 1988.
Fones-Wolf, Ken. "Caught between Revolutions: Wheeling Germans in the Civil War Era." In *Transnational West Virginia: Ethnic Communities and Economic Change, 1840–1940*, edited by Ken Fones-Wolf and Ronald L. Lewis, 19–40. Morgantown: West Virginia University Press, 2003.
Fones-Wolf, Ken, and Ronald L. Lewis. "Introduction: Networks Large and Small." In *Transnational West Virginia: Ethnic Communities and Economic Change, 1840–1940*, edited by Ken Fones-Wolf and Ronald L. Lewis, ix-xiii. Morgantown: West Virginia University Press, 2003.
Ford, Bridget. *Bonds of Union: Religion, Race, and Politics in a Civil War Borderland*. Chapel Hill: University of North Carolina Press, 2016.
Fox-Genovese, Elizabeth. *Within the Plantation Household: Black and White Women of the Old South*. Chapel Hill: University of North Carolina Press, 1988.
Frankel, Noralee. *Freedom's Women: Black Women and Families in Civil War Era Mississippi*. Bloomington: Indiana University Press, 1999.
Fredette, Allison. "Breaking Vows: Divorce and Separation in the Postrevolutionary United States." In *A Cultural History of Marriage in the Age of Enlight-

enment, edited by Edward Behrend-Martinez, 103-14. London: Bloomsbury Academic, 2020.

Fredette, Allison Dorothy. *Marriage on the Border: Love, Mutuality, and Divorce in the Upper South during the Civil War*. Lexington: University Press of Kentucky, 2020.

Garrison, Zachary Stuart. *German Americans on the Middle Border: From Antislavery to Reconciliation, 1830-1877*. Carbondale: Southern Illinois University, 2019.

Genovese, Eugene. "'Our Family, White and Black': Family and Household in the Southern Slaveholders' World View." In *In Joy and in Sorrow: Women, Family, and Marriage in the Victorian South, 1830-1900*, edited by Carol Bleser, 69-87. New York: Oxford University Press, 1991.

Giesberg, Judith. *Army at Home: Women and the Civil War on the Northern Home Front*. Chapel Hill: University of North Carolina Press, 2012.

Ginzberg, Lori D. *Women and the Work of Benevolence: Morality, Politics, and Class in the Nineteenth-Century United States*. New Haven, Conn.: Yale University Press, 1990.

Glymph, Thavolia. *Out of the House of Bondage: The Transformation of the Plantation Household*. New York: Cambridge University Press, 2008.

———. *The Women's Fight: The Civil War's Battles for Home, Freedom, and Nation*. Chapel Hill: University of North Carolina Press, 2020.

Goodheart, Lawrence B., Neil Hanks, and Elizabeth Johnson. "'An Act for the Relief of Females . . .': Divorce and the Changing Legal Status of Women in Tennessee, 1796–1860, Part 1." *Tennessee Historical Quarterly* 44, no. 3 (Fall 1985): 318-39.

Griswold, Robert L. "Divorce and the Legal Redefinition of Victorian Manhood." In *Meanings for Manhood: Construction of Masculinity in Victorian America*, edited by Mark Carnes and Clyde Griffin, 205–11. Chicago: University of Chicago Press, 1990.

———. *Family and Divorce in California, 1850–1890: Victorian Illusions and Everyday Realities*. Albany: State University of New York Press, 1982.

Grossberg, Michael. *Governing the Hearth: Law and the Family in Nineteenth-Century America*. Chapel Hill: University of North Carolina Press, 1985.

———. "Who Gets the Child? Custody, Guardianship, and the Rise of a Judicial Patriarchy in Nineteenth-Century America." *Feminist Studies* 9 (1983): 235–60.

Hartog, Hendrik. *Man and Wife in America: A History*. Cambridge, Mass.: Harvard University Press, 2000.

Henwood, Dawn. "Slaveries 'in the Borders': Rebecca Harding Davis's 'Life in the Iron Mills' in Its Southern Context." *Mississippi Quarterly* 52, no. 4 (Fall 1999): 567–592.

Hodes, Martha. *White Women, Black Men: Illicit Sex in the Nineteenth-Century South*. New Haven, Conn.: Yale University Press, 1997.

Hoff, Joan. *Law, Gender, and Injustice: A Legal History of U.S. Women*. New York: New York University Press, 1991.

Howe, Barbara J. "Patient Laborers: Women at Work in the Formal Economy of West(ern) Virginia." In N*either Lady nor Slave: Working Women in the Old*

South, edited by Susanna Delfino and Michele Gillespie, 121–51. Chapel Hill: University of North Carolina, 2002.

Hunter, Tera. *Bound in Wedlock: Slave and Free Black Marriage in the Nineteenth Century*. Cambridge, Mass.: Harvard University Press, 2017.

———. *To 'Joy My Freedom: Southern Black Women's Lives and Labors after the Civil War*. Cambridge, Mass.: Harvard University Press, 1998.

Janney, Caroline. *Burying the Dead but Not the Past: Ladies' Memorial Associations and the Lost Cause*. Chapel Hill: University of North Carolina Press, 2012.

Johansen, Shawn. *Family Men: Middle-Class Fatherhood in Early Industrializing America*. New York: Routledge, 2001.

Jones, Jacqueline. *Labor of Love, Labor of Sorrow: Black Women, Work, and the Family from Slavery to the Present*. New York: Vintage, 1985.

———. *Soldiers of Light and Love: Northern Teachers and Georgia Blacks, 1865–1873*. Chapel Hill: University of North Carolina Press, 1980.

Jones, Mary Somerville. *An Historical Geography of the Changing Divorce Law in the United States*. New York: Garland, 1987.

Jones-Rogers, Stephanie. *They Were Her Property: White Women as Slave Owners in the American South*. New Haven, Conn.: Yale University Press, 2019.

Kann, Mark E. *A Republic of Men: The American Founders, Gendered Language, and Patriarchal Politics*. New York: New York University Press, 1998.

Kelley, Mary. *Learning to Stand and Speak: Women, Education, and Public Life in America's Republic*. Chapel Hill: University of North Carolina Press, 2006.

Kerber, Linda K. "Separate Spheres, Female Worlds, Woman's Place: The Rhetoric of Women's History." *Journal of American History* 75 (June 1988): 9–39.

———. *Women of the Republic: Intellect and Ideology in Revolutionary America*. Chapel Hill: University of North Carolina Press, 1980.

Kolb, Robert. "Martin Luther." In *Christian Theologies of the Sacraments: A Comparative Introduction*, edited by Justin S. Holcomb and David A. Johnson, 132–51. New York: New York University Press, 2017.

Kurlansky, Mark. *The Big Oyster: History on the Half Shell*. New York: Random House, 2007.

Lasch, Christopher. "The Family as a Haven in a Heartless World." *Salmagundi* 35 (Fall 1976): 42–55.

Lawson, Andrew. *Downwardly Mobile: The Changing Fortunes of American Realism*. New York: Oxford University Press, 2012.

Lebsock, Suzanne. *Free Women of Petersburg: Status and Culture in a Southern Town, 1784–1860*. New York: Norton, 1984.

———. "Radical Reconstruction and the Property Rights of Southern Women." *Journal of Southern History* 43 (May 1977): 195–216.

Lee, Erika. *America for Americans: A History of Xenophobia in the United States*. New York: Basic Books, 2019.

Lerner, Gerda. "The Meaning of Seneca Falls." *Dissent* 45, no. 4 (Fall 1998): 35–41.

Link, William A. *Roots of Secession: Slavery and Politics in Antebellum Virginia*. Chapel Hill: University of North Carolina Press, 2003.

Massey, Mary Elizabeth. *Bonnet Brigades: American Women and the Civil War*. New York: Knopf, 1966.
McCurry, Stephanie. *Masters of Small Worlds: Yeoman Households, Gender Relations, and the Political Culture of the Antebellum South Carolina Low Country*. New York: Oxford University Press, 1995.
Meehan, Thomas R. "'Not Made Out of Levity: Evolution of Divorce in Pennsylvania." *Pennsylvania Magazine of History and Biography* 92, no. 4 (October 1968): 441–64.
Molloy, Marie S. "'An Illicit and Criminal Intercourse': Adultery and Marital Breakdown in the Slaveholding South." *American Nineteenth Century History* (January 2022): 1–17.
Monroe, Elizabeth. *The Wheeling Bridge Case: Its Significance in American Law and Technology*. Boston: Northeastern University Press, 1992.
Morgan, Jennifer. *Laboring Women: Reproduction and Gender in New World Slavery*. Philadelphia: University of Pennsylvania Press, 2004.
Morsman, Amy Feely. *The Big House after Slavery: Virginia Plantation Families and Their Postbellum Domestic Experiment*. Charlottesville: University of Virginia Press, 2010.
Nadelhaft, Jerome. "'The Public Gaze and the Prying Eye': The South and the Privacy Doctrine in Nineteenth-Century Wife Abuse Cases." *Cardozo Journal of Law and Gender* 14 (Summer 2008): 549–607.
"National Register of Historic Places Nomination for DeQueen and Eastern Railroad Machine Shoppe." National Register of Historic Places Nomination Form. Washington, D.C.: U.S. Department of the Interior, National Park Service, 1996.
Newman, Louise. *White Women's Rights: The Racial Origins of Feminism in the United States*. New York: Oxford University Press, 1999.
Norton, Mary Beth. *Founding Mothers and Fathers: Gendered Power and the Forming of American Society*. New York: Knopf, 1996.
Pascoe, Peggy. *What Comes Naturally: Miscegenation Law and the Making of Race in America*. New York: Oxford University Press, 2010.
Penningroth, Dylan C. "African American Divorce in Virginia and Washington, D.C., 1865–1930." *Journal of Family History* 33 (January 2008): 21–35.
Perrone, Giuliana. "'Back into the Days of Slavery': Freedom, Citizenship, and the Black Family in the Reconstruction-Era Courtroom." *Law and History Review* 37:1 (February 2019): 125–61.
Phillips, Christopher. *The Rivers Ran Backward: The Civil War and the Remaking of the American Middle Border*. New York: Oxford University Press, 2016.
Rable, George C. *Civil Wars: Women and the Crisis of Southern Nationalism*. Urbana: University of Illinois Press, 1989.
Rice, Connie Park. "Caldwell, Alfred." In *Dictionary of Virginia Biography*, vol. 2, edited by Sara B. Bears, John T. Kneebone, J. Jefferson Looney, Brent Tarter, and Sandra Gioia Treadway, 504-5. Richmond: Library of Virginia, 2001.
Rice, Otis K. *West Virginia: A History*. Lexington: University Press of Kentucky, 1985.

Riley, Glenda. *Divorce: An American Tradition*. New York: Oxford University Press, 1991.

———. "Legislative Divorce in Virginia, 1803–1850." *Journal of the Early Republic* 11, no. 1 (Spring 1991): 51–67.

Rothman, Joshua D. *Notorious in the Neighborhood: Sex and Families across the Color Line in Virginia, 1787–1861*. Chapel Hill: University of North Carolina Press, 2003.

———. "'To Be Freed from Thate Curs and Let at Liberty': Interracial Adultery and Divorce in Antebellum Virginia." *Virginia Magazine of History and Biography* 106, no. 4 (Autumn 1998): 443–81.

Rotundo, E. Anthony. *American Manhood: Transformations in Masculinity from the Revolution to the Modern Era*. New York: Basic Books, 1993.

Ryan, Mary. *Cradle of the Middle Class: The Family in Oneida County, New York, 1790–1865*. Cambridge: Cambridge University Press, 1981.

Sachs, Honor. "The Myth of the Abandoned Wife: Married Women's Agency and the Legal Narrative of Gender in Eighteenth-Century Kentucky." *Ohio Valley History* 3, no. 4 (Winter 2003): 3–20.

Sager, Robin. *Marital Cruelty in Antebellum America*. Baton Rouge: Louisiana State University Press, 2016.

Salmon, Marylynn. *Women and the Law of Property in Early America*. Chapel Hill: University of North Carolina Press, 1986.

Schultz, Jane E. *Women at the Front: Hospital Workers in Civil War America*. Chapel Hill: University of North Carolina Press, 2005.

Schwalm, Leslie A. *Emancipation's Diaspora: Race and Reconstruction in the Upper Midwest*. Chapel Hill: University of North Carolina Press, 2009.

———. *A Hard Fight for We: Women's Transition from Slavery to Freedom in South Carolina*. Urbana: University of Illinois Press, 1997.

Schwartzberg, Beverly. "'Lots of Them Did That': Desertion, Bigamy, and Marital Fluidity in Late-Nineteenth-Century America." *Journal of Social History* 37, no. 3 (Spring 2004): 573–600.

Schweninger, Loren. *Families in Crisis in the Old South: Divorce, Slavery, and the Law*. Chapel Hill: University of North Carolina Press, 2012.

Scott, Anne Firor. *The Southern Lady: From Pedestal to Politics, 1830–1930*. Chicago: University of Chicago Press, 1970.

Shammas, Carole. "Re-assessing the Married Women's Property Acts." *Journal of Women's History* 6, no. 1 (Spring 1994): 9–30.

Shapiro, Henry D. *Appalachia on Our Mind: The Southern Mountains and Mountaineers in the American Consciousness, 1870–1920*. Chapel Hill: University of North Carolina Press, 1995.

Silkenat, David. *Moments of Despair: Suicide, Divorce and Debt in Civil War Era North Carolina*. Chapel Hill: University of North Carolina Press, 2011.

Sklar, Kathryn. *Catherine Beecher: A Study in American Domesticity*. New Haven, Conn.: Yale University Press, 1973.

Smith-Rosenberg, Carroll. "The Female World of Love and Ritual: Relations between Women in Nineteenth-Century America." *Signs* 1, no. 1 (Autumn 1975): 1–29.

Snell, Mark A. *West Virginia and the Civil War*. Stroud, UK: History Press, 2011.
Stanley, Amy Dru. *From Bondage to Contract: Wage, Labor, Marriage, and the Market in the Age of Slave Emancipation*. Cambridge: Cambridge University Press, 1998.
Stansell, Christine. *City of Women: Sex and Class in New York, 1789–1860*. Urbana: University of Illinois Press, 1987.
Stealey, John Edmund, III. "Slavery and the Western Virginia Salt Industry." *Journal of Negro History* 59, no. 2 (April 1974): 105–31.
"St. James Evangelical Lutheran Church." Ohio County Public Library, Wheeling, W.Va. https://www.ohiocountylibrary.org/research/wheeling-history/5360. Accessed June 15, 2021.
Stone, Lawrence. *Road to Divorce: England, 1530–1987*. Oxford: Oxford University Press, 1990.
Strasser, Susan. *Never Done: A History of American Housework*. New York: Pantheon Books, 1982.
Sword, Kristen. *Wives Not Slaves: Patriarchy and Modernity in the Age of Revolutions*. Chicago: University of Chicago Press, 2021.
Taylor, Amy Murrell. *The Divided Family in Civil War America*. Chapel Hill: University of North Carolina Press, 2005.
———. *Embattled Freedom: Journeys through the Civil War's Slave Refugee Camps*. Chapel Hill: University of North Carolina Press, 2020.
Thomas, Tracy A. *Elizabeth Cady Stanton and the Feminist Foundations of Family Law*. New York: New York University Press, 2016.
Tosh, John. *A Man's Place: Masculinity and the Middle-Class Home in Victorian England*. New Haven, Conn.: Yale University Press, 1999.
Towers, Frank. *The Urban South and the Coming of the Civil War*. Charlottesville: University of Virginia, 2004.
The United States Postal Service: An American History. Washington, D.C.: United States Postal Service, 2020.
Warbasse, Elizabeth Bowles. *The Changing Legal Rights of Married Women: 1800–1861*. New York: Garland, 1987.
Welter, Barbara. "The Cult of True Womanhood: 1820–1860." *American Quarterly* 18, no. 2, part 1 (Summer 1966): 151–74.
"Wheeling Iron and Nail Co." Ohio County Public Library, Wheeling, W.Va. https://www.ohiocountylibrary.org/research/wheeling-history/3040. Accessed June 15, 2021.
Whisnant, David. *All That Is Native and Fine: The Politics of Culture in an American Region*. Chapel Hill: University of North Carolina Press, 1983.
White, Deborah Gray. *Ar'n't I a Woman?: Female Slaves in the Plantation South*. New York: Norton, 1985.
Whites, Lee Ann. *The Civil War as a Crisis in Gender: Augusta, Georgia, 1860–1890*. Athens: University of Georgia Press, 1995.
Williams, John Alexander. *Appalachia: A History*. Chapel Hill: University of North Carolina Press, 2001.
———. *West Virginia: A Bicentennial History*. New York: Norton, 1976.
Wilson, Joan Hoff. "The Illusion of Change: Women and the American Rev-

olution." In *The American Revolution: Explorations in the History of American Radicalism*, edited by Alfred Young, 383–446. DeKalb: Northern Illinois University Press, 1976.

Wright, Danaya C. "*De Manneville v. De Manneville*: Rethinking the Birth of Custody Law under Patriarchy." *Law and History Review* 17, no. 2 (Summer 1999): 247–307.

Wyatt-Brown, Bertram. *Southern Honor: Ethics and Behavior in the Old South*. New York: Oxford University Press, 1982.

Zagarri, Rosemarie. *Revolutionary Backlash: Women and Politics in the Early American Republic*. Philadelphia: University of Pennsylvania Press, 2008.

Zainaldin, Jamil S. "The Emergence of a Modern American Family Law: Child Custody, Adoption, and the Courts, 1796–1851." *Northwestern University Law Review* 73 (1979): 1038–89.

Zeigler, Sara L. "Uniformity and Conformity: Regionalism and the Adjudication of the Married Women's Property Acts." *Polity* 28, no. 4 (Summer 1996): 467–95.

Index

abandonment: during Civil War, 35, 114; examples of, 77–93, 95–96, 134–35, 167–202; by gender, 3, 26, 40; as grounds for divorce, 20, 26–27, 264–69. *See also* adultery; divorce

absolute divorce, 18n68, 20–21, 27, 53n12, 78n4; granted by court, 53, 63, 69, 73, 76, 117, 121, 190; grounds for, 264; requested by plaintiff, 55, 64–65, 74, 97n6, 133. *See also* adultery; divorce

abuse. *See* cruelty

adultery: examples of, 49–76, 97n6, 114, 119, 125–66; as grounds for divorce, 17, 20, 26–27, 78n4, 264–68; interracial cases of, 37–38; in Ohio County, 18n68, 21, 24. *See also* abandonment; divorce; interracial sex

affidavit of non-residency, 61

alcohol, 2, 52n10, 127, 211n13, 245, 250. *See also* intemperance

alimony, 19–22, 265, 268; granted by court, 93, 141, 173, 190; requests for, 74n45, 88, 135, 148, 169, 205–7, 222–27, 235. *See also* divorce

Allegheny County, Pa., 119, 187

Altpeter, Catharine, 117–21

Altpeter, Frederick, 117–21

Anglican Church, 14

Appalachia, 42–43

Arkansas, 147–48

Australia, 95, 98

bail, 73–74

Bailey, Georgiana, 33

Baltimore, Md., 70, 72, 96, 228–30

Baltimore and Ohio Railroad, 9, 62, 129n10; house, 144, 146; shop, 90. *See also* railroad

Bank of Wheeling, 95

Baptist Church, 59

bar. *See* tavern

barbers, 186

Bardaglio, Peter, 29

Barr, Robert G., 169, 180

Bauman, Lizzette, 142–46

Belmont County, Ohio, 51n8, 60, 130, 162, 254n35

Belmont Iron Mill, 194

Berkshire, Ralph Lazier, 113, 117

Beshor, Catherine (Altpeter), 117–21

bigamy, 185, 263, 266. *See also* adultery

boarders: affairs at boarding houses, 67, 147–54; families' history of being, 89–91, 262; testimony from, 52, 139, 162, 208–9, 228

boarding houses, affairs at, 67, 147–54. *See also* boarders

boiler, 93, 171

Bole, Margaret, 39–40, 94–105

Bole, William, 39–40, 94–105

book binding, 157

bookkeeper, 225

border South, definition and importance of, 4–5, 8–9, 11–13. *See also* Ohio County; slavery; Wheeling

Boyer, Christina, 69–73

Boyer, John, 69–73

Brareton, Caroline, 38n120, 113–17

Brareton, Enoch, 38n120, 113–17

brewer, 38, 70–72

Brooke County, W.Va., 125n2, 244n29

brothel, 55–56, 58, 65, 164. *See also* prostitution

butcher, 147n33, 150–51

Caldwell, Alfred, 51, 70, 78, 84

Caldwell, Elbert Halsted, 125, 132, 134, 136, 141, 167, 174

283

California, 29, 82–83, 85
Calvinists, 14
carpenter: family members, 41, 87n21, 135, 174n14, 179–84; witnesses, 63
Catholicism, 60; adherents to, 37, 50–52, 67; doctrinal issues in, 14; prejudice against, 42, 98
Centre Wheeling, 118n13, 121, 146, 194, 199–200
Chalk, Catherine, 40, 55–57
chambermaid, 187
chancery courts, definition of, 49
Chandler, John G., 142
Chapman, Mary Jane (Wehner), 37–38, 49–53
Charleston, W.Va., 36
childbirth: abuse after, 39, 100–105, 204–30; death due to, 62n27; scandal after, 37, 50–53
Christian, Joseph, 33
Cincinnati, Ohio, 42, 71, 75, 119n15, 198
Civil War: impact on households, 2, 31–33; in Ohio County, 30–37
—soldiers: in general, 30–37, 145, 198; in Iowa regiments, 60; in Ohio regiments, 35, 131–32, 172; in Virginia regiments, 254n34, 255n38; in West Virginia regiments, 1, 41, 125–28, 147n31, 176, 191n43
Cochran, Robert, 135n18, 148, 161, 185, 192, 205, 236, 253
Coleman, Peter, 114, 118–21
collusion, 81, 263, 267–68
Columbus, Ohio, 131
common law, 14–15, 49n2. *See also* divorce
companionate marriage, 23, 26, 29
conductors, 149, 157–58
confectioners, 129, 143
Conrad, Francisca, 43, 141–46
Conrad, Frederick, 43, 141–46
constitutional convention, 12–13, 36. *See also* statehood
contractualism, 5, 17–18. *See also* divorce
coverture, 15–16, 78n5, 79; versus feme sole, 78, 87. *See also* divorce; married women's property laws
Cranmer, Gibson L., 119, 126, 133, 175, 196, 199
cruelty: examples of, 94–105, 147, 203–62; by gender, 26–27, 30; as grounds for divorce, 20, 267; mental, 26, 80–81, 95, 103, 204–27, 234–48, 256–62; neighbors' testimony about, 30, 43. *See also* abandonment; adultery; divorce
Cummins, James, 224
Cummins, Robert, 53, 230, 256
custody, 19–22, 264–65, 268; granted by court to father, 121; granted by court to mother, 105, 146, 173, 190, 197, 207, 232; remaining with father, 51, 198; remaining with mother, 52, 118; requested by father, 119; requested by mother, 169, 191–92, 236n26. *See also* alimony; divorce

Daugua, Christiana (Wells), 40, 64–69
Davenport, George, 142, 255
Davis, Hester, 61–63
Davis, James, 61–63
Davis, Rebecca Harding, 11
Debold, Ferdinand, 161–66
debt: on behalf of husband, 40, 64, 96, 101, 134, 204–5; on behalf of wife, 255. *See also* gender roles; neglect
Delfino, Susanna, 39
Democratic Party, 54n15
Dennis, Charles, 114–17
divorce: in antebellum America, 17–18; in Civil War era, 4–7; in colonial America, 14–16; documents and deception, 20–21; legislative, 14–15, 18–19; "no-fault," 19–20, 24, 81n12, 119n16; process of, 19–23; in Reconstruction Era, 19; religion and, 14; requirements for, 20–21; slavery and, 17–18; in West Virginia, 13–14, 18–19, 21–24; women's rights movement and, 15–16. *See also* emancipation; gender roles
divorce *a mensa et thoro*. *See* separation from bed and board
divorce *a vinculo matrimonii*. *See* absolute divorce
dock hand, 38, 71
doctors: childbirth and, 50–53, 104, 212–30; impotency and, 21; opiates and, 256; treating sexually transmitted disease, 164
domesticity, 25–29. *See also* gender roles
dower rights, 51, 53. *See also* married women's property laws

Edwards, Laura, 18
emancipation: impact on households, 2–3, 28, 31–33; reunification of Black families, 2; in West Virginia, 12, 36
engineer, 38, 61, 63, 71
England, immigrants from, 6, 54n16, 77n1. *See also* immigration

factories, 10, 38–42, 80, 86, 262; urban South, 3–4, 37–44. *See also* industrialization
farms, 38–39, 87n21, 182–83, 203n2, 253; as contested property, 92–93, 235, 243–47
feme covert. *See* coverture
feme sole, 78, 87. *See also* coverture
Fifth Ward. *See under* Wheeling
fireman, 75
Fitzhugh, Edward Henry, 97
Fourth Ward (Wheeling), 134n17, 194
France, immigrants from, 161n40, 167n3, 169
Fry, Joseph L., 49, 55, 56n21, 65, 74

gender roles, 24–30; after Civil War, 2–3; as "good" husband, 50, 113, 118–21, 133, 151, 160–65, 180, 255, 262; as "good" wife, 147, 168, 185–88, 204–13, 219, 224–29, 234, 245; of husband as provider, 25–26, 32, 118, 133, 151, 198, 248, 259; masculinity, 3, 26, 32; of wife as obedient, 25–26, 29–32, 78, 95, 103, 209
German Lutheran Church, 69, 71, 168; Germany United Evangelical Church, 119–20, 168n4; Lutheran Church, 132, 198. *See also* Germany, immigrants from
German United Evangelical Church, 119–20, 168n4; Lutheran Church, 132, 198. *See also* German Lutheran Church; Germany, immigrants from
Germany, immigrants from, 6, 41–43; in divorce cases, 1, 69–70, 118n11–13, 125–31, 141–46, 167–68, 174–77, 197n52. *See also* immigration
Gillespie, Michele, 39
Goods, M. C., 62
Goudy, Elizabeth, 35, 41–42, 87n21, 174–79
Goudy, Isaac, 42, 86–87
Goudy, James, 35, 41–42, 87n21, 174–79
Grafton, W.Va., 145

Green, Annie, 38n120, 184–97
Green, Augustus, 38n120, 184–97
Greene County, Pa., 61–63, 179, 182
Griffith, Charles, 53n11, 203–33
Griffith, Maggie, 53n11, 203–33
guns, 99, 163, 228, 238

Hamilton, Virginia, 159–66
Hamilton, William, 159–66
Hill, Mary (Mary Jane Work), 86–93
Hornbrook, Rachel (McGinnis), 40–43, 54–61
hotels, 53n11, 126, 128–29, 131, 144
house of ill fame. *See* brothel
Hubbard, Chester D., 136
Hubbard, William, 135–36, 161
Hunter, John. 1, 24, 126–31

immigration, 6, 11, 37–38, 41–43, 53; from England, 6, 54n16, 77n1; nativism, 41–42, 175–78. *See also* France, immigrants from; Germany, immigrants from
imprisonment: as grounds for divorce, 21, 106–9, 264, 267; of husbands, 66–68; for threats and abuse, 72–73, 226–33
Indiana, as "divorce haven," 17
individualism, 5; contractualism and, 17–18
industrialization: box factories, 147n32; brick manufacturing, 10, 131; glass production, 10, 254n34, 262; iron factories, 10, 80, 82n14, 171, 194, 197n52; pulp and paper mills, 10, 130; in Wheeling, 10–11, 37–44. *See also* factories
insanity, 255; mental illness, 263, 266
intemperance: as grounds for divorce, 27; by husband, 64, 101–2, 147, 204–33, 234–52; nativism and, 42; by wife, 256–62. *See also* alcohol; cruelty
International Organisation of Good Templars, 211–12
interracial marriage, 263, 266
interracial sex, 37–38, 50–52, 115–16, 228. *See also* adultery
Iowa, 60, 88, 90–93, 235

jail. *See* imprisonment
jealousy, 66, 82–85, 181–82, 249–52

Kentucky, 11, 86, 185–86; divorce in, 17, 20, 27

Kerr, James, 179–84
Kerr, Louisa, 179–84
Kiefer, Mary, 167–73
Kiefer, Xavier, 167–73
knives, 95, 99, 162, 227, 241–49
Kyriakoudes, Louis M., 39

Ladies' Memorial Association, 3
Lamb, Daniel, 13, 119n15
laudanum, 255–62
Leasure, Elizabeth, 53n11, 224n16, 254–62
Leasure, James, 53n11, 224n16, 254–62
lewdness, charges of; as grounds for divorce, 20, 24; against husband, 57–59, 65–67, 75; against wife, 126, 132–33, 161. *See also* adultery; divorce; prostitution
Lindemuth, Augusta, 197–202
Lindemuth, Louis, 197–202
liquor. *See* alcohol
Long, Lewis, 35, 132–33
Long, Rosanna, 35, 132–33
Louis, Louisa (Kerr), 179–84
Louisville, Ky., 86, 115
Luther, Martin, 14
Lutheran Church, 132, 198. *See also* German Lutheran Church

Maine, 234n21
manufacturing. *See* industrialization
married women's property: land and buildings, 168–71, 203–9; material goods, 235, 250–51; wages, 40, 96
married women's property laws, 13–17, 49n2, 64, 78n5. *See also* women's rights movement
Marriott, Elizabeth (Rogers), 43, 77–86
Marshall County, W.Va., 62, 87n21, 125n2
Martins Ferry, Ohio, 131, 188, 197
masculinity, 3, 26, 32. *See also* gender roles
mason, 171, 244, 246
Massachusetts, 4, 15, 43, 77–80
McGinnis, Dorrance, 40–43, 54–61
McGinnis, Rachel, 40–43, 54–61
mechanic, 10, 38, 70, 80, 162, 179
Melvin, Thayer, 147, 160, 179, 184, 191, 203, 231, 234
mental illness, 263, 266; insanity, 255
merchant, 206, 220, 222

Methodist Church, 165
Methodist Episcopal Church, 108n4, 109, 133
Milleger, Elizabeth. *See* Goudy, Elizabeth
milliner, 40, 45, 64, 147n33. *See also* married women's property laws; women: working
miner, 191n42
Missouri, 60
Mitchell, Anne, 136–41
Monongalia County, W.Va., 113, 202n59

nail factory, 10, 86n17, 93, 171n8
National Road, 4, 8–9
nativism, 41–42, 175–78. *See also* immigration
neglect, 40–41; on behalf of husband, 26–27, 35, 64, 78, 81–82, 87–93, 134, 147, 177–78, 187, 194–96, 210; on behalf of wife, 26, 50, 80, 151, 161, 257–58, 261; of child, 104, 191, 231, 258; forcing wife to work, 40, 74, 96, 168–70, 185, 187–89, 191, 235, 251. *See also* abandonment; cruelty; divorce; gender roles; intemperance; separation from bed and board
Nelson, M., 88
New Jersey, 15, 54n17, 69–71
New York, 40–43, 94–97, 142–44, 191–93; married women's property law and, 13, 17. *See also* married women's property law
next friend, 35, 39–42, 267; as used by wives, 54, 64, 73, 86, 94, 106, 134–36, 167, 174; wife's failure to use, 79
Norman, John, 233–53
Norman, Mary, 233–53
North Carolina, 15, 33
North Wheeling, 56, 164
nurses: after childbirth, 103, 212–18, 231; during Civil War, 3, 134n17

obedience. *See* gender roles
O'Brien, Annie, 40, 65–69
Ohio County: divorce in, 6–7, 18–19, 20–21, 23–24; history of, importance of, 4, 6, 8–13, 24. *See also* Wheeling
Ohio River, 4–6, 8, 11, 43, 61, 74
opium, 254–59

paper mill, 10, 130
patriarchy, 29–30, 32, 35
Paull, James, 55, 65, 74
Pease, Ohio, 202
Peck, Daniel, 135–36, 148–49, 185–86, 192–94, 205, 236, 253
peddler, 199n58
Pendleton, Joseph Henry, 255
Peninsula Cemetery, 61, 262
penitentiary. *See* imprisonment
Peters Run, 161
Philadelphia, 52, 96, 173, 190
physicians. *See* doctors
pilot, 130
pistol. *See* guns
Pittsburgh, 8–10, 36, 126
Presbyterian Church, 63, 77n3, 189, 202n59
printing office, 152
prostitution, 40–41, 72–75; charges against wives of, 24, 27, 130–31, 234, 267; husbands' use of, 55, 57–60, 65–67, 164. *See also* adultery; lewdness, charges of
public house. *See* tavern

Quakers, 54n17

race, 28–29
railroad, 99, 101, 145, 157. *See also* Baltimore and Ohio Railroad
Reconstruction, 19, 31–33, 36. *See also* Civil War; emancipation
regional identity, 27–29
Reininger, Rosanna (Long), 35, 132–33
remarriage: court forbidding, 20–23, 78n4, 119, 121, 136n19; rules governing, 265; spouse requesting court to forbid, 119. *See also* absolute divorce; separation from bed and board
Republican Party, 19, 52n8
Restored State of Virginia, 11, 107n3, 119n15
Richmond, Va., 6, 10, 38, 54n15, 97n8
Riddle, Mary, 147–59
Rippets, Louisa, 136
Ritchietown, 115–16, 118, 120–21, 132–33. *See also* South Wheeling
riverboats, 6, 43; engineer, 38, 61, 63, 71; working on, 61, 71, 74–75, 130n11, 187–90, 193
river man. *See* engineer

Rogers, Elizabeth, 43, 77–86
Rogers, Thomas, 43, 77–86
rolling mill, 82–83, 86, 114, 161n40, 197n51. *See also* industrialization
Roney's Point, 163–64, 235–36, 245
Ruffner, Henry, 10
Russell, Charles Wells, 97

saloon. *See* tavern
saw mill, 58, 166
Scatterday, Emeline, 123, 133–41
Scatterday, Pulaski, 123, 133–41
Scottish immigrant, 83–85
seamstresses, 41, 174n13, 251
secession. *See under* statehood
Second Ward. *See under* Wheeling
separation from bed and board, 20, 78n4; granted by court, 93, 105; grounds for, 264–65, 267–69; requested by plaintiff, 88, 135, 255. *See also* abandonment; cruelty; divorce
servants: abuse toward, 217–20; failure of husband to provide, 95, 100, 231; as litigants, 186; presence of, 233n18; relationship with, 50, 53n11. *See also* slavery
Seventh Ward (Wheeling), 131, 139
sexuality, 27–28. *See* prostitution
sexually transmitted disease, 27, 40, 164
sheriff, 100–101, 224, 231–32; papers served by, 21, 49, 179
Sistersville, W.Va., 97n7
Sixth Ward (Wheeling), 161n40
slavery, 26–27, 29–32, 38–39; at constitutional convention, 12–13; family separation during, 10; judges and, 49n1; labor and, 38–39; lawyers and, 51n8, 97n8, 107n3; petitioners and, 203n2; rhetoric about, 103; in Wheeling, 4, 10–12
Sly, Mary Ann (Annie Green), 38n120, 184–97
Snider, Isaac, 73–76
Snider, Mary, 73–76
sobriety, as character defense, 162. *See also* gender roles; intemperance; neglect
soldiers. *See* Civil War
Somer, Mary (Kiefer), 167–73
South Carolina, 15, 17, 19

South Wheeling, 77, 80–82, 86, 168, 170–73. *See also* Ritchietown
Stansell, Christine, 43
Stanton, Elizabeth Cady, 5n15, 16–17
statehood, 31, 35–36; secession, 1, 11–12, 97, 113
statehood convention, 54n15, 107n3, 113n1, 119n15
steamboats. *See* riverboats
stepfamilies, 89–93, 191–92
Steubenville, Ohio, 89, 140
Stewart, Maggie (Griffith), 53n11, 203–33
St. Louis, Mo., 42, 75
stores, 57, 68, 144, 146; boot and shoe, 39, 95, 98–105; grocery, 35, 194, 259; hat and cap, 213; pharmacy, 208, 259; tobacco, 211, 214, 222–24; urban South, 3–4, 37–44
Stroble, Ellen, 1–4, 24, 125–31
Stroble, Jacob, 1–3, 24, 125–31
Switzerland, 35, 172

tavern: as site of affair, 2, 56–58, 127–29; work at, 37–38, 50–52, 84, 125n3
Taylor, Belvidere, 190–97
Taylor, Frank, 190–97
Taylor, Samuel Oliver, 169, 180
teacher, 3, 233n19
Thompson, George, 9n26, 54, 61, 64, 69, 73, 79, 87, 94, 106, 113n1
tobacco, 100; sale of, 38, 62, 157, 204–23. *See also* stores
Top Mill, 162, 171
Trenton, N.J., 69–72
Triadelphia (Wheeling), 161, 165–66

United Daughters of the Confederacy, 3
unmarried name, wife's use of, 22, 60, 69, 93, 133, 195n46
urban South, importance of, 3–4, 37–44. *See also* border South, definition and importance of; Ohio County; slavery; Wheeling

venereal disease, 27, 40, 164

Washington County, Pa., 157–58, 169, 178–83; marriages in, 43, 58, 63, 73, 76, 113, 125–26, 161n41, 165, 174, 234

watchman, 171
Watkins, Ellen. *See* Stroble, Ellen
weapons. *See* guns; knives
Wehner, John Michael, 37–38, 49–53
Wehner, Mary Jane, 37–38, 49–53
Welch, Connor, 147–59
Welch, Elizabeth, 147–59
Wells, Christina, 40, 64–69
Wells, Levi, 40, 64–69
Wellsburg, W.Va., 144, 147n33, 150–54
West Alexander, Pa. *See* Washington County, Pa.
Wheat, James Sanders, 107
Wheeler and Wilson Sewing Machine Company, 165
Wheeling: as capital, 11, 36; Fifth Ward, 93, 118n13, 142n26, 174n12; Fourth Ward, 134n17, 194; history and importance of, 3–4, 8–13; Second Ward, 94n2, 184n29, 49n1; Seventh Ward, 131, 139; Sixth Ward, 161n40. *See also* Ohio County
Wheeling and Belmont Bridge Company, 9, 139
Wheeling Argus, 77
Wheeling Daily Register, 141, 167, 174
Wheeling Daily Times and Gazette, 106
Wheeling Intelligencer, 53n13, 133, 179, 184
Wheeling Island, 9, 57, 60, 137–40. *See also* Wheeling Suspension Bridge
Wheeling Suspension Bridge, 9, 38, 57n23, 60, 139–40. *See also* Wheeling Island
Whig Party, 42, 55n21
whiskey, 2, 127, 163, 171, 229, 255–58. *See also* alcohol; intemperance
widow, 53, 141; affair with, 137; at time of marriage, 54n16, 91, 148, 254n35
widower, 108, 134, 148, 202
Willey Amendment, 12–13. *See also* slavery; statehood
Williams, Mary, 106–9
Williams, William George, 106–9
women: after Civil War, 2–3; sexuality, 27–28; working, 25–26, 28–29, 38–40. *See also* Civil War; emancipation
women's rights movement, 3–5, 13–18, 23, 30–33, 39
Work, Alexander, 86–93
Work, Mary Jane, 86–93

NEW PERSPECTIVES ON THE CIVIL WAR ERA

Practical Strangers: The Courtship Correspondence of Nathaniel Dawson and Elodie Todd, Sister of Mary Todd Lincoln
EDITED BY STEPHEN BERRY AND ANGELA ESCO ELDER

The Greatest Trials I Ever Had: The Civil War Letters of Margaret and Thomas Cahill
EDITED BY RYAN W. KEATING

Prison Pens: Gender, Memory, and Imprisonment in the Writings of Mollie Scollay and Wash Nelson, 1863–1866
EDITED BY TIMOTHY J. WILLIAMS AND EVAN A. KUTZLER

William Gregg's Civil War: The Battle to Shape the History of Guerrilla Warfare
EDITED AND ANNOTATED BY JOSEPH M. BEILEIN JR.

Seen/Unseen: Hidden Lives in a Community of Enslaved Georgians
EDITED BY CHRISTOPHER R. LAWTON, LAURA E. NELSON, AND RANDY L. REID

Radical Relationships: The Civil War–Era Correspondence of Mathilde Franziska Anneke
TRANSLATED BY VICTORIJA BILIC
EDITED BY ALISON CLARK EFFORD AND VIKTORIJA BILIC

Private No More: The Civil War Letters of John Lovejoy Murray, 102nd United States Colored Infantry
EDITED BY SHARON A. ROGER HEPBURN

Heartsick and Astonished: Divorce in Civil War–Era West Virginia
EDITED BY ALLISON DOROTHY FREDETTE

www.ingramcontent.com/pod-product-compliance
Lightning Source LLC
Chambersburg PA
CBHW030526230426
43665CB00010B/778